TIME ZONES

TEACHER'S BOOK | THIRD EDITION

COLLEEN SHEILS
CARMELLA LIESKE
DAVID BOHLKE
JENNIFER WILKIN
ANDREW BOON

NATIONAL
GEOGRAPHIC
LEARNING

Australia · Brazil · Mexico · Singapore · United Kingdom · United States

NATIONAL GEOGRAPHIC LEARNING

National Geographic Learning,
a Cengage Company

Time Zones Teacher's Book 4 Third Edition

Colleen Sheils, Carmella Lieske, David Bohlke,
Jennifer Wilkin, and Andrew Boon

Publisher: Andrew Robinson

Managing Editor: Derek Mackrell

Associate Development Editor: Yvonne Tan

Additional Editorial Support: Jacqueline Eu

Director of Global Marketing: Ian Martin

Senior Product Marketing Manager: Anders Bylund

Heads of Regional Marketing:
    Charlotte Ellis (Europe, Middle East and Africa)
    Irina Pereyra (Latin America)

Senior Production Controller: Tan Jin Hock

Associate Media Researcher: Jeffrey Millies

Senior Designer: Lisa Trager

Operations Support: Rebecca G. Barbush,
    Hayley Chwazik-Gee

Manufacturing Planner: Mary Beth Hennebury

Composition: Symmetry Creative Production, Inc.

For permission to use material from this text or product,
submit all requests online at **cengage.com/permissions**
Further permissions questions can be emailed to
permissionrequest@cengage.com

ISBN-13: 978-0-357-42647-0

National Geographic Learning
200 Pier 4 Boulevard
Boston, MA 02210
USA

Locate your local office at **international.cengage.com/region**

Visit National Geographic Learning online at **ELTNGL.com**
Visit our corporate website at **www.cengage.com**

Printed in Mexico
Print Number: 4   Print Year: 2023

CONTENTS

SCOPE AND SEQUENCE

UNIT	FUNCTIONS	GRAMMAR	VOCABULARY	PRONUNCIATION	READ, WRITE, & WATCH
1 I LOVE MIXING MUSIC!					**PAGE 6**
	Talking about hobbies and interests **Real English:** *Tell me about it!*	**Using verb + -ing:** *Do you like playing chess?* *I enjoy doing jigsaw puzzles.* *Baking is a lot of fun.*	Hobbies Interests Nouns and verbs: *effect* vs. *affect*, *advice* vs. *advise*, *council* vs. *counsel*	Question intonation	**Reading:** Turning Hobbies into Cash **Writing:** Description **Video:** Robot Games
2 HOW LONG HAVE YOU BEEN DOING ARCHERY?					**PAGE 18**
	Identifying different sports Talking about sports and exercise **Real English:** *Give it a try.*	**Present perfect progressive:** *He's been playing tennis.* *I've been going to the gym.* **Adverbs of time:** *lately, recently, for, since*	Sports Collocations with *record*	Review: weak form of *been*	**Reading:** Running a Marathon **Writing:** Biography **Video:** Life Rolls On
3 WHAT SHOULD I DO?					**PAGE 30**
	Asking for and giving advice Talking about possible careers **Real English:** *On top of that, …*	**Modals for giving advice:** *should, could* **Verbs with *try*:** *try talking, try asking* **Other expressions:** *Why don't you … ?* *If I were you, …*	Problems and advice Phrasal verbs with *make*	Weak forms of *could* and *should*	**Reading:** Vision of Hope **Writing:** Informal letter **Video:** Eco-Fuel Africa
4 THE KOALA WAS TAKEN TO A SHELTER					**PAGE 42**
	Talking about animal rescue **Real English:** *It's up to you.*	**Passive voice without an agent:** *The dog was left at the shelter.* *Tags are being attached to the birds.* *How often are the animals fed?*	Wild animals Animal rescue Transitive and intransitive verbs	Intonation in a series	**Reading:** Bear Rescue **Writing:** News article **Video:** Raising Pandas
5 HOW ARE THEY MADE?					**PAGE 54**
	Describing manufacturing processes **Real English:** *I don't get it.*	**Passive voice with an agent:** *The wood is cut by a machine.* *The colors were chosen by the customer.* *The shoes have been customized by the store.*	Manufacturing and assembly Collocations with *global*	Contrastive stress	**Reading:** Where Is the iPhone Made? **Writing:** Descriptive paragraph **Video:** Prosthetic Legs
6 LOOK AT THOSE NARWHALS!					**PAGE 66**
	Talking about the importance of conserving marine animals and their habitats **Real English:** *You're telling me …*	**Non-defining relative clauses:** *The narwhal, which is a type of whale, has a long tusk.* *My uncle, who visits us every summer, is a marine biologist.*	Marine animals Coral reefs Approximation expressions	Pausing in relative clauses	**Reading:** Cities in the Sea **Writing:** Formal email **Video:** Boneless Beauties

Welcome to the updated and expanded edition of *Time Zones*.

WHAT IS *TIME ZONES*?

Time Zones is a five-level, four-skills series that combines a communicative approach to learning English with up-to-date National Geographic content. It is designed to be engaging for all young students, from pre-teens to young adults.

HOW IS THE BOOK ORGANIZED?

Time Zones follows a familiar grammatical syllabus, with simple structures introduced in the lower levels, followed by increasingly complex structures in later levels. However, *Time Zones* also follows a rich, thematic content syllabus. Real-world content is used as a springboard for introducing the language that students need to become effective communicators in English.

As with the grammatical syllabus, *Time Zones* teaches the highest-frequency vocabulary in the earlier stages of the course, with relatively lower-frequency vocabulary appearing only in the higher levels of the series. Along the way, more specialized vocabulary is occasionally introduced so that students can develop a meaningful understanding of it, as well as be able to talk about the real-world topics and issues introduced in *Time Zones*. Key vocabulary is recycled systematically throughout the series.

The vocabulary and grammar is well integrated throughout the series. For example, students might learn the grammatical structure *can* to talk about abilities in a unit on animals—learning to talk about what animals can and can't do—before going on to personalize the language and talk about themselves and their own abilities.

Ideally, the units of *Time Zones* will be taught in order, and no units will be skipped. However, if your students have some background in English, you may wish to skip the **Starter Level**, which consolidates some of the core English that young students might have already encountered if they have been exposed to English learning before.

WHAT ARE THE PRINCIPLES BEHIND THE SERIES?

1. ENGLISH FOR INTERNATIONAL COMMUNICATION

Students today are living in an increasingly globalized world, with English continuing to become an important lingua franca. The distinction between "native" and "non-native" speakers of English is becoming even less distinct than in the past. In fact, the majority of communication in English is between two so-called "non-native" English speakers. While *Time Zones* uses standard American English as its basis—in terms of lexis and grammar—it also acknowledges, and embraces, the fact that English is a global language.

Time Zones positions students to be effective communicators in English in a world where English is a common means of international communication. Because of this, the *Time Zones* audio program includes speakers from other countries with a range of real-world accents. This allows students to become comfortable listening to speakers from around the world and encourages them to speak themselves. Additionally, this emphasis on global accents better prepares students for common international exams, which increasingly focus on various international English accents.

2. AUTHENTIC, REAL-WORLD CONTENT

Time Zones is built on the belief that authentic, real-world content is more motivating and more relevant to students than content that is contrived or artificial. Stories, photographs, and video from National Geographic and other real sources tap into student curiosity, motivate them to learn about the world, and get students talking in English as early in their studies as possible.

At the same time, this focus on authenticity provides students with many opportunities for personalization. Throughout the program, students apply the language they learn as they develop the ability to talk about the world, as well as about themselves and their own lives. For example, students may learn about climate change—how human activity is increasing global temperatures—but will also be able to use this language to talk about what they can do in their own lives to deal with climate change.

3. GLOBAL CITIZENSHIP AND VALUES

Time Zones encourages students to think deeply about the values that all global citizens share. Throughout reading, listening, and video lessons, students of *Time Zones* learn about the world around them and its many varied cultures, as well as about global issues and events affecting everyone—including historical discoveries, scientific developments, and the health of the environment and the planet's inhabitants. Real stories about National Geographic Explorers and real-life global citizens prompt students to consider the effects of their own thoughts, beliefs, and actions on the whole world, and act as a springboard for short projects that go beyond the textbook.

4. ESSENTIAL SKILLS FOR SUCCESS

Students need more than strong communication skills to be successful. *Time Zones* recognizes that students need to be able to understand information presented in different ways—text, audio, video, charts, maps, and graphs—and be able to communicate about them in different settings and contexts. They also need to be able to work collaboratively in pairs and in group settings. Explicit and frequent practice in higher-order thinking skills are critical to future success in the classroom. Students using *Time Zones* will be exposed to all of these skills woven into each unit of the program.

Time Zones also acknowledges that many students today are balancing long-term communication goals with the immediate need for exam preparation. Throughout the program, students are exposed to task types commonly found on international exams. This helps students practice test-taking strategies and builds their confidence before taking these high-stakes exams.

WHAT'S NEW IN *TIME ZONES*, THIRD EDITION?

- Two videos in every unit help students see more of the world and make personal connections with the unit theme.
- More grammar and vocabulary activities in each unit deliver more guided language practice for in-class use.
- Clear unit goals and review activities encourage learner independence and self-assessment.
- Audio recordings with a range of international accents expose learners to natural English.
- Updated technology resources make *Time Zones* easy to use in and out of the classroom.
- Different activities in the Workbook and Online Practice offer more practice opportunities out of the classroom.
- An expanded Starter Combo level with six complete units is ideal for short courses for true beginners.

TAKE A TOUR OF *TIME ZONES* TEACHER'S BOOK

The Teacher's Book of *Time Zones* is full of suggestions on how to get the most out of your class time. The following pages will help you understand the vast resources at your disposal. (Don't forget to read about the other components on page xix.)

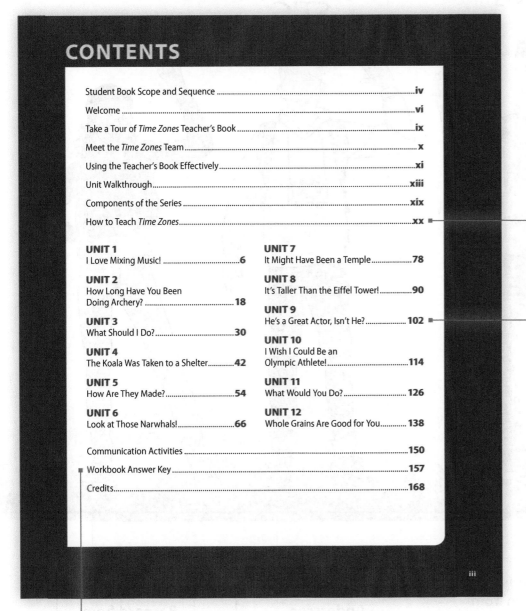

CONTENTS

iii

The **How to Teach *Time Zones*** section introduces techniques and tips to help you teach *Time Zones* more effectively.

Every level of *Time Zones* is divided into **12 units**. Each twelve-page unit is based on a particular theme, allowing students to learn about the world around them as they develop language skills.

The **Workbook** is an effective way for students to practice the language learned in *Time Zones*. Page xix gives more information about the Workbook. Answer keys for all of the Workbook activities are on pages 157–167.

MEET THE *TIME ZONES* TEAM

MAYA

MING

STIG

NADINE

This is **Maya Santos** from Rio de Janeiro, in Brazil. She's into music, singing, and shopping.

This is **Ming Chen** from Shanghai, in China. He likes sports and animals.

This is **Stig Andersson** from Stockholm, in Sweden. He loves food, photography, and sports.

This is **Nadine Barnard** from Cape Town, in South Africa. She loves nature, movies, and music.

The **reduced Student's Book pages** show answers for each activity. "Answers will vary." is used when there is no single correct answer for a particular question or activity.

The **CONTENT AREA** box summarizes key vocabulary and the grammar point in the unit. It also gives optional suggestions for things you may want to prepare before class.

Other useful vocabulary is related to the topic of the unit and is particularly helpful for students who are slightly more advanced and need a further challenge.

The **End of Unit Project** section provides a suggestion for a bigger project that students can do either inside or outside of class. The project extends and personalizes both the content and the language from the unit.

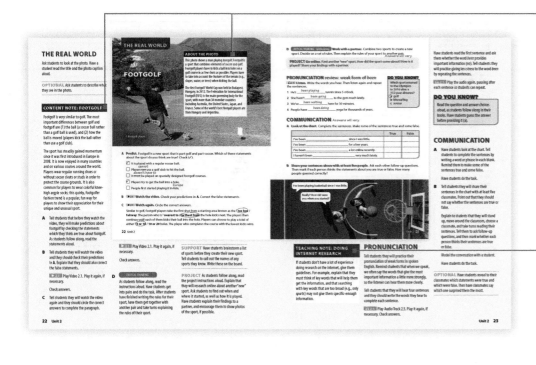

Both the **CONTENT NOTE** boxes and the **ABOUT THE PHOTO** boxes give additional details about the content being studied and the photos. This information can be shared with students to widen their knowledge.

The **TEACHING NOTE** boxes contain tips for teachers, additional activity explanations, and explanations of language acquisition concepts. These notes are in easy-to-understand language so that they can be used to explain the concepts to students.

Three sections give suggestions for differentiated instruction. **SUPPORT** sections provide ideas to make the activities more accessible for lower-level students. **CHALLENGE** sections include ways to expand the learning or make the activities more difficult (for stronger students). **OPTIONAL** sections expand the activities, providing more practice.

Additional Activities to Use with the Reading suggest various activities to expand the content, including reinforcing vocabulary, increasing students' awareness of the way vocabulary is used, expanding on the grammar used in the reading, personalizing the material, and practicing the unit's pronunciation point. You can select the activities that best meet your students' needs and your time constraints.

The **CHALLENGE** sections allow you to expand on the Student's Book material, adding additional learning and challenge. These are particularly appropriate for students who are finding the material a little too easy. In mixed-level classes, for example, while other students finish the Student's Book activity, you can ask fast-finishing pairs and groups to work on these activities.

The **SUPPORT** sections provide suggestions for further explanation for students who are finding the Student's Book material a little challenging. These additional procedures help students review previously studied material and explore Student's Book material in more detail. These sections also provide additional practice of the language.

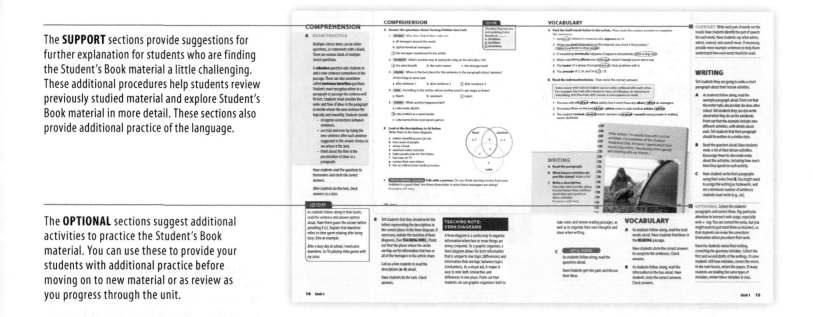

The **OPTIONAL** sections suggest additional activities to practice the Student's Book material. You can use these to provide your students with additional practice before moving on to new material or as review as you progress through the unit.

UNIT WALKTHROUGH

Time Zones, Third Edition uses amazing photography, updated videos, and inspiring stories of global citizens to encourage teenage learners to explore the world in English.

Through teacher-tested language lessons, carefully scaffolded practice activities, and teaching resources that keep classrooms engaged, *Time Zones*, Third Edition delivers the skills and language that learners need for wherever they're going next.

High-interest photography introduces the unit topic and target vocabulary, stimulates students' interest, and sparks classroom discussion.

Each **Preview** section includes a listening activity that provides authentic speaking models so students can improve their pronunciation and general communication skills.

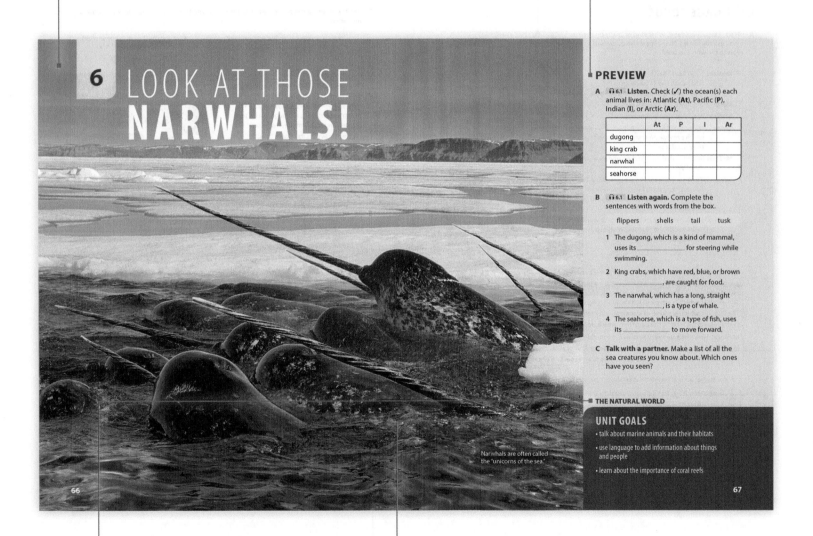

6 LOOK AT THOSE NARWHALS!

Narwhals are often called the "unicorns of the sea."

66

PREVIEW

A ⓝ 6.1 **Listen.** Check (✓) the ocean(s) each animal lives in: Atlantic (**At**), Pacific (**P**), Indian (**I**), or Arctic (**Ar**).

	At	P	I	Ar
dugong				
king crab				
narwhal				
seahorse				

B ⓝ 6.1 **Listen again.** Complete the sentences with words from the box.

flippers   shells   tail   tusk

1 The dugong, which is a kind of mammal, uses its _____ for steering while swimming.

2 King crabs, which have red, blue, or brown _____, are caught for food.

3 The narwhal, which has a long, straight _____, is a type of whale.

4 The seahorse, which is a type of fish, uses its _____ to move forward.

C **Talk with a partner.** Make a list of all the sea creatures you know about. Which ones have you seen?

■ THE NATURAL WORLD

UNIT GOALS

• talk about marine animals and their habitats

• use language to add information about things and people

• learn about the importance of coral reefs

67

Time Zones features real-world information from **four content areas**: People and Places, History and Culture, the Natural World, and Science and Technology.

The **Unit Goals** box tells students what they are going to learn in the unit. This can be particularly helpful for students who might otherwise focus on the details without seeing how they are related to one another.

The unit's target language is introduced through an entertaining conversation featuring the *Time Zones* team. Students can repeat the conversation, varying vocabulary and the speaker parts, to build fluency and confidence.

The **Real English** box highlights a functional phrase or discourse marker from the dialog that is commonly spoken by fluent speakers of English.

The **Language Focus** activities practice and reinforce the unit's grammar and language, moving from controlled and contextualized practice to freer practice.

Most **Language Focus** sections have a listening component, allowing students to become more comfortable with the language before producing it.

LANGUAGE FOCUS

A 🎧6.2 **Listen and read.** What kind of shells do hermit crabs usually live in? Then repeat the conversation and replace the words in **bold**.

Nadine: Look! **That shell is moving!**
(**That shell has something in it** /
There's something inside that shell)

Ming: Oh, that's just a hermit crab.

Nadine: I've never seen one before.

Ming: They usually live in abandoned snail shells, which **provide** protection. (**they use for** /
they need for)

Nadine: Really? Do they live in the same shell all their lives?

Ming: No, they change shells. It's **incredible** to watch. If they don't like their new shell, they go back to their old one. (**amazing** /
fascinating)

Nadine: So, you're telling me they want the **most fashionable** shell-ter! (**most stylish** /
coolest-looking)

B 🎧6.3 **Look at the chart.** Then circle the correct answers below.

ADDING INFORMATION TO A SENTENCE (USING NON-DEFINING RELATIVE CLAUSES)
The narwhal, **which is a type of whale**, has a long tusk.
The dugong, **which is a kind of mammal**, is sometimes called a sea cow.
Last weekend we went to the aquarium, **which now has a collection of seahorses**.
My uncle, **who visits us every summer**, is a marine biologist.
My cousin Lisa, **who is a scuba diving instructor**, knows a lot about coral reefs.
If you have questions, ask the tour guide, **who is an expert on ocean conservation**.

1 A clause that adds extra information about a person begins with *which* / *who*.

2 A clause that adds extra information about a thing begins with *which* / *who*.

3 We use **commas** / **semicolons** to separate a non-defining relative clause from the rest of the sentence.

C 🎧6.4 **Complete the paragraph.** Use the phrases in the box (a–d). Then listen and check your answers.

a which is where they find all their food
b which they gather with their tentacle-like feet
c which means they're active at night
d which are related to starfish and sea urchins

Sea cucumbers, [1] _____, are one of the ocean's most interesting creatures. There are over 1,200 known species, and they come in a variety of colors. They are typically 10 to 30 centimeters long, although the largest species can reach 3 meters. Most sea cucumbers live on the ocean floor, [2] _____. They eat algae, tiny sea creatures, and even waste materials, [3] _____. When threatened, some sea cucumbers shoot sticky threads out of their bottoms to trap their enemies. Sea cucumbers are nocturnal creatures, [4] _____.

A sea cucumber

D **Rewrite these sentences.** Use *which* or *who*.

1 Alice is writing a research paper on narwhals. She's a marine biologist.
Alice, who's a marine biologist, is writing a research paper on narwhals.

2 The *Titanic* is now an underwater shelter for marine life. It sank in 1912.
_____

3 My friend Jada is coming to visit this weekend. She's studying medicine in Toronto.
_____

4 Rio de Janeiro is an interesting place to live. It has a population of more than six million.
_____

5 My science teacher is very patient and friendly. He's from Australia.
_____

E **Play a chain game.** Work in groups of three. One student says a sentence. The other two students add more information to the sentence using *which* or *who*.

Jun is from Seoul.

Jun, who is our classmate, is from Seoul.

Jun, who is our classmate, is from Seoul, which is …

The final activity in each Language Focus is an open-ended communicative activity, such as a game, role-play, or survey.

The Real World uses a short video to introduce students to more general knowledge about the world through personal stories and experiences of National Geographic Explorers, recent discoveries and research, scientific experiments, and more.

Do You Know? quizzes provide students with fun, real-world facts related to the content.

The **Pronunciation** section helps to build student confidence, using a listen-notice-repeat sequence. This section introduces and practices features of spoken English that are appropriate to students at each level.

Project suggestions encourage students to personalize what they've learned in the lesson and go beyond the book to do research online, in their neighborhood, or in the classroom.

THE REAL WORLD

LEARNING FROM HUMPBACKS

Humpback whales have inspired new wind turbine technology (inset).

A ▶6.1 **Watch the video.** What characteristic of humpback whales has inspired scientists to create more efficient wind turbines?

a the blowholes on the top of a humpback's head

b the structure of a humpback's flippers

c the shape of a humpback's head

B ▶6.1 **Watch again.** Circle the correct answers.

1 The drag on something makes it move more **slowly / quickly**.

2 Wind turbines with tubercles experience **more / less** drag.

3 Researchers are considering adding tubercles to **the bottom of ships / airplane wings** to increase speed and improve safety.

DO YOU KNOW?

The nose of Japan's Shinkansen bullet trains is modeled after _____ .

a a kingfisher's beak

b a narwhal's tusk

c the head of a fish

C **Read the definition of biomimicry below.** Then check (✓) the options that are examples of biomimicry.

> **biomimicry** (*n.*): the science of copying designs from nature in human engineering and invention

☐ putting bird feathers in a jacket to stay warm in cold weather

☐ inventing a multilegged robot that can move through tight spaces like a spider

☐ sticking pieces of shark skin onto swimwear to help people swim faster

☐ developing a bat-inspired drone that can fly around in the dark by itself

☐ designing a prosthetic arm that looks and functions like an octopus tentacle

D **CRITICAL THINKING** Applying **Talk with a partner.** What other traits or abilities of animals or plants do you think would be useful to copy? In what situations might these traits or abilities be useful to humans?

PROJECT Go online. Find another example of biomimicry. Make some notes about it and share with a partner.

PRONUNCIATION pausing in relative clauses

🎧6.5 **Listen.** Mark the pauses in these sentences with a slash (/). Then listen again and repeat the sentences.

1 My friend Maria / who runs the aquarium / is interested in marine conservation.

2 Saltwater crocodiles, which are very dangerous, are the largest living reptiles.

3 The scientists, who work for WhalePower, are studying humpback whales.

4 Sea otters, which live in the Pacific Ocean, are very playful animals.

COMMUNICATION

Play a guessing game. Work in groups. **Group A:** Turn to page 155. **Group B:** Turn to page 156. Follow the instructions on the page.

> This animal, which can live up to 23 years, lives in the Pacific Ocean.

> Is it a whale shark?

> No, sorry. The next animal, which ...

The **Communication** section is the longest communicative task of the unit. These pair or group activities allow students to use the language they have learned in a less structured speaking activity. These sections include activities such as games, surveys, information gap activities, and questionnaires.

Critical Thinking questions provide an opportunity for students to engage critically with the content by asking and answering questions related to the content.

The **Reading** section starts with a photograph and a pre-reading activity to engage students, introduce the topic, and activate prior knowledge and language. Students also practice skimming, scanning, prediction, and other skills that are essential for effective reading.

Audio recordings of each passage help students practice their listening, understand the pronunciation of new words, and study natural rhythm and intonation.

READING

A **Read paragraph A.** What are *polyps*?
  a small creatures that can cause coral reefs to become sick
  b tiny organisms that form the structure of coral reefs
  c large fish that depend on coral reefs for survival

B **Skim the article.** Add these headings (1–4) to the correct places.
  1 Reefs in Trouble   3 Super-Sized Cities
  2 What Can We Do?   4 Why Are Reefs Important?

C **Scan the article.** Underline all the things that are threatening the health of coral reefs.

The Great Barrier Reef, Australia

72 Unit 6

CITIES IN THE SEA

A 🎧 6.6 They may be small, but they build big things! Coral polyps, which live in the warm, **shallow** parts of the ocean, are probably the biggest builders on the planet. Each polyp uses calcium from seawater to build itself a hard limestone skeleton. When a polyp dies, its skeleton **remains**. Young polyps attach themselves to the old skeletons and make new skeletons. Over time, strange and wonderful shapes are slowly built up into amazing coral reefs.

B _____ Some coral reefs are huge, and the Great Barrier Reef in Australia is the largest of them all. It covers nearly 350,000 square kilometers.

C Scientists sometimes think of coral reefs as underwater cities. A quarter of all known ocean species live in and on reefs—there are nearly a thousand coral species. Reefs are also home to millions of sea creatures, like fish, crabs, turtles, and sharks.

D _____ Humans don't live in coral reef cities, but we benefit from them. Reefs create jobs for people in the fishing industry and other related businesses. They also supply us with food. Reefs protect our coasts—the coral slows down waves and protects beaches from erosion.

E Coral reefs are also **popular** with divers—many countries benefit from the tourists they **attract**. Finally, chemicals from reef creatures are used to create new medicines, which help doctors treat different illnesses.

F _____ Coral reefs are important, yet we don't take good care of them. About 20 percent of the world's reefs are already dead. Some experts **warn** that all reefs may be gone by 2050.

G Why are reefs in such trouble? For one thing, people catch too many reef fish and often **damage** the reefs—divers sometimes break off pieces of coral. Many people make and sell coral jewelry, too.

H Polluted water also causes problems because a certain type of algae grows in dirty water. This type of algae harms the reefs. Another type of algae is good for the reefs. But global warming is causing warmer ocean temperatures, which can cause polyps to lose this helpful algae. Without it, coral turns white. This is called "coral bleaching."

I _____ Can we save coral reefs? Experts say yes—if we make hard choices. More than 100 countries have created marine protected areas, where fishing is limited or banned. Another important step is fighting pollution.

J Humans and coral polyps are very different, but both build amazing cities. All of us will benefit if we protect our beautiful oceans.

Unit 6 73

High-interest readings feature real-world information that has been adapted from National Geographic or other reliable sources. The reading passage introduces new vocabulary; however, the length and language level of each passage is carefully graded and controlled to ensure student understanding with little or no teacher support.

Activity A of the Comprehension section features multiple-choice questions to check students' basic comprehension. The multiple-choice questions follow the same format as many common international exams. Question types include main idea, purpose, detail, inference, cohesion, vocabulary, and understanding reference words.

Activity A of the Vocabulary section gives students more practice with target lexicon from the Reading passage.

Activity B explains and practices real-world, commonly used expressions such as phrasal verbs, collocations, and synonyms.

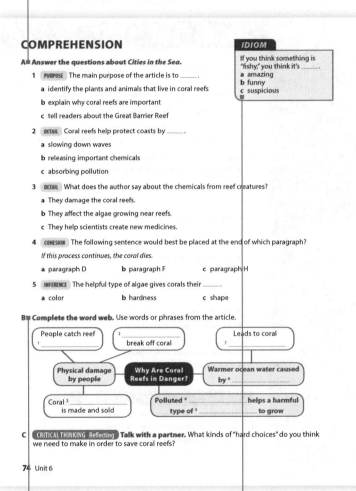

COMPREHENSION

A Answer the questions about *Cities in the Sea.*

1 PURPOSE The main purpose of the article is to _____.

  a identify the plants and animals that live in coral reefs

  b explain why coral reefs are important

  c tell readers about the Great Barrier Reef

2 DETAIL Coral reefs help protect coasts by _____.

  a slowing down waves

  b releasing important chemicals

  c absorbing pollution

3 DETAIL What does the author say about the chemicals from reef creatures?

  a They damage the coral reefs.

  b They affect the algae growing near reefs.

  c They help scientists create new medicines.

4 COHESION The following sentence would best be placed at the end of which paragraph?

  If this process continues, the coral dies.

  a paragraph D   b paragraph F   c paragraph H

5 INFERENCE The helpful type of algae gives corals their _____.

  a color   b hardness   c shape

B Complete the word web. Use words or phrases from the article.

- People catch reef 1 _____
- 2 _____ break off coral
- 7 _____ Leads to coral
- Physical damage by people
- **Why Are Coral Reefs in Danger?**
- Warmer ocean water caused by 6 _____
- Coral 3 _____ is made and sold
- Polluted 4 _____ helps a harmful type of 5 _____ to grow

C CRITICAL THINKING Reflecting Talk with a partner. What kinds of "hard choices" do you think we need to make in order to save coral reefs?

IDIOM

If you think something is "fishy," you think it's _____.

a amazing
b funny
c suspicious

74 Unit 6

VOCABULARY

A Find the bold words below in the article. Then circle the correct answers.

1 A lake that is **shallow** is *very big / not deep.*

2 If something **remains**, it *continues to exist / disappears.*

3 Things that are **popular** are enjoyed by *very few / many* people.

4 If something **attracts** people, it has features that cause people to *come to it / go away.*

5 When you **warn** someone about something, you tell them that something *good / bad* may happen.

6 When you **damage** an object, you *break or destroy / fix or improve* it.

B Read the information below. Then draw an arrow from the **bold** word or phrase to where it should go in each sentence (1–5).

When we don't know the exact number or wish to be vague, we can use expressions to give approximate numbers:

  about …   around …   more than …   nearly …   … or so

1 The Great Barrier Reef covers an area of 350,000 square kilometers. **nearly**

2 It contributes 70,000 jobs to the Australian economy. **around**

3 It consists of 3,000 individual coral reefs. **about**

4 It's home to 1,500 species of fish. **more than**

5 The reef grows a centimeter each year. **or so**

WRITING

A Read the email.

B What can the government do to help protect coral reefs? Note some ideas.

C Write a formal email using your notes from B. Persuade a government official to help protect coral reefs in your country.

New message

To | governmentofficial@mail.com
Subject | Help protect coral reefs

Dear Sir or Madam,

I am writing about the state of our country's coral reefs. There are beautiful reefs near our beaches, which many tourists currently enjoy, but these reefs have suffered a lot of damage recently from fishermen and divers. I feel that we can protect our coral reefs by …

Unit 6 75

Activity B contains graphic organizers, such as charts, word webs, and diagrams. These help students develop their critical thinking skills and help students gain a deeper understanding of the reading passage.

The **Idiom** box presents an idiom related to the unit topic. The idioms are all commonly used expressions, and understanding them will increase students' communicative ability.

In the **Writing** section, students demonstrate their newly gained language skills through a variety of writing tasks, including writing emails, blog posts, and reports. A clear model is provided for each writing activity to support students as they create their own piece of personalized writing.

Each unit includes a short **Video** related to the unit theme. The video is scripted to be level-appropriate and to recycle the unit's target language.

The **Before You Watch** section is a pre-watching task that introduces the topic, engages students, and activates prior knowledge.

The **While You Watch** section helps students understand the video. These activities can be used to assess students' understanding and determine how many times to show the video.

The **Review** page allows students to show that they understand the grammar and main vocabulary that was introduced in the unit.

ABOUT THE VIDEO Jellyfish are among the ocean's most fascinating creatures.

BONELESS **BEAUTIES**

Before You Watch

Take a quiz. What do you know about jellyfish? Circle **T** for true or **F** for false.

1 Jellyfish appeared on the Earth before dinosaurs.   **T**   **F**

2 Jellyfish are a type of fish.   **T**   **F**

3 Some jellyfish stings can kill a human.   **T**   **F**

4 Jellyfish have no hearts, blood, or brains.   **T**   **F**

5 A group of jellyfish can cover hundreds of square kilometers.   **T**   **F**

While You Watch

A   ▶6.2 **Watch the video.** Check your answers to the quiz above. Is any of the information surprising?

B   ▶6.2 **Watch again.** Circle the correct answers.

1 Another name for jellyfish is **sea jellies** / **jelly bells**.

2 The Australian box jellyfish is considered to be the **longest** / **most venomous** marine animal in the world.

3 Jellyfish are **60** / **95** percent water.

4 Groups of jellyfish—called **schools** / **blooms**—have been known to damage **ships** / **coral reefs**.

C   **Look at these possible impacts of jellyfish.** Are they positive or negative? Or could they be both? Write **P** (positive), **N** (negative), or **B** (both). Then compare with a partner and discuss reasons for your answers.

1 Jellyfish use up much of the oxygen that farmed fish require. _____

2 Jellyfish provide shelter for younger fish that live within their tentacles. _____

3 Jellyfish are an additional food source for certain communities. _____

4 Jellyfish discourage tourism because beachgoers avoid going into the water. _____

5 Large groups of jellyfish block the water pipes of seaside power plants. _____

■ **After You Watch**

Talk with a partner. Look back at all the marine animals you have learned about in this unit. Which animal do you find most interesting? Why?

Sea nettle jellyfish

A   **Complete the sentences.** Use the words in the box. Two words are extra.

feathers	flippers	shells	tails	tusks

1 Oysters, mussels, and snails all live inside _____ .

2 Cats, dogs, and mice all have _____ .

3 An elephant has two _____ , but a narwhal has just one.

B   **Rewrite these sentences.** Use *which* or *who*.

1 The sea otter lives along the Pacific coast. It uses rocks to break open shellfish.
   The sea otter, which uses rocks to break open shellfish, lives along the Pacific coast.

2 My teacher loves diving. She has a degree in oceanography.
   _____
   _____

3 Fur seals have large eyes. These allow them to see well underwater.
   _____
   _____

C   **Correct the error in each sentence.**
                                    about six
1 We spent six about weeks at the research center.

2 He's 40 years around old.

3 We saw or so 30 fish while snorkeling.

4 There nearly are 20 people in the queue.

■ **SELF CHECK**   Now I can ...

☐ talk about marine animals and their habitats

☐ add information about things and people

☐ discuss the importance of coral reefs

The **After You Watch** activities allow students to respond to the video by analyzing and personalizing what they've learned.

Self Check *I can* statements allow students to assess their own learning and help teachers evaluate learner confidence.

COMPONENTS OF THE SERIES

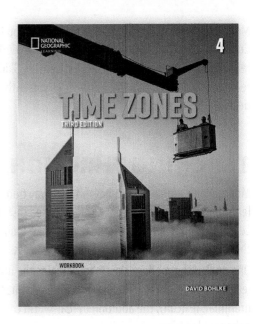

WORKBOOK

Reinforce Student's Book lessons with additional practice in the print Workbook. You may use the Workbook as additional class practice or set it as homework.

ONLINE PRACTICE & LEARNING MANAGEMENT PLATFORM

Keep students engaged with mobile-responsive Online Practice, including audio, video, and practice activities. Manage your classroom and track students' Online Practice progress.

STUDENT'S EBOOK

Access the Student's Book content digitally, with embedded audio and video.

CLASSROOM PRESENTATION TOOL

Enrich your classroom lessons with interactive Student's Book and Workbook pages with embedded audio, video, and interactive activities on the Classroom Presentation Tool.

EXAMVIEW® ASSESSMENT SUITE

Track learner progress with exam questions for every unit, plus mid-year and end-of-year tests.

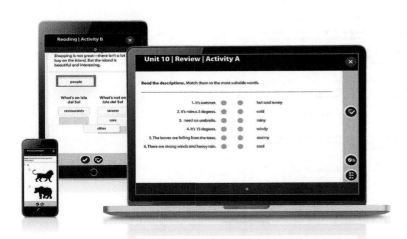

HOW TO TEACH *TIME ZONES*

More than ever before, students need to develop **C**ritical thinking, **C**reative thinking, the ability to **C**ommunicate with speakers from around the world, and the ability to work **C**ollaboratively. Often referred to as the **Four Cs**, these 21st Century Skills are essential for all students, and because of its real-world content, *Time Zones* provides you with amazing opportunities to help your students develop these skills.

TEACHING THROUGH CONTENT

Modern language teaching has moved away from discreet, non-contextual drills to context-based learning, utilizing ideas from Content-based Instruction (CBI) and Content and Language Integrated Learning (CLIL). In addition, the flipped classroom and active learning emphasize the importance of the student in the language acquisition process.

One goal of the modern classroom remains the utilization of class time and the maximization of learning, but there is an increased awareness that rather than only focusing on the language (e.g., grammar, lexicon), the addition of real-world content and subject matter via a foreign language enhances learning.

Although the primary aim of *Time Zones* is to introduce the student to English, the language is always contextualized so that the student develops an appreciation and understanding of topics which are essential in the 21st Century, including world cultures, the environment, health, history, science, and sociology.

A few ideas for utilizing the content include:

• Make full use of the National Geographic images to help students understand more about their world. Have students describe what they see in the photographs. Encourage them to make connections between the photographs and the content of the unit.

• Have students look up country or city names on a map to help develop their geographical awareness.

• Have students find out more about the content you are teaching them. This could be given as homework (e.g., find out one fact about a polar bear and share with the class the next week).

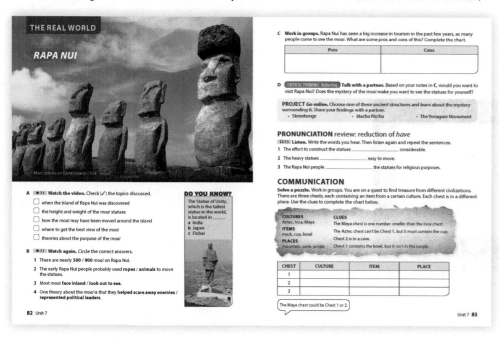

CONTENT TO DEVELOP GLOBAL CITIZENS

TIP

Encourage learners to think critically by comparing and contrasting content with their own cultures.

Teaching through content helps students see a real need or purpose for using the language. Furthermore, using topics or content that can stimulate the interest of the students can make learning the language a much more enjoyable experience. For example, imagine you prepare a lesson about "School." Your students can learn:

- about education around the world.
- country names (e.g., Indonesia, China, Colombia).
- about schools and children around the world.
- questions (e.g., *Where do you live? How do you travel to school?*).
- to share information about their own culture (e.g., *The school year starts in April.*).
- to talk about their own lives (e.g., *I travel to school by bus.*).

By becoming global students, your students will understand more about the world they inhabit. Global students will:

- develop a deeper understanding of the world as a whole.
- develop a deeper understanding, tolerance, and respect for other cultures.
- develop a deeper understanding and appreciation of their own culture within the context of a more global perspective.
- develop a greater understanding of the issues the world faces.
- think creatively about responding to global issues.
- develop the skills needed to function in an ever-increasing global society.
- realize a need for bilingualism or multilingualism and increase their motivation to study the target language.

TEACHING VOCABULARY

Successfully knowing a word requires a student to understand its meaning, its form, and its usage. In this respect, *Time Zones* provides students with the opportunity to encounter new words through incidental learning, repeated exposure to key vocabulary in different contexts, and by encouraging students to produce the vocabulary in communication activities.

Vocabulary is first introduced in the Preview tasks. It is expanded in the **Language Focus** and reinforced in the listening, **Reading**, **Vocabulary**, and **Video** activities.

Throughout each unit, students are given opportunities to practice using the words for themselves via both spoken and written activities. Some tips for vocabulary learning include:

• Have students keep a vocabulary notebook. Students write the word, the part of speech, a definition in English, and an example sentence using the word (e.g., *I like playing tennis.*).

• Review the vocabulary at the end of the unit. Give teams blank pieces of paper. Have them write words from the unit on each piece of paper. Put the pieces in a pile and shuffle. One student takes the first word, and then puts the paper on his or her forehead so the other group members can see the word but the student holding the paper cannot. Group members try to get the student to say the word by giving hints in English (e.g., *hobby*—"*My _____ is music. I like playing the guitar.*" "*Is the word* hobby?" "*Yes, that's correct.*"). Repeat with the next student until all the words have been guessed.

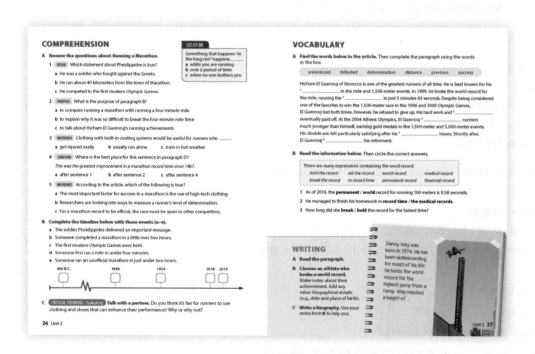

TEACHING GRAMMAR COMMUNICATIVELY

LANGUAGE FOCUS

A 🎧 9.2 **Listen and read.** What don't Nadine and Maya want to miss? Then repeat the conversation and replace the words in **bold**.

REAL ENGLISH Same here.

Nadine: I've been waiting **so long** to see this movie. **(forever / a long time)**

Maya: Same here. The poster looks great, doesn't it?

Nadine: Yeah, it does. You know, I really love the actors in this movie.

Maya: And I've heard the **costumes are gorgeous. (plot is really interesting / special effects are stunning)**

Nadine: Everyone says the opening scene is **spectacular. (amazing / incredible)**

Maya: So let's hurry! I don't want to miss it.

Nadine: Hey, what's this?

Maya: Oh, no! **We must be** in the wrong theater! **(I think we're / It looks like we're)**

B 🎧 9.3 **Look at the chart.** Then circle the correct answers below.

ASKING FOR CONFIRMATION OR INFORMATION (USING TAG QUESTIONS)	
Leonardo DiCaprio **is** a good actor, **isn't he**?	Yes, he is.
That TV show **was** amazing, **wasn't it**?	Yes, it was.
You **liked** the ending of the movie, **didn't you**?	Yeah, I did.
You **haven't** been to the new movie theater, **have you**?	No, I haven't.
Meryl Streep **will** star in a new TV series next year, **won't she**?	Actually, she won't.
You **can't** see that movie until you're 18, **can you**?	No, I can't.

1 We use tag questions when we expect the listener to **agree** / **disagree** with us.

2 When a statement is in the affirmative, the question tag is in the **affirmative** / **negative**.

3 When a statement is in the negative, the question tag is in the **affirmative** / **negative**.

104 Unit 9

C **Complete the tag questions.** Then ask and answer the questions with a partner.

1 Special effects make movies more exciting, _don't they_ ?

2 You didn't watch TV last night, _____?

3 You haven't seen every *Star Wars* movie, _____?

4 Most romantic comedies are really predictable, _____?

5 You don't like action movies very much, _____?

6 You're not a fan of superhero movies, _____?

D 🎧 9.4 **Complete the conversation.** Write appropriate tag forms and answers. Then listen and check.

Sam: Do you like the actress Scarlett Johansson?

Kylie: She was in the *Avengers* movies, ¹ _____?

Sam: Yes, ² _____. She played Black Widow.

Kylie: Yeah, I think she's really talented. By the way, I'm taking my nephew out for a movie tomorrow. Do you have any suggestions?

Sam: Hmm … He likes animated movies, ³ _____?

Kylie: Yeah, ⁴ _____. What do you have in mind?

Sam: How about the latest *Lego* movie? He hasn't seen that yet, ⁵ _____?

Kylie: I don't think so. Maybe we'll watch that. Thanks for the suggestion.

E **Work in groups.** Talk about the topics below. Ask follow-up questions.

favorite actors/actresses   action movies   movie soundtracks   animated movies
science fiction movies   favorite books   new TV shows   pop music

You like action movies, don't you?

Of course!

Have you seen the new Keanu Reeves movie?

Unit 9 105

Conversation

Communicative activity

Language chart

One of the important goals of the 21st Century English language classroom is to develop each student's communicative competence. This can be facilitated by:

• getting students to communicate with one another in the target language.

• providing active, meaningful tasks—tasks in which students need to use the target language.

• using content and language that is important and meaningful to the students.

• allowing students to make errors, particularly when working on activities to increase fluid speaking.

The aim of teaching grammar is therefore to equip students with the skills to communicate with the target language in a meaningful way.

In *Time Zones*, grammar is introduced in the **Language Focus** section of each unit. First, the grammar is contextualized within a **conversation**, making it meaningful for students. Next, they focus on form. Students are then guided through the structures in several controlled activities until they communicate with one another in a final free **communicative activity**.

Tips for increasing communicative grammar teaching include:

• Have students personalize the language to make it more meaningful.

• Have students think of other contexts in which they can use the language (e.g., *How often do you go to school? What do you do on weekends?*).

• Think of interesting ways to get students to use the language (e.g., talking about a friend's hobbies and interests; comparing their interests with a partner's).

TEACHING WATCHING AND LISTENING COMMUNICATIVELY

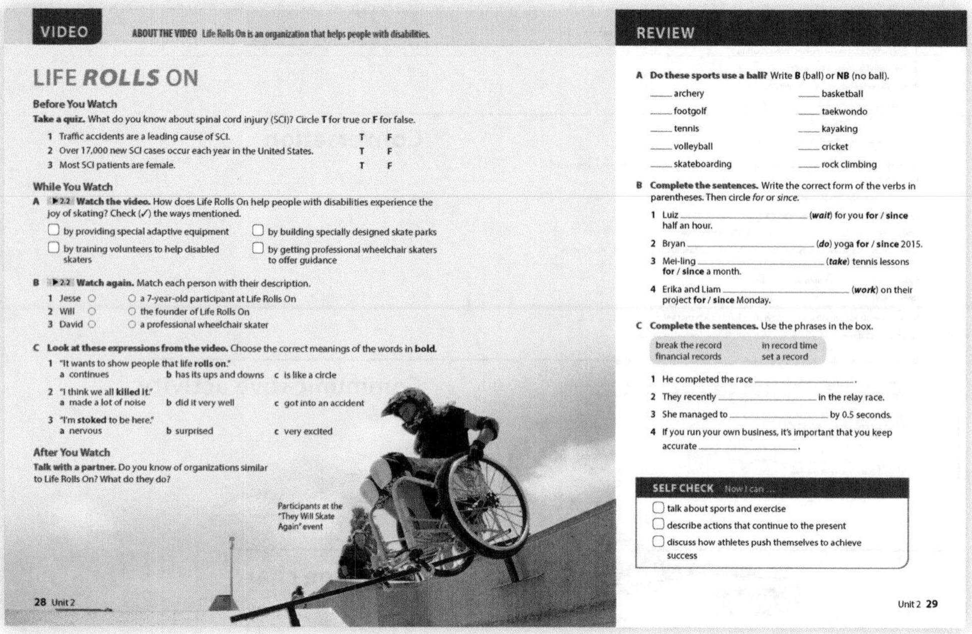
VIDEO ABOUT THE VIDEO Life Rolls On is an organization that helps people with disabilities.

LIFE ***ROLLS*** ON

Before You Watch

Take a quiz. What do you know about spinal cord injury (SCI)? Circle **T** for true or **F** for false.

1 Traffic accidents are a leading cause of SCI. T F
2 Over 17,000 new SCI cases occur each year in the United States. T F
3 Most SCI patients are female. T F

While You Watch

A ▶2.2 **Watch the video.** How does Life Rolls On help people with disabilities experience the joy of skating? Check (✓) the ways mentioned.

☐ by providing special adaptive equipment
☐ by building specially designed skate parks
☐ by training volunteers to help disabled skaters
☐ by getting professional wheelchair skaters to offer guidance

B ▶2.2 **Watch again.** Match each person with their description.

1 Jesse ○ ○ a 7-year-old participant at Life Rolls On
2 Will ○ ○ the founder of Life Rolls On
3 David ○ ○ a professional wheelchair skater

C **Look at these expressions from the video.** Choose the correct meanings of the words in **bold**.

1 "It wants to show people that life **rolls on**."
a continues b has its ups and downs c is like a circle
2 "I think we all **killed it**."
a made a lot of noise b did it very well c got into an accident
3 "I'm **stoked** to be here."
a nervous b surprised c very excited

After You Watch

Talk with a partner. Do you know of organizations similar to Life Rolls On? What do they do?

Participants at the "They Will Skate Again" event

28 Unit 2

REVIEW

A **Do these sports use a ball?** Write **B** (ball) or **NB** (no ball).

____ archery ____ basketball
____ footgolf ____ taekwondo
____ tennis ____ kayaking
____ volleyball ____ cricket
____ skateboarding ____ rock climbing

B **Complete the sentences.** Write the correct form of the verbs in parentheses. Then circle *for* or *since*.

1 Luiz ________ (***wait***) for you **for / since** half an hour.
2 Bryan ________ (***do***) yoga **for / since** 2015.
3 Mei-ling ________ (***take***) tennis lessons **for / since** a month.
4 Erika and Liam ________ (***work***) on their project **for / since** Monday.

C **Complete the sentences.** Use the phrases in the box.

break the record | in record time | financial records | set a record

1 He completed the race ________.
2 They recently ________ in the relay race.
3 She managed to ________ by 0.5 seconds.
4 If you run your own business, it's important that you keep accurate ________.

SELF CHECK Now I can ...
☐ talk about sports and exercise
☐ describe actions that continue to the present
☐ discuss how athletes push themselves to achieve success

Unit 2 29

VIDEO

Video can add a new and exciting dimension to classroom learning. There are many advantages to video. First, students can be exposed to a range of authentic content and encounter the target language in a natural context. Second, students are aided in their comprehension of the content with the use of visual cues as well as audio ones. In addition, video can accommodate students with different learning styles—both visual and auditory. Fourth, students' lives, including their free time, are filled with video. Video is part of their world, and it is a part of an authentic, motivating classroom. Finally, it is essential for 21st Century learners to understand and analyze various types of media, including video.

Both listening and watching are, by their nature, receptive skills, and many students benefit from a receptive period and working alone before being asked to communicate. Here are some ideas you can use to expand the video activities in *Time Zones* and make them more communicative:

- Have students look at the photo and predict what the video is about.
- Tell students to describe the photo in as much detail as possible.
- Ask students questions that activate their schemata so they think about the topic they will listen to.
- Have your students make and ask each other questions. You could provide a word list and have students make questions using specific words that will appear in the video (e.g., *fruits—What fruits do you like? What fruits don't you like?*).
- Encourage students to enjoy the video.
- The first time you play the video, allow students to watch it without doing a task. Have students watch and share what they saw with a partner.
- Have students check their answers with a partner after each task.
- Expand activities and games. For example, in Student's Book 1, Unit 4, students learn vocabulary for describing their extended family. Have students describe their own families to one another and have partners draw the other person's family tree.

USING VIDEO IN THE CLASSROOM

ADDITIONAL IDEAS FOR USING VIDEO IN THE CLASSROOM

BEFORE THE LESSON

Watch the video yourself. Make a note of language you feel may be difficult for your learners. Prepare activities to pre-teach the language.

BEFORE STUDENTS WATCH

Pre-teach any difficult language. For example, give students a handout where they match target words to definitions. Another idea is to make a list of questions that contain the target words for students to ask one another (e.g., *Have you ever been bird watching?*).

Have students predict the content of the video they are going to watch. For example, show students pictures that are related to the video and have students guess what the topic is.

Activate students' schemata and background knowledge of the topic of the video by discussing the photo and predicting the content (e.g., *I think the video is about people selling clothes.*).

WHILE STUDENTS WATCH

Preview the video without doing any Student's Book activities. Have students get into pairs. Play the video without sound. Have Student A watch the first half of the video while Student B turns his/her back. Student A should explain what he/she is seeing. Have students swap roles halfway through the video.

AFTER STUDENTS WATCH

Have students retell what they saw and heard in the video.

Have students make a dialog about the content.

TIP

Encourage learners to think critically by doing role-plays based on the video.

MAKING READING MORE COMMUNICATIVE

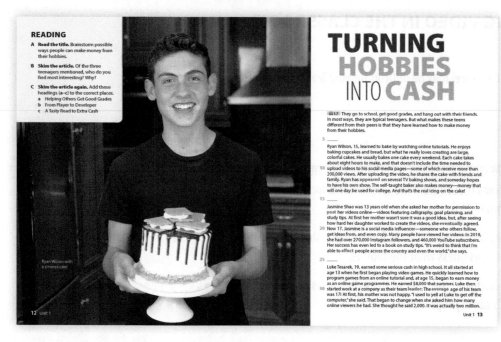

Although reading is a receptive skill, it is very useful as a springboard to discussion in the communicative classroom. Here are some ideas you can use to get students communicating:

- Activate students' schemata by writing the title of the reading on the board. Have students predict what they will read about.

- Have students discuss what they see in the photograph (e.g., *a boy holding a cake*).

- Photocopy the article and cut it into separate paragraphs. Before students study the passage, have students get into groups. Have each member read one of the paragraphs silently. Then have students explain the paragraph they have read to their group.

- Photocopy the article (or part of it) and cut it into separate sentences. After students have studied the passage, have students get into groups. Have each member take turns reading a sentence. Students then have to put the sentences in the correct order.

- Make the comprehension questions a race between groups. Elect one member of the group as the writer and give him/her a piece of chalk. Group members shout out the answers to their writer, who writes the answers on the board. The first team with all answers correct is the winner.

- The Critical Thinking task aims to get students talking about what they have read. Encourage students to give reasons for their answers.

GETTING STUDENTS TO COMMUNICATE

Students can be shy, reticent, afraid of making mistakes, fearful of appearing foolish in front of their classmates, and unwilling to take risks. As a result, students can be reluctant to produce the language and try to speak English in the classroom. The following are suggestions that may help you avoid too much teacher-talk and student silence:

• Create a classroom environment in which students feel safe and willing to take risks.

• Treat errors as a natural part of the learning process.

• Try to provide individual correction privately. In class, focus your discussion on mistakes that many students have been making, without singling out any students.

• When students are developing fluency, don't correct mistakes.

• Bring the students' own personal experiences into the tasks whenever possible.

• Incorporate movement into the classroom. Moving around can help students stay focused, engaged, and alert.

• Use the classroom space in innovative ways. Get your students to stand facing each other in a line. Have them do the speaking task and then physically move to the next person. Have them repeat the speaking task with a new partner (e.g., *What's your favorite hobby?*). Swap partners again and continue the activity.

• Regularly assign students different partners. This reduces complacency, increases social interaction, and develops flexibility to deal with various speakers.

• Encourage friendly competition among groups (e.g., *Which group can keep the conversation going the longest? Which group is the first to get survey answers from 10 different students?*).

GETTING STUDENTS TO WRITE

Each unit of *Time Zones* has one short writing task that encourages students to reproduce the key language they have learned through a piece of writing. This helps develop students' communicative competence as they need to remember the vocabulary, spelling, and language structures while at the same time developing writing techniques such as cohesion, coherence, and paragraph structure. The writing task also gives students the opportunity to personalize the language, making it more meaningful to them. Some tips include:

- Develop students' critical thinking as they deduce the type of information needed. For example, if students must write a short email describing their hobbies, have students study the example and decide what kind of information should be included (e.g., a greeting, their hobbies, a closing remark).

- Have students write a first draft with their textbooks closed. Then have students open their textbooks, look at the model writing as a guide, and write a second draft.

- Have students work with a partner, exchange first drafts, and read them. Have students write a comment under the partner's writing (e.g., *Wow! You play piano every morning? That's amazing!*).

- Have students read their first drafts to a partner or group of students. Encourage students to ask questions to clarify anything they did not understand. Have students write their second drafts while considering this feedback.

- Have students get into groups and share their writing. Then have a quiz about the group's writing (e.g., *What is Takashi's hobby? He likes playing the guitar.*).

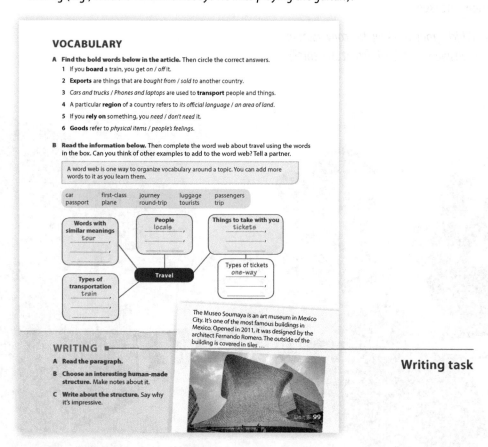

Writing task

GOING BEYOND THE CLASSROOM

Homework is a great way to get students to think about what they have learned in class, to review lessons, and to practice the language outside of the classroom. This gives students more time for actually using the language.

As an example, let's take examples from Unit 1 in *Time Zones* Student's Book 4, I Love Mixing Music!

- Students could write new words they have learned from the unit in their vocabulary notebook.
- Students could practice the Language Focus conversations at home, with friends, in front of a mirror, or in front of their pet dog!
- Students could do research about popular hobbies in other countries.
- Students could do a survey about favorite hobbies with friends from other classes.
- Students could write a short paragraph to describe a family member's or friend's hobby.
- Students could watch the unit video again, make some quiz questions, and test the class by asking them in the next lesson.
- Students can do activities from the Workbook.

> **TIP**
>
> Encourage students to think critically by offering them a choice of homework tasks (e.g., a piece of writing, internet research, or video task).

I LOVE MIXING MUSIC!

CONTENT AREA:
PEOPLE AND PLACES

Topic: hobbies and interests

Vocabulary: hobbies and activities: drawing, gardening, cooking, Instagramming, mixing music, dancing, reviewing videos, making videos, reading comic books and fantasy novels, doing jigsaw puzzles; **other words:** not very good at, don't really like, pretty bad at, enjoy, like, love, appear, post, eventually, affect, leader, average

Grammar: verb + -ing

Extra material: photos of different board games

Other useful vocabulary:
hobbies: surfing, photography, fishing, skateboarding, writing a blog, building models, collecting comic books; **activities:** shopping, going out to eat, going to the beach, going to the movies, going to school events

END OF UNIT PROJECT Have students work in groups to write a business plan for a hobby that can be turned into a business.

If necessary, remind students that in the **READING** section they learned about three teenagers who are making money off their hobbies. Tell students to use these three teenagers and their business ideas as inspiration.

Ask students to work in groups of three to make a plan for a business based on one of their hobbies.

1
I LOVE MIXING MUSIC!

PREVIEW

A 🎧 **1.1 Listen.** Circle each person's hobby.

		Hobby	When
1	Sun-hee	⟨drawing⟩/ gardening	on Sunday afternoons
	Andy	cooking /⟨Instagramming⟩	after school
2	Eric	⟨mixing music⟩/ dancing	on weekends
6	Megan	reviewing videos /⟨making videos⟩	on Saturday mornings

Tell students that groups will present their business ideas to the class. Explain that the class is a group of investors who are going to decide which business idea to give funding to. Tell students to include the following details in their business plans:

- a description of what the hobby is
- an explanation of how the hobby can be turned into cash
- a description of the market who will use the service or buy the item(s) being sold
- reasons why the business will be successful

Tell groups to brainstorm, discuss, and take notes together. Ask them to use visuals in their presentation, such as pictures, posters, or graphic organizers, when explaining their business idea.

After all the groups have completed their presentations, have the class take a secret vote by writing their favorite business idea on a piece of paper. Collect the votes and tally them. Announce the winning business idea.

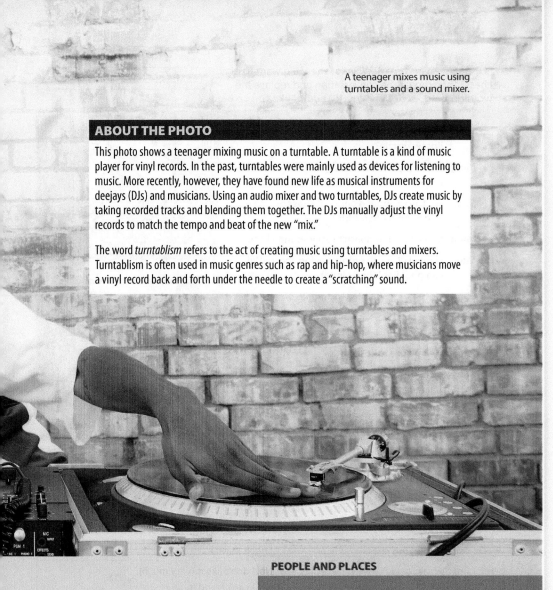

A teenager mixes music using turntables and a sound mixer.

ABOUT THE PHOTO

This photo shows a teenager mixing music on a turntable. A turntable is a kind of music player for vinyl records. In the past, turntables were mainly used as devices for listening to music. More recently, however, they have found new life as musical instruments for deejays (DJs) and musicians. Using an audio mixer and two turntables, DJs create music by taking recorded tracks and blending them together. The DJs manually adjust the vinyl records to match the tempo and beat of the new "mix."

The word *turntablism* refers to the act of creating music using turntables and mixers. Turntablism is often used in music genres such as rap and hip-hop, where musicians move a vinyl record back and forth under the needle to create a "scratching" sound.

B 🎧 1.1 **Listen again.** When does each person do their hobby? Fill in the **When** column in **A**.

C **Talk with a partner.** What are your hobbies? Ask follow-up questions.
Answers will vary.

PEOPLE AND PLACES

UNIT GOALS

- describe your hobbies and interests
- use language for talking about things people like doing
- learn about teenagers who are making money from their hobbies

7

A Tell students that they will hear two conversations. Explain that they should listen and circle each person's hobby.

🎧 1.1 Play Audio Track 1.1. Tell students they can confirm their answers as they listen to the audio again in **B**.

B Tell students they will listen to the conversations again and they should write when each person does their hobby in the *When* column in **A**.

🎧 1.1 Play Audio Track 1.1. Play it again, if necessary.

Check answers for **A** and **B**.

OPTIONAL Encourage students to connect what they heard in the conversations to their own lives. Ask students if any of them enjoy any of the same hobbies as the speakers.

CHALLENGE Have the class brainstorm a list of other hobbies they know. (See **Other useful vocabulary**.)

C Tell students they are going to get into pairs and take turns asking and answering questions about each other's hobbies. Encourage students to learn more about their classmates.

Have students do the task.

CHALLENGE Have students ask at least three questions about their partner's hobby. Have students then take turns introducing their partner's hobby to the class.

UNIT GOALS

Direct students' attention to the **UNIT GOALS** box. Explain that these are some of the things students will learn in this unit. Point out that this unit is about people and places. As students follow along, read each of the unit goals to the class. Explain any words students do not know. Remind students that at the end of the unit there is a self check that allows them to see if they have accomplished each goal.

TEACHING NOTE: EXPECTATIONS IN CLASS

During the first few weeks of class, tell your students about your expectations for the class. For example:
- Ask students to take notes and be active learners.
- Encourage them to speak in English.
- Remind students to not text during class.

- If you do not allow students to use their phones in class (e.g., to search for words and information), tell them to put their cell phones and other devices away so they will not get distracted.

PREVIEW

Have students read the unit title and the photo caption to themselves as you read it aloud. Explain that in this unit they will learn to talk about their hobbies and interests, and things people like doing.

LANGUAGE FOCUS

A Tell students they will listen to a conversation between Stig and Ming.

1.2 Play Audio Track 1.2 as students listen and follow along in their books.

As students follow along, read the question, *Why doesn't Ming want to play chess?* Have students answer.

Have students work in pairs and practice the conversation once. Point out the bold words. Tell students to practice the conversation two more times, changing the bold words each time and swapping roles after the first time.

OPTIONAL Have students name some other board games, for example, checkers, Clue, LIFE, Othello, or Go. If you brought photos of different board games, show them to the students. Tell them what each game is and have them guess how it is played.

The earliest version of chess began in India around the sixth century. In the game, two players move pieces of different colors, often black and white, on a checkered board with 64 light and dark squares. The goal is to get the other player's most important piece, the king, into a position where it cannot avoid being captured.

The board game Monopoly was first sold by the American company Parker Brothers in 1935. The game involves buying, selling, and developing property in an effort to bankrupt other players until only one player remains.

Scrabble is a board game in which players make words using square-shaped tiles with letters on them, and get points based on the difficulty and placement of their words on the board. The game continues until all the tiles are used, and then the player with the highest score wins.

LANGUAGE FOCUS

A **1.2** **Listen and read.** Why doesn't Ming want to play chess? Then repeat the conversation and replace the words in **bold**. *It doesn't really sound like fun to him.*

> **REAL ENGLISH** Tell me about it!

Stig:	It's so hot today. Do you feel like doing a jigsaw puzzle?
Ming:	Not really. **I'm not very good at** puzzles. (**I don't really like / I'm pretty bad at**)
Stig:	Well, how about a game of **chess**? (**Monopoly / Scrabble**)
Ming:	Sorry, but that doesn't really sound like fun.
Stig:	I know! We both **enjoy** playing sports. We can go skiing! (**like / love**)
Ming:	I love skiing! But it's the middle of summer.
Stig:	Give me just a second …
Ming:	Skiing **sure takes a lot of energy**! (**is so exhausting / is such good exercise**)
Stig:	Tell me about it! Is it time for a break yet?

B **1.3** **Look at the chart.** Then circle the correct answers below.

TALKING ABOUT HOBBIES AND INTERESTS (USING VERB + *-ING*)	
What are your hobbies? What do you **like doing** in your free time?	I **love reading** comic books and fantasy novels. I **enjoy doing** jigsaw puzzles.
Do you **like playing** chess?	Yes, I love it! Yes, I like it (a lot). ☺
	I don't mind it. 😐
	No, I don't like it (very much). No, I can't stand it. ☹
Skiing is such good exercise!	**Gardening** is kind of boring.

1 After *enjoy*, we use *to + base verb* / **base verb + *-ing***
2 Base verb + *-ing* at the beginning of a sentence acts as a **noun** / verb.
3 If you hate doing something, you say *I don't mind it* / **I can't stand it**

REAL ENGLISH

Direct students' attention to the expression in the **REAL ENGLISH** box. Explain that *Tell me about it!* is a casual and friendly way to say that you agree with something that has been said. Explain that the speaker is not really asking the listener to tell them about anything. Instead, it means the opposite: nothing more needs to be added because we are both already in agreement. For example:

A: That test was so hard. I don't think I'll pass.

B: Tell me about it! I didn't even finish.

B Ask students to look at the chart. Explain that they will study how to talk about hobbies and interests using verb + *-ing*.

1.3 Have students follow along as they listen to Audio Track 1.3.

As students follow along in their books, read the first two questions and the responses aloud. Point out that the responses talk about liking an activity and have nothing to do with being good at the activity. Explain that *love* is stronger than *like*, and that *enjoy* and *like*

C 🎧1.4 **Complete the conversation.** Use the correct form of the verbs in the box. Then listen and check your answers.

dance	hike	play	sing	stay	watch

Kara: Hey, Paulo. Have you signed up for any after-school activities yet?

Paulo: No, not yet. I love ¹ __singing__ , so I might join the musical theater club.

Kara: That would be fun! You have a great voice.

Paulo: Thanks. The problem is I don't like ² __dancing__ very much. I find it hard to remember all the steps. Hey! Maybe you should try out too. You enjoy ³ __playing__ the guitar.

Kara: Me? No way! Performing in front of people makes me nervous.

Paulo: Well, there's the Classic Film Club.

Kara: I don't really like ⁴ __watching__ old movies. Plus, ⁵ __staying__ inside even longer after school doesn't sound like fun!

Paulo: So why don't you join an outdoors club? Do you like ⁶ __hiking__ ?

Kara: That's a great idea! I love the outdoors.

D 🎧1.5 **Listen to the conversation.** What does each person think of these activities? Write 😊, 😐, or 😦.

	baking	playing tennis	singing	playing video games
Lucia	😊	😐	😊	😦
Wes	😦	😊	😦	😊

E **Talk with a partner.** Look at the activities below. Do you like doing them? Why or why not?

singing	baking	drawing	playing video games	watching TV
gardening	reading	dancing	listening to music	doing puzzles

Answers will vary.

> I like singing a lot. I've always been good at it.

> I like singing too. I also enjoy …

Unit 1 **9**

C Have students complete the conversation using the correct form of the verbs in the box. Tell students they will listen and check their answers.

🎧1.4 Play Audio Track 1.4. Play it again, if necessary. Check answers.

OPTIONAL Have students get into pairs and practice the conversation twice, swapping roles after the first time.

D Tell students they will listen to a conversation and they should write the correct symbol to match how each speaker feels about each activity.

🎧1.5 Play Audio Track 1.5. Play it again, if necessary. Check answers as a class.

E Tell students they are going to work in pairs to talk about the activities in the box. Call on a few students to read the activities aloud.

Model the conversation with a student.

Tell students they should say what's true for them, and that it is OK to have different opinions than their classmates.

Have students do the task.

TEACHING NOTE: MAKING PAIRS

At the beginning of the school year, before students in your class know each other well, it can be helpful to use short games for making random pairs. One idea is to have a deck of cards with sets of matching pairs. Shuffle and hand out one card to each student. Then have them circulate to find the student with the matching card who will be their partner.

---

are similar. Have students make a rule about how to form sentences using these words, providing the answer if necessary. (After the word, they should use the *-ing* form of the verb.)

Read the third question and the responses aloud. Point out to students that the responses have been put in order from *like the most* to *like the least* (*love, like, don't mind, don't like, can't stand*).

Read the two sentences at the bottom of the chart aloud. Point out the subject of each sentence (*Skiing, Gardening*). Remind students that the subject of a sentence is always a noun or a pronoun. Tell students that a base verb + *-ing* at the beginning of a sentence acts as a noun.

Draw students' attention to the three statements under the chart. Have students circle the correct answers. Check answers.

THE REAL WORLD

Ask students to look at the photo. Have a student read the title and the photo caption aloud.

A Tell students they will make predictions about four activities before watching a video about how American teenagers spend their time. Have students mark their predictions for each activity using ↑ or ↓.

B Tell students they will watch the first part of the video and they should check their predictions in **A**.

▶ 1.1 Play Video 1.1. Play it again, if necessary.

Ask students to share any surprising information they heard in the video and give reasons why they found the information surprising.

C Tell students they will watch the second part of the video and they should complete the pie chart by writing the letters that represent the activities in the correct boxes. Have students read the question and activities (**a–d**) silently. Then give them a moment to look at the pie chart and read the note beside it.

▶ 1.2 Play Video 1.2. Play it again, if necessary.

Check answers.

OPTIONAL Have students compare the daily activities of American teenagers to teenagers in their own countries. Ask, *Are the activities mostly the same? If not, which ones are different?*

D CRITICAL THINKING

Read the two questions aloud. Have students get into pairs and discuss their ideas. Tell pairs to come up with at least three activities that they think will be popular with teenagers in 10 years.

THE REAL WORLD

ABOUT THE PHOTO

This photo shows a group of teens using their cell phones. The rapid advancement in communications technology has resulted in many teens spending more and more time in front of a screen—for both school and leisure activities. According to a 2019 study on media use by tweens and teens in the U.S., American teens spend an average of seven hours a day on screen media for entertainment purposes. One popular activity is viewing content on online platforms such as YouTube. Smartphone ownership has increased as well, with almost 70 percent of kids owning a smartphone by age 12.

A group of teens hang out and use their cell phones.

A **Predict.** Do you think American teenagers today spend more time (↑) or less time (↓) on these activities compared to teens 10 years ago?

____ doing homework ____ sleeping ____ socializing face-to-face ____ working for pay

B ▶ 1.1 **Watch Part 1 of the video.** Check your predictions in **A**. Is any of the information surprising?

C ▶ 1.2 **Watch Part 2 of the video.** How does a typical American teenager spend their day? Complete the pie chart with these activities (**a–d**).

a face-to-face socializing
b unpaid work
c online leisure activities
d offline leisure activities

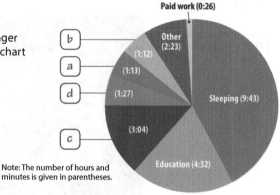

Paid work (0:26)
Other (2:23)
b (1:12)
a (1:13)
d (1:27)
Sleeping (9:43)
(3:04)
c
Education (4:32)

Note: The number of hours and minutes is given in parentheses.

10 Unit 1

Remind them that they should give reasons for their predictions.

PROJECT As students follow along, read the project instructions aloud. Give students time to write out their individual schedules before creating their pie charts.

You might want to assign the pie chart as homework.

In class, have students take turns introducing their daily schedules, using their pie charts as visual aids.

PRONUNCIATION

Tell students they will practice intonation patterns for questions.

Explain that when we ask questions, we often use an upward intonation at the end of the question, but sometimes we use a downward intonation instead.

Tell students that they will hear four questions and they should mark each question with the intonation pattern they hear.

🔊 1.6 Play Audio Track 1.6. Play it again, if necessary.

D CRITICAL THINKING Predicting **Talk with a partner.** How do you think teenagers 10 years from now will spend their time? What do you think they will do more or less of? Give reasons for your predictions. Answers will vary.

> **PROJECT Create a pie chart.** How do you spend a typical 24 hours? Note the number of hours and minutes you spend on each activity.

PRONUNCIATION question intonation

🎧 1.6 **Listen.** Mark each question with the intonation pattern ↗ or ↘. Then listen again and repeat the questions.

1 Do you like hiking?

2 Do you enjoy doing jigsaw puzzles?

3 Do you prefer playing board games or video games?

4 What sport do you like playing?

> **DO YOU KNOW?**
>
> People in _____ spend the most amount of time on leisure activities.
> a the United States
> b Spain
> c New Zealand

COMMUNICATION

A Look at the chart below. Complete the sentences with information that is true for you. Then interview a classmate. Write their name and responses. Answers will vary.

	Name: _____
I like watching _____ movies.	
I enjoy hanging out at _____.	
I don't mind spending time _____.	
I don't like playing _____.	
I enjoy listening to _____ music.	
I love _____ on weekends.	

Do you like watching horror movies?

No, I don't. I prefer watching sci-fi movies.

Where do you enjoy hanging out?

B Work in groups. Tell your group members the answers in your chart. Answers will vary.

Check answers. Explain to students that questions beginning with words like *Who, What, Where, Why,* and *When* use falling intonation.

🎧 1.6 Play the audio again, pausing after each question so students can repeat.

OPTIONAL Have students get into pairs and take turns asking and answering the questions. Tell them to focus on their intonation when asking the questions. Ask the other partner to answer with information that is true for them.

DO YOU KNOW?

Read the sentence and answer choices aloud, as students follow along in their books. Have students guess the answer before providing it (b).

CONTENT NOTE: LEISURE TIME

According to a study done by the Organization for Economic Co-operation and Development (OECD), an intergovernmental organization based in Paris, people in Spain spend an average of 316 minutes a day on leisure activities that include sunbathing at the beach and visiting historical sites.

In comparison, people in the United States spend an average of 283 minutes a day on leisure activities, while those in New Zealand spend an average of 301 minutes a day on leisure activities.

COMMUNICATION

A Direct students' attention to the chart. Tell students that they should complete each sentence in the first column with information that is true for them.

After they have completed the sentences, explain that they will interview a classmate. Point out that they should write the classmate's name at the top of the column on the right.

Model the conversation with a student.

Explain that each sentence should be turned into a question. Point out that students can ask either a *Do you …* question or a question starting with *What/ Where/When*.

Have them do the task. Walk around the classroom, providing assistance as necessary.

SUPPORT Before doing the activity, have students turn the sentences in the chart into questions. Write them on the board.

B Tell students that they are going to get into groups and share the answers in their chart. Have students get into groups and take turns sharing their answers.

Walk around the classroom as students share about themselves and their classmates. Comment on any interesting information you hear. To help your class get to know you better, share any information that is also true for you.

READING

Ask a student to read the title aloud. Have students guess what it means to *turn something into cash* (make money from it).

A Ask students to brainstorm ways people can make money from their hobbies. Randomly call on students to share their ideas. Write the ideas on the board.

B Tell students that they should skim the article and answer the questions. If necessary, review what skimming is. (See **TEACHING NOTE**.)

Have students do the task.

Then have students get into pairs and compare answers.

TEACHING NOTE: SKIMMING

Skimming is a reading technique. It is not the same as reading because you read more quickly than in regular reading. You do not read every word. You look for key words to get the main idea(s) of the text. You can also use skimming to decide if you want to read the text more closely. Skimming is not searching for specific information.

Hints for skimming:
1 Read the title.
2 Look at the photos.
3 Read the headings and notice how the text is arranged.
4 In longer texts, read the first and last sentences of each paragraph.
5 Try to notice key words.

C Tell students they will skim the article again and write the letters representing the headings in the correct places.

As students follow along, read the headings (**a–c**) aloud. If necessary, remind students that headings are like road signs, dividing a text into smaller sections, making it easier for the reader to understand the important ideas.

READING

A **Read the title.** Brainstorm possible ways people can make money from their hobbies. Answers will vary.

B **Skim the article.** Of the three teenagers mentioned, who do you find most interesting? Why?
    Answers will vary.

C **Skim the article again.** Add these headings (**a–c**) to the correct places.
   a Helping Others Get Good Grades
   b From Player to Developer
   c A Tasty Road to Extra Cash

ABOUT THE PHOTO

This photo shows Ryan Wilson, a teenager from San Francisco. He is a self-taught baker with his own YouTube channel—Baking with Ryan. Since 2013, Ryan has been uploading baking videos to his YouTube channel, which has more than 40,000 subscribers. In each video, he demonstrates how to bake and decorate a particular cake. Ryan's cakes are colorful and creative. He makes all kinds of cakes, such as animal-themed cakes, and cakes with chocolate and candy. Some of his popular cake creations include Oreo Cake, Cereal Cake, and Rainbow Rosette Cake. Ryan also shares his recipes on his website (www.bakingwithryan.com).

Ryan Wilson with a s'mores cake

12 Unit 1

Explain that headings are titles for the sections of a text and they help us understand how a text is organized and what is coming next.

After completing the task, give students the opportunity to read the article in more detail so they can answer the **COMPREHENSION** questions.

OPTIONAL The text can also be used as a listening activity. Have students close their books. Tell students they will listen to the passage.

🔊 1.7 Play Audio Track 1.7. Ask students to get into pairs and discuss what information they heard. Then have them read the article more carefully.

TURNING HOBBIES INTO CASH

🎧 **1.7** They go to school, get good grades, and hang out with their friends. In most ways, they are typical teenagers. But what makes these teens different from their peers is that they have learned how to make money from their hobbies.

5 _c_

Ryan Wilson, 15, learned to bake by watching online tutorials. He enjoys baking cupcakes and bread, but what he really loves creating are large, colorful cakes. He usually bakes one cake every weekend. Each cake takes about eight hours to make, and that doesn't include the time needed to
10 upload videos to his social media pages—some of which receive more than 200,000 views. After uploading the video, he shares the cake with friends and family. Ryan has **appeared** on several TV baking shows, and someday hopes to have his own show. The self-taught baker also makes money—money that will one day be used for college. And that's the real icing on the cake!

15 _a_

Jasmine Shao was 13 years old when she asked her mother for permission to **post** her videos online—videos featuring calligraphy, goal planning, and study tips. At first her mother wasn't sure it was a good idea, but, after seeing how hard her daughter worked to create the videos, she **eventually** agreed.
20 Now 17, Jasmine is a social media influencer—someone who others follow, get ideas from, and even copy. Many people have viewed her videos: In 2019, she had over 270,000 Instagram followers, and 460,000 YouTube subscribers. Her success has even led to a book on study tips. "It's weird to think that I'm able to **affect** people across the country and even the world," she says.

25 _b_

Luke Tesarek, 19, earned some serious cash in high school. It all started at age 13 when he first began playing video games. He quickly learned how to program games from an online tutorial and, at age 15, began to earn money as an online game programmer. He earned $8,000 that summer. Luke then
30 started work at a company as their team **leader**: The **average** age of his team was 17! At first, his mother was not happy. "I used to yell at Luke to get off the computer," she said. That began to change when she asked him how many online viewers he had. She thought he said 2,000. It was actually two million.

Unit 1 **13**

Additional Activities to Use with the Reading

Additional Comprehension Questions—True/False Questions

1 Each of the individuals featured in the passage started making money online as a teenager. (True.)

2 Ryan Wilson learned how to bake cakes from his grandmother. (False. He learned by watching online tutorials.)

3 Ryan sells his cakes after he makes them. (False. He shares them with friends and family.)

4 A *social media influencer* is someone who posts often online, has a lot of followers, and often affects other people's choices. (True.)

5 Jasmine Shao's book is about how to do calligraphy. (False. It's about study tips.)

6 Luke Tesarek earned $8,000 in one year when he was a teenager. (False. He did it in one summer.)

7 Luke has two million online viewers. (True.)

Discussion and Making Predictions

Have a class discussion about the three individuals in the article. Ask students to share which individual they think is the most interesting. Ask them to support their opinions with reasons.

Continue the class discussion by asking students to predict what each of the teenagers will choose to do after high school. Ask, *Will they go to college? Will they continue their businesses? Will they go to work for a company related to their hobbies?*

Developing Fluency

If necessary, explain shadowing to students. (See **TEACHING NOTE**.) Have students listen to the passage to confirm pronunciation.

🎧 **1.7** Play Audio Track 1.7.

Tell students they will listen again and they should pay attention to the delivery, including pausing and emotion.

🎧 **1.7** Play Audio Track 1.7. Play it again, as necessary, until students feel comfortable attempting to shadow it.

Emphasize that they may not be able to mimic the audio perfectly but they are developing fluency through the activity.

🎧 **1.7** Play Audio Track 1.7, having students practice shadowing.

TEACHING NOTE: SHADOWING

Shadowing is a technique that helps students practice their pronunciation, rhythm, and intonation. With shadowing, students listen to a passage at least once. Students then listen and try to simultaneously mimic (repeat) what they are hearing. They usually look at the script while doing this.

COMPREHENSION

A EXAM PRACTICE

Multiple-choice items can be either questions, or statements with a blank. There are various kinds of multiple-choice questions.

A **cohesion** question asks students to add a new sentence somewhere in the passage. These are also sometimes called **sentence insertion** questions. Students must recognize where in a paragraph or passage the sentence will fit best. Students must consider the order and flow of ideas in the paragraph to decide where the new sentence fits logically and smoothly. Students should:

- recognize connections between sentences.
- use trial and error by trying the new sentence after each sentence suggested in the answer choices to see where it fits best.
- think about the flow in the presentation of ideas in a paragraph.

Have students read the questions to themselves and circle the correct answers.

After students do the task, check answers as a class.

IDIOM

As students follow along in their books, read the sentence and answer options aloud. Have them guess the answer before providing it (c). Explain that *downtime* refers to time spent relaxing after being busy. Give an example:

After a busy day at school, I need some downtime. So I'm playing video games with my sister.

COMPREHENSION

A **Answer the questions about *Turning Hobbies into Cash*.**

1 **REFERENCE** Who does *They* in line 1 refer to?
   a all teenagers around the world
   b typical American teenagers
   c the teenagers mentioned in the article ⓒ

2 **VOCABULARY** What's another way of saying the *icing on the cake* (line 14)?
   ⓐ the extra benefit   b the main reason   c the strange result

3 **COHESION** Where is the best place for this sentence in the paragraph about Jasmine?
   All this brings in extra cash.
   a after sentence 1   b after sentence 2   ⓒ after sentence 3

4 **DETAIL** According to the article, whose mother used to get angry at them?
   a Ryan's   b Jasmine's   ⓒ Luke's

5 **SEQUENCE** Which activity happened last?
   a Luke made $8,000.
   ⓑ Luke worked as a team leader.
   c Luke learned how to program games.

B **Look at the descriptions (a–h) below.** Write them in the Venn diagram.

a makes something you can eat
b led a team of people
c wrote a book
d watched online tutorials
e helps people plan for the future
f has been on TV
g creates their own videos
h has an online/social media presence

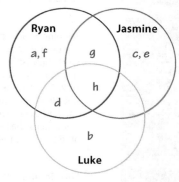

C **CRITICAL THINKING Evaluating** **Talk with a partner.** Do you think earning money from your hobbies is a good idea? Are there downsides to what these teenagers are doing? Answers will vary.

IDIOM

The time that you are not working is also known as ____.
a slowtime
b backtime
ⓒ downtime

B Tell students that they should write the letters representing the descriptions in the correct places in the Venn diagram. If necessary, explain the function of Venn diagrams. (See **TEACHING NOTE**.) Point out that the places where the circles overlap are for information that two or all of the teenagers in the article share.

Call on a few students to read the descriptions (**a–h**) aloud.

Have students do the task. Check answers.

TEACHING NOTE: VENN DIAGRAMS

A Venn diagram is a useful way to organize information when two or more things are being compared. As a graphic organizer, a Venn diagram allows for both information that is unique to one topic (differences) and information that overlaps between topics (similarities). As a visual aid, it makes it easy to note both similarities and differences in one place. Point out that students can use graphic organizers both to

VOCABULARY

A Find the bold words below in the article. Then circle the correct answers to complete the sentences.

1 A(n) _actor_ / director is someone who **appears** on TV.

2 When you **post** information on the internet, you _check it for accuracy /_ _make it available to other people_

3 If something **eventually** happens, it happens _immediately /_ _after a long time_

4 When something **affects** you, it _changes_ / doesn't change you in some way.

5 The **leader** of a group of people _controls_ / finds problems with it.

6 The **average** of 5, 20, and 50 is _25_ / 75.

B Read the information below. Then circle the correct answers.

> Some nouns and verbs in English can be easily confused with each other. For example, the verb _affect_ means to have an influence on someone or something, and the noun _effect_ means a consequence or result.

1 The new rule will _affect_ / **effect** adults, but it won't have any **affect** / _effect_ on teenagers.

2 The instructions on the box _advise_ / **advice** users to seek medical **advise** / _advice_

3 The student **counsel** / _council_ wants teachers to _counsel_ / **council** young people in making career decisions.

WRITING

A Read the paragraph.

B What leisure activities do you like doing? Make a list.

C Write a description.
Describe what you like doing in your leisure time, and how much time you spend on these activities.
Answers will vary.

> After school, I'm usually busy with my club activities. I'm a member of the Outdoor Adventure Club. At home, I spend about four hours a day online. I like playing online games and chatting with my friends. I ...

Unit 1 **15**

take notes and review reading passages, as well as to organize their own thoughts and ideas when writing.

C ⬤ CRITICAL THINKING

As students follow along, read the questions aloud.

Have students get into pairs and discuss their ideas.

VOCABULARY

A As students follow along, read the bold words aloud. Have students find them in the **READING** passage.

Have students circle the correct answers to complete the sentences. Check answers.

B As students follow along, read the information in the box aloud. Have students circle the correct answers. Check answers.

WRITING

Tell students they are going to write a short paragraph about their leisure activities.

A As students follow along, read the example paragraph aloud. Point out that the writer talks about what she does after school. Tell students they can also write about what they do on the weekends. Point out that the example includes two different activities, with details about each. Tell students that their paragraph should be written in a similar style.

B Read the question aloud. Have students make a list of their leisure activities. Encourage them to also make notes about the activities, including how much time they spend on each activity.

C Have students write their paragraphs using their notes from **B**. You might want to assign the writing as homework, and set a minimum number of sentences students must write (e.g., six).

Have the students revise their writing, correcting the grammar mistakes. Collect the first and second drafts of the writings. If some students still have mistakes, correct the errors. In the next lesson, return the papers. If many students are making the same types of mistakes, review these mistakes in class.

VIDEO

Give students a moment to study the photo. Have a student read the caption aloud. Tell students they are going to watch a video called "Robot Games." As students follow along in their books, read the sentence about the video aloud.

BEFORE YOU WATCH

Tell students they will get into pairs and talk about robots. As students follow along, read the two questions aloud. Have students do the task.

OPTIONAL Randomly call on pairs to share their ideas with the class. Have them say one thing robots can do now and one thing they would like robots to do for them.

By thinking about what they already know about some of the content of the video, students activate prior topic knowledge and think about the vocabulary, which helps them more easily understand the video.

WHILE YOU WATCH

A Tell students they will watch the video and they should check the things that they see robots do. Before playing the video, have students read the items listed.

▶ 1.3 Play Video 1.3. Play it again, if necessary. Check answers.

B Explain to students that they will watch the video again and they should circle the correct answers to complete the sentences. Before playing the video, have students read the sentences.

▶ 1.3 Play Video 1.3. Play it again, if necessary. Check answers.

ROBOT GAMES

Before You Watch

Talk with a partner. What are some things that robots can do? What would you like a robot to do for you? Answers will vary.

While You Watch

A ▶ 1.3 **Watch the video.** Check (✓) all the things you see robots do.

- ☐ speak
- ☐ cook something
- ☑ move forward
- ☑ hang something
- ☑ carry something
- ☐ go underwater

B ▶ 1.3 **Watch again.** Circle the correct answers.

1 The FIRST Robotics Competition is for high school students from **all over the world** / **the United States**.

2 FIRST was started by Dean Kamen, a famous **athlete** / **inventor**.

3 Kamen had the idea for the competition after seeing how much kids enjoy **sports** / **robotics**.

4 A(n) **adult** / **student leader** guides each team.

C **Rank.** How well do you think robots would do in these sports? Rank them from **1** (the best) to **4** (the worst). Then share your ranking and reasons with a partner. Answers will vary.

_____ golf   _____ skiing

_____ swimming   _____ weightlifting

After You Watch

Talk with a partner. Every year, the events at the FIRST Robotics Competition are changed to create new challenges. Make a list of challenging tasks you would like to see robots do in the competition. Answers will vary.

Participants at the FIRST Robotics Competition

16 Unit 1

OPTIONAL Tell students that *FIRST* stands for *For Inspiration and Recognition of Science and Technology*. Have them talk about what this means and why the organization chose this name (e.g., to encourage young people to be excited about and want to work in the fields of science and technology).

C Tell students they will think about how well robots would do in certain sports and rank them from 1 (the best) to 4 (the worst). As students follow along in their books, read the question and the list of sports aloud.

Have them do the task. Then have them get into pairs and share their ranking and reasons with their partner.

SUPPORT Review useful questions for sharing their ranking and reasons. Ask students for some ways to ask each other about the rankings. For example: *What did you rank as number one/two/three/four? Why did you rank weightlifting as four?*

ABOUT THE PHOTO

This photo shows two high school participants at a FIRST Robotics Competition. The FIRST (For Inspiration and Recognition of Science and Technology) Robotics Competition is an international high school robotics competition. It is organized by FIRST—a non-profit founded by Dean Kamen (the inventor of the Segway) in 1989. The goal of FIRST is to inspire more students to become interested in science and technology. In addition to educating and training students in STEM (science, technology, engineering, and mathematics), FIRST's programs also help young people develop self-confidence and other life skills.

The FIRST Robotics Competition takes place every year. Teams are issued a challenge, and they have to design and build a robot using a specific set of resources within a specified time period. Each team usually has a mentor who guides the students and offers advice.

A Match the verbs with the correct nouns to form hobbies.

1 bake — cakes
2 mix — jigsaw puzzles
3 read — comic books
4 do — music
5 watch — movies

B Complete the sentences. Use the correct form of the verbs in the box.

cook   dance   hike   sing   spend   watch

1 I enjoy _spending_ time with my friends on the weekend.
2 I can't stand _watching_ black-and-white movies. They're so boring.
3 I love _singing_. My music teacher says I have a great voice.
4 I don't mind _hiking_, but it's not my favorite outdoor activity.
5 _Cooking_ is a lot of fun, but no one wants to eat my food!
6 I don't like _dancing_ very much. People say I have two left feet!

C Complete the sentences. Use the words in the box. Two words are extra.

advice   advise   affect   council   counsel   effect

1 Can I give you some _advice_?
2 His injury had no _effect_ on his performance.
3 The town _council_ is having a meeting right now.
4 How will the new rules _affect_ you?

SELF CHECK   Now I can ...

☐ describe my hobbies and interests
☐ talk about things people like doing
☐ talk about teenagers who are making money from their hobbies

Unit 1 17

REVIEW

Explain to students that they are going to review the material from the unit and this will help them remember what they have studied.

A Explain that activity **A** reviews vocabulary from the unit. Explain that they should match the verbs on the left with the correct nouns on the right to form hobbies.

Have students do the task. Check answers as a class.

B Explain that activity **B** reviews the grammar from the unit. Tell students they should use the correct form of the verbs in the box to complete the sentences.

Have students do the task. Check answers.

C Point out that activity **C** reviews words from **VOCABULARY** activity **B**.

Tell students to use the words in the box to complete the sentences and questions. Point out that two words are extra and won't be used.

Have students do the task. Check answers.

SELF CHECK

These *I can* statements provide vital feedback on students' perceived ability to use the language from the unit. If you find students are reluctant to check they can do the skills, consider asking them to rate themselves from 1 (not very confident) to 3 (very confident).

OPTIONAL Have students complete the **SELF CHECK** before doing the **REVIEW** activities. After reviewing the unit, have students once again check their confidence for each statement.

AFTER YOU WATCH

Tell students they will get into pairs and talk about the video.

As students follow along in their books, read the instructions aloud.

Have them do the task.

CHALLENGE Have students make their own discussion questions about the video. For example: *Do you think the competition looks exciting? Would you like to be part of one of the teams? Would you like to build a robot?* Give students time to write their questions. Then have them get into pairs and take turns asking and answering questions.

CONTENT NOTE: COMPETITION THEMES

Every year, FIRST announces a new theme for their robotics competition. Teams must then build robots connected to this theme.

Past themes were related to topics such as renewable energy, deep space, steamworks, and recycling.

HOW LONG HAVE YOU BEEN DOING ARCHERY?

CONTENT AREA: HISTORY AND CULTURE

Topic: sports and exercise; routines

Vocabulary: sports: cricket, archery, volleyball, taekwondo, tennis, basketball, skateboarding; **other words:** defeat, announce, distance, success, determination, previous

Grammar: present perfect progressive

Extra material: photos of cricket, volleyball, taekwondo; picture of human anatomy to show spinal cord; a world map

Other useful vocabulary: sports that use no verb or can be used with *go*: running, skiing, bowling, rock climbing, snowboarding; **sports that use *do*:** karate, weightlifting, judo, yoga; **sports that use *play*:** soccer, baseball, golf

END OF UNIT PROJECT Have students write a report about a new sport and then share their findings with their classmates.

Remind students that in the project for **THE REAL WORLD**, they did research online about a "new" sport. Explain that they should now write a short paragraph introducing it. Remind students that they should include information like how the sport came about and how it is played.

Tell students they can include other information and should do more research online, if necessary.

2 HOW LONG HAVE YOU BEEN DOING ARCHERY?

PREVIEW

A 🎧 **2.1 Listen.** Match the people with the sports they do.

	Sports	How long
1 Lucy has been	playing cricket	for about two years.
2 Nathan has been	doing archery	for a year.
3 Claudia has been	playing volleyball	since she was five.
4 Jin-soon has been	doing taekwondo	since middle school.

18

Emphasize that the report should be in the students' own words, and they should not copy what they have read on the internet.

Tell students that at the end of their report, they should list the internet site(s) they used to do their research. Point out that they should write the name of the website, the date they looked at that page, and the web address.

Give an example:
Resources
TopEndSports. Accessed February 28, 2020. http://www.topendsports.com/sport/new/list.htm

In the next lesson, have students get into small groups and share their information.

CONTENT NOTE: SPORTS

Cricket is said to have started as early as the thirteenth century. Two teams of 11 people play on an oval field that has two sets of

An archery lesson just outside of Dublin, Ireland

B 🎧 2.1 **Listen again.** Match the people's sports in **A** with how long they have been doing them.

C **Talk with a partner.** Which sports in **A** have you done before? Which have you never done? Answers will vary.

HISTORY AND CULTURE

UNIT GOALS

• talk about sports and exercise

• use language to describe actions that continue to the present

• learn about how athletes push themselves to achieve success

19

wickets (sticks) at the ends. The sport is particularly loved in Britain, Australia, India, Pakistan, and the West Indies.

Volleyball was invented in 1895 in Massachusetts, U.S.A. It was originally created as a game for businessmen who found basketball to be too exhausting. It is a game played by two teams of six people.

Taekwondo is a Korean martial art characterized by its use of head-height kicks and jumping spinning kicks.

PREVIEW

Have students read the unit title to themselves as you read it aloud. Explain that in this unit they will learn to talk about playing sports, and things they started doing in the past and continue to do now.

Have students look at the photo. Ask a student to read the photo caption aloud.

OPTIONAL Have students find Ireland on a world map.

A Tell students that they will hear four short conversations, and they should match the people with the sports they do.

🎧 2.1 Play Audio Track 2.1. Don't check answers yet.

SUPPORT If you brought in photos of cricket, volleyball, and taekwondo, show them to the students.

B Tell students they will listen to the conversations again, and they should match the people's sports in **A** with how long they have been doing them.

🎧 2.1 Play Audio Track 2.1. Play it again, if necessary.

Check answers for **A** and **B**.

C Have students get into pairs and take turns asking and answering questions about the sports in **A** that they have or have not done. Encourage students to ask their partners follow-up questions.

OPTIONAL Having students classify new vocabulary is an important critical thinking skill. Have students name other sports that use no extra verb or can be used with *go*, and sports that use *do* or *play*. (See **Other useful vocabulary**.) Then have students talk about which ones they have tried.

UNIT GOALS

Direct students' attention to the **UNIT GOALS** box. Explain that these are some of the things students will learn in this unit. Point out that this unit is about history and culture. As students follow along, read each of the unit goals to the class. Explain any words students do not know. Remind students that at the end of the unit there is a self check that allows them to see if they have accomplished each goal.

LANGUAGE FOCUS

A Tell students they will listen to a conversation between Nadine and Stig.

🎧 **2.2** Play Audio Track 2.2 as students listen and follow along in their books.

As students follow along, read the question, *What three pieces of equipment does Stig show Nadine?* Have students answer.

Have students work in pairs and practice the conversation once. Point out the bold words. Tell students to practice the conversation two more times, changing the bold words each time and swapping roles after the first time.

CONTENT NOTE: GYM EQUIPMENT

The three pieces of equipment mentioned in the conversation are common ones found in a weightlifting gym.

The rowing machine (in the top picture, Stig is using it) mimics the action of rowing a boat. It helps work muscles throughout the body, as it requires the rower to use about 85 percent of their body's muscles at once. It also gives a low-impact cardio workout and helps with posture.

A traditional bench press (in the top picture, it is behind the rowing machine) is a flat bench that users lie down on to lift a heavy barbell up and down, pushing from their chest.

When using a chest press (bottom picture), users sit upright and press the weights outward. It has similar movement and benefits to the bench press except the user is sitting upright.

LANGUAGE FOCUS

A 🎧 **2.2** **Listen and read.** What three pieces of equipment does Stig show Nadine? Then repeat the conversation and replace the words in **bold**.
a rowing machine, a bench press, and a chest press

REAL ENGLISH Give it a try.

Nadine:	Thanks for showing me around the gym.
Stig:	No problem. I've been coming here **for months**, so I know all the equipment. (**since October / for a long time**)
Nadine:	What's this?
Stig:	It's a rowing machine. It's great for working out your whole body.
Nadine:	You've been using it for 10 minutes. Can I **give it a try**? (**have a turn / try it**)
Stig:	Oh, and this bench press is good for your **upper body**. (**arms / shoulders**)
Stig:	And here's my favorite—a chest press.
Nadine:	Um, Stig, I think you're **sitting on it backward**. (**facing the wrong way / using it incorrectly**)

B 🎧 **2.3** **Look at the chart.** Then circle the correct answers below.

DESCRIBING ACTIONS THAT CONTINUE TO THE PRESENT (USING PRESENT PERFECT PROGRESSIVE)		
Sandra looks tired. She**'s been working** hard lately.		
Nick and Tina are in great shape. They**'ve been going** to the gym a lot recently.		
How long **have** you **been doing** archery?	I**'ve been doing** it	**for** a year. **since** last year.
What **have** you **been doing** all day?	I**'ve been watching** TV.	

1 With the present perfect progressive tense, the action is **completed** / (**not completed**)

2 We use **for** / (**since**) to indicate when an action started.

3 We use (**for**)/ **since** to indicate how long an action has been taking place.

REAL ENGLISH

Direct students' attention to the expression in the **REAL ENGLISH** box. Explain that the phrase *Give it a try* is used to encourage someone to try something. For example:

A: Wow, that yoga pose looks really difficult.

B: Actually, it's not so bad. Give it a try.

Tell students that they can use *Why don't you give it a try?* to make the suggestion more polite. Point out that in Nadine's third turn, *Can I give it a try?* is used to ask for a chance to try something.

B Ask students to look at the chart. Tell them that they will study how to talk about actions that started in the past and still continue now. Explain that this verb form is called the present perfect progressive or present perfect continuous. Remind students that *continuous* means "goes on over a period of time."

🎧 **2.3** Have students follow along as they listen to Audio Track 2.3.

Read the sentences in the first part of the chart aloud. Explain that *lately* and *recently* are used in these sentences to

C **Rewrite these sentences.**

1 John began doing karate when he was five years old. He's still doing it now.

John _____*has been doing karate since*_____ he was five years old.

2 The snow started last night. It's still snowing now.

It _____*has been snowing since*_____ last night.

3 May and Etsuko started playing tennis two hours ago. They're still playing now.

May and Etsuko _____*have been playing tennis for*_____ two hours.

4 The kids began doing their homework three hours ago. They're still doing it now.

The kids _____*have been doing their homework for*_____ three hours.

5 Jessica started kayaking at 3 o'clock. She hasn't stopped yet.

Jessica _____*has been kayaking since 3 o'clock*_____ .

D 🎧 **2.4** **Complete the conversations.** Circle the correct words. Then listen and check your answers.

1 **Penny:** You're really good at tennis, Carlos. Can you give me some lessons?

Carlos: Sure, but ¹ I'm only / (I've only been) playing ² (for) / since a year. How long ³ are you / (have you been) playing?

Penny: ⁴ (I've been) / I was taking lessons ⁵ for / (since) last month.

Carlos: Well, ⁶ (I'm) / I've been going to be here tomorrow at 2 o'clock. Why don't you stop by then?

Penny: Great, thanks!

2 **Ying:** You look busy, Brian. What ⁷ (are) / were you doing?

Brian: I'm uploading some photos to my blog.

Ying: Oh, ⁸ are you / (have you been) blogging long?

Brian: Not really. ⁹ I only did / (I've only been doing) it ¹⁰ (for) / since a month or so.

Ying: ¹¹ (I had) / I've been having a sports blog in high school. I should start it up again sometime.

E **Talk with a partner.** Find out about the sports your partner does. Then share the information with another classmate. *Answers will vary.*

> Janet likes rock climbing. She's been rock climbing for three years. She goes to an indoor climbing gym every weekend.

Unit 2 **21**

SUPPORT Direct students' attention to the second question in the chart. Ask students whether this pattern would be identical if the subject were changed to *she*. (No, the verb *have* would become *has*.)

OPTIONAL Remind students that *lately* and *recently* discuss time but are not as specific as *since* and *for*. Have students rewrite the sentences in the first part of the chart using *for* or *since*, providing a period of time (e.g., *Sandra looks tired. She's been working hard for the past two weeks.*).

Draw students' attention to the three statements under the chart. Have students circle the correct answers. Check answers.

C Tell students to read the sentences, then rewrite them using the present perfect progressive.

Have students do the task. Check answers.

D Have students circle the correct words to complete the conversations. Explain to students they will then listen and check their answers.

🎧 **2.4** Play Audio Track 2.4. Check answers as a class.

OPTIONAL Have students get into pairs and practice the conversations twice, swapping roles after the first time.

E Tell students they are going to work in pairs to talk about sports they do. Explain that they should remember their partner's answers so they can tell another classmate what they learned.

Model the example.

Have students interview their partner first, then share what they learned about each other with another pair.

talk about something that started not long ago (e.g., the last few weeks or months).

Read the two questions and the responses in the rest of the chart aloud. Have students formulate a pattern for the questions and responses, providing the answer if necessary.

The questions have the following pattern: *Wh-* question word + *has/have* + subject + *been -ing* verb + additional detail.

The responses follow this pattern: subject + *has/have been -ing* verb (+ preposition + additional detail).

Explain that *since* is used with a specified point in time. Have students give examples (e.g., since 2010, since yesterday). Tell students that *for* is used with a specified period of time. Have them give examples (e.g., for two days, for eight months, for 10 years).

THE REAL WORLD

Ask students to look at the photo. Have a student read the title and the photo caption aloud.

OPTIONAL Ask students to describe what they see in the photo.

CONTENT NOTE: FOOTGOLF

Footgolf is very similar to golf. The most important differences between golf and footgolf are (1) the ball (a soccer ball rather than a golf ball is used), and (2) how the ball is moved (players kick the ball rather than use a golf club).

The sport has steadily gained momentum since it was first introduced in Europe in 2008. It is now enjoyed in many countries and on various courses around the world. Players wear regular running shoes without soccer cleats or studs in order to protect the course grounds. It is also common for players to wear colorful knee-high argyle socks; this quirky footgolfer fashion trend is a popular, fun way for players to show their appreciation for their unique and unusual sport.

A Tell students that before they watch the video, they will make predictions about footgolf by checking the statements which they think are true about footgolf. As students follow along, read the statements aloud.

B Tell students they will watch the video and they should check their predictions in **A**. Explain that they should also correct the false statements.

▶2.1 Play Video 2.1. Play it again, if necessary.

Check answers.

C Tell students they will watch the video again and they should circle the correct answers to complete the paragraph.

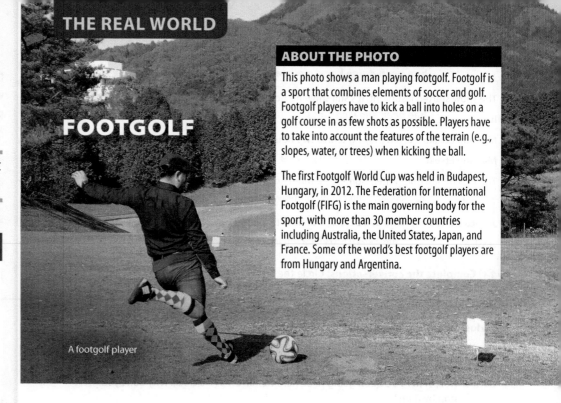

THE REAL WORLD

FOOTGOLF

A footgolf player

ABOUT THE PHOTO

This photo shows a man playing footgolf. Footgolf is a sport that combines elements of soccer and golf. Footgolf players have to kick a ball into holes on a golf course in as few shots as possible. Players have to take into account the features of the terrain (e.g., slopes, water, or trees) when kicking the ball.

The first Footgolf World Cup was held in Budapest, Hungary, in 2012. The Federation for International Footgolf (FIFG) is the main governing body for the sport, with more than 30 member countries including Australia, the United States, Japan, and France. Some of the world's best footgolf players are from Hungary and Argentina.

A Predict. Footgolf is a new sport that is part golf and part soccer. Which of these statements about the sport do you think are true? Check (✓).

☑ It is played with a regular soccer ball.

cannot
☐ Players ~~can~~ use a golf club to hit the ball.

doesn't have to
☐ It ~~must~~ be played on specially designed footgolf courses.

☑ Players try to get the ball into a hole.

Europe
☐ People first started playing it in ~~Asia~~.

B ▶2.1 **Watch the video.** Check your predictions in **A**. Correct the false statements.

C ▶2.1 **Watch again.** Circle the correct answers.

Similar to golf, footgolf players take the first shot from a starting area known as the ¹ (**tee box**)/ **fairway**. The person who is ² **nearest to** / (**farthest from**) the hole kicks next. The players then continue until each of them kicks their ball into the hole. Players can choose to play a total of either ³ (**9 or 18**) / **10 or 20** holes. The player who completes the course with the fewest kicks wins.

▶2.1 Play Video 2.1. Play it again, if necessary.

Check answers.

D CRITICAL THINKING

As students follow along, read the instructions aloud. Have students get into pairs and do the task. After students have finished writing the rules for their sport, have them get together with another pair and take turns explaining the rules of their sport.

SUPPORT Have students brainstorm a list of sports before they create their new sport. Tell students to call out the names of any sports they know. Write these on the board.

PROJECT As students follow along, read the project instructions aloud. Explain that they will research online about another "new" sport. Ask students to find out when and where it started, as well as how it is played. Have students explain their findings to a partner, and encourage them to show photos of the sport, if possible.

D CRITICAL THINKING Synthesizing **Work with a partner.** Combine two sports to create a new sport. Decide on a set of rules. Then explain the rules of your sport to another pair.
Answers will vary.

PROJECT Go online. Find another "new" sport. How did the sport come about? How is it played? Share your findings with a partner.

PRONUNCIATION review: weak form of *been*

🎧 2.5 **Listen.** Write the words you hear. Then listen again and repeat the sentences.

1 He's ___been playing___ tennis since 5 o'clock.

2 She hasn't ___been going___ to the gym much lately.

3 We've ___been waiting___ here for 30 minutes.

4 People have ___been doing___ yoga for thousands of years.

DO YOU KNOW?

Which sport returned to the Olympics in 2016 after a 112-year absence?
a golf
b kitesurfing
c soccer

COMMUNICATION Answers will vary.

A Look at the chart. Complete the sentences. Make some of the sentences true and some false.

	True	False
I've been _____ since I was little.		
I've been _____ for a few years.		
I've been _____ a lot online recently.		
I haven't been _____ very much lately.		

B Share your sentences above with at least five people. Ask each other follow-up questions. Then mark if each person thinks the statements about you are true or false. How many people guessed correctly?

I've been playing basketball since I was little.

Really? How old were you when you started?

Unit 2 **23**

TEACHING NOTE: DOING INTERNET RESEARCH

If students don't have a lot of experience doing research on the internet, give them guidelines. For example, explain that they must think of key words that will help them get the information, and that searching with key words that are too broad (e.g., only *sports*) may not give them specific-enough information.

PRONUNCIATION

Tell students they will practice their pronunciation of weak forms in spoken English. Remind students that when we speak, we often say the words that give the most important information a little more strongly, so the listener can hear them more clearly.

Tell students that they will hear four sentences and they should write the words they hear to complete each sentence.

🎧 2.5 Play Audio Track 2.5. Play it again, if necessary. Check answers.

Have students read the first sentence and ask them whether the word *been* provides important information (no). Tell students they will practice giving less stress to the word *been* by repeating the sentences.

🎧 2.5 Play the audio again, pausing after each sentence so students can repeat.

DO YOU KNOW?

Read the question and answer choices aloud, as students follow along in their books. Have students guess the answer before providing it (a).

COMMUNICATION

A Have students look at the chart. Tell students to complete the sentences by writing a word or phrase in each blank. Remind them to make some of the sentences true and some false.

Have students do the task.

B Tell students they will share their sentences in the chart with at least five classmates. Point out that they should not say whether the sentences are true or false.

Explain to students that they will stand up, move around the classroom, choose a classmate, and take turns reading their sentences. Tell them to ask follow-up questions, and then mark whether each person thinks their sentences are true or false.

Model the conversation with a student.

Have students do the task.

OPTIONAL Have students reveal to their classmates which statements were true and which were false. Then have classmates say which one surprised them the most.

READING

Ask students to look at the photo and follow along as you read the title and the caption aloud.

OPTIONAL Ask students what they know about marathons or long-distance running (e.g., the official distance of a full marathon is 42.195 kilometers; a marathon is usually run as a road race).

A Tell students they will get into pairs and talk about runners. As students follow along in their books, read the two questions aloud.

Have students do the task.

B Have students locate paragraph C. Tell students that they will skim it to check if any of their ideas from **A** are mentioned. Remind them that skimming involves quickly moving through the text (not scanning for specific information).

Have students do the task.

C Read the question aloud. Tell students to scan the article to find the answer to the question. Remind students that scanning involves reading quickly to find specific information. If necessary, review scanning. (See **TEACHING NOTE**.)

Have students do the task. Check answers.

After completing the task, give students the opportunity to read the article in more detail so they can answer the **COMPREHENSION** questions.

OPTIONAL The text can also be used as a listening activity. Have students close their books. Tell students they will listen to the passage.

♩ 2.6 Play Audio Track 2.6. Ask students to get into pairs and discuss what information they heard. Then have them read the article more carefully.

READING

A **Talk with a partner.** What are some things that can affect a runner's time? Why do you think runners today are faster than ever? Answers will vary.

B **Skim paragraph C.** Are any of your ideas from **A** mentioned? Answers will vary.

C **Scan the article.** What is the official marathon world record time as of 2019? 2 hours, 1 minute, and 39 seconds

24 Unit 2

TEACHING NOTE: SCANNING

Remind students that scanning is a reading technique in which you look for specific information, or find information in a list (e.g., a phone number, the time a TV show starts, the page of an item in a catalog). When scanning, it is not important to understand or read every word.

Hints for scanning:
1 Don't read every word.
2 Think about the type of information. Is it a date? Is it a measurement with specific units, such as kilometers?
3 Think about the order of the information. Is it by date (chronological)? Is it alphabetical? Is it by time (like a bus schedule)?

RUNNING A MARATHON

Eliud Kipchoge crosses the finish line to win the 2018 Berlin Marathon.

A 🎧 2.6 It's 490 B.C. The Greek army has just **defeated** a much larger Persian army at the town of Marathon, Greece. A Greek soldier named Pheidippides runs to Athens, about 40 kilometers away, to **announce** the victory. After he delivers the message, he collapses and dies. To honor his run, the marathon race was included in the first modern Olympic Games, in 1896. Since then, humans have been asking themselves how fast we can run this **distance**.

B At one point, it was believed that a runner could never run a mile (1.6 kilometers) in under four minutes. But it happened, way back in 1954. In the nearly 70 years since, the mile record has been lowered by nearly 17 seconds. In 1999, Morocco's Hicham El Guerrouj set the world record for running a mile in 3 minutes 43 seconds. As of 2019, his record still stands. Similarly, the record for running a marathon has continued to fall over the past few decades, as runners today are faster than ever.

C Researchers know what allows top runners to perform at their best. These things include a healthy diet, muscle building, pacing, and training in an ideal environment. More recently, researchers have been working to improve runners' clothing and shoes. For example, there are new socks that provide better air flow and greater foot support. Special pads on the bottom of lighter shoes help push runners forward. A new type of tape that attaches to the sides of a runner's arms and legs helps cut through the air. There is even talk of designing clothing with built-in cooling systems.

D While these things certainly help, a runner's **success** may depend on something much more difficult to measure: their level of **determination**. Kenya's Eliud Kipchoge knows this to be true. As of 2019, he is the marathon world record holder, with an official time of 2 hours, 1 minute, and 39 seconds. He set this record in 2018, breaking the **previous** record by 1 minute 18 seconds. In October 2019, Kipchoge ran the marathon distance in just under two hours; however, this did not count as an official record as the race was not an open competition. Nevertheless, Kipchoge believes it is only a matter of time before someone officially breaks the two-hour marathon barrier.

Unit 2 **25**

---

4 When possible, use titles and headings to help you find the information quickly. With longer texts, use header words at the top of sections, pages, and columns.

5 When searching for names or places, scan for capital letters.

6 When searching for a statistic or other numerical value, look for numbers in the text.

Additional Activities to Use with the Reading

Additional Comprehension Questions

1 What is the origin of the word *marathon*? (It is the name of the town that the Greek soldier ran from [toward Athens], in order to deliver a message of victory.)

2 When was the quickest one-mile race run? (1999)

3 Where is Eliud Kipchoge from? (Kenya)

4 Before Eliud Kipchoge broke the marathon world record, what was the previous record? (2 hours, 2 minutes, and 57 seconds)

Content Discussion

Read the last sentence of the passage aloud. Ask students to explain in their own words what this means. Tell them to explain the "two-hour marathon barrier" and discuss why Kipchoge is certain it will be broken (e.g., one reason is the technological advancements in running gear, but a bigger reason is the ever-increasing determination of runners to break records, run faster, and do better than the last record-holder).

Listening and Pronunciation (Focused)

Ask students to underline all instances of *been* in the article (last sentence in paragraph A; third sentence in paragraph B; third sentence in paragraph C). Explain that they will listen to the text and should note how *been* has a weak stress.

🎧 2.6 Play Audio Track 2.6. Play it again, pausing so that students can repeat each sentence with *been*.

Have students practice saying each of the sentences with *been*. Give students time to practice reading the entire passage aloud.

Play the audio a final time, having students read along while trying to maintain the speed and rhythm of the recording.

Vocabulary Reinforcement

Have students write all the new words in a vocabulary notebook, including easy explanations for the words and example sentences.

COMPREHENSION

A EXAM PRACTICE

Multiple-choice items can be either questions or statements with a blank. There are various kinds of multiple-choice questions.

The answers to **inference** items are not stated in the passage. Instead, students must use reason to analyze the hints in part or all of the passage and make an educated guess. Students must:

- recognize unstated assumptions.
- speculate (e.g., on the author's motivation or unspoken feelings).
- produce a conclusion based on the provided information.
- deduce additional details based on the passage.

Students should make sure that their inference does not contradict any part of the passage.

Have students read the questions to themselves and circle the correct answers.

After they have finished, check answers as a class.

COMPREHENSION

A Answer the questions about *Running a Marathon*.

1 DETAIL Which statement about Pheidippides is true?

   a He was a soldier who fought against the Greeks.

   (b) He ran about 40 kilometers from the town of Marathon.

   c He competed in the first modern Olympic Games.

2 PURPOSE What is the purpose of paragraph B?

   (a) to compare running a marathon with running a four-minute mile

   b to explain why it was so difficult to break the four-minute mile time

   c to talk about Hicham El Guerrouj's running achievements

3 INFERENCE Clothing with built-in cooling systems would be useful for runners who _____.

   a get injured easily   b usually run alone   (c) train in hot weather

4 COHESION Where is the best place for this sentence in paragraph D?

   This was the greatest improvement in a marathon record time since 1967.

   a after sentence 1   b after sentence 2   (c) after sentence 4

5 INFERENCE According to the article, which of the following is true?

   a The most important factor for success in a marathon is the use of high-tech clothing.

   b Researchers are looking into ways to measure a runner's level of determination.

   (c) For a marathon record to be official, the race must be open to other competitors.

B Complete the timeline below with these events (a–e).

a The soldier Pheidippides delivered an important message.

b Someone completed a marathon in a little over two hours.

c The first modern Olympic Games were held.

d Someone first ran a mile in under four minutes.

e Someone ran an unofficial marathon in just under two hours.

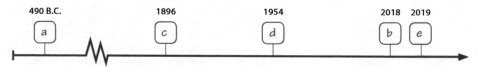

C CRITICAL THINKING Evaluating **Talk with a partner.** Do you think it's fair for runners to use clothing and shoes that can enhance their performance? Why or why not? Answers will vary.

26 Unit 2

VOCABULARY

A Find the words below in the article. Then complete the paragraph using the words in the box.

> announced   defeated   determination   distance   previous   success

Hicham El Guerrouj of Morocco is one of the greatest runners of all time. He is best known for his ¹ __success__ in the mile and 1,500-meter events. In 1999, he broke the world record for the mile, running the ² __distance__ in just 3 minutes 43 seconds. Despite being considered one of the favorites to win the 1,500-meter race in the 1996 and 2000 Olympic Games, El Guerrouj lost both times. However, he refused to give up. His hard work and ³ __determination__ eventually paid off. At the 2004 Athens Olympics, El Guerrouj ⁴ __defeated__ runners much younger than himself, earning gold medals in the 1,500-meter and 5,000-meter events. His double win felt particularly satisfying after his ⁵ __previous__ losses. Shortly after, El Guerrouj ⁶ __announced__ his retirement.

B Read the information below. Then circle the correct answers.

> There are many expressions containing the word *record*:
>
> | hold the record | set the record | world record | medical record |
> |---|---|---|---|
> | break the record | in record time | permanent record | financial record |

1 As of 2019, the **permanent** / (**world**) record for running 100 meters is 9.58 seconds.

2 He managed to finish his homework in (**record time**) / **the medical records**.

3 How long did she **break** / (**hold**) the record for the fastest time?

WRITING

A Read the paragraph.

B Choose an athlete who broke a world record. Make notes about their achievement. Add any other biographical details (e.g., date and place of birth).

C Write a biography. Use your notes from **B** to help you.
Answers will vary.

Danny Way was born in 1974. He has been skateboarding for most of his life. He holds the world record for the highest jump from a ramp. Way reached a height of ...

Unit 2 **27**

C [CRITICAL THINKING]

As students follow along, read the questions aloud.

Have students get into pairs and discuss their ideas. Then discuss as a class.

CHALLENGE Divide the class into two teams, for and against clothing and shoes that enhance a runner's performance. Have each team come up with arguments to support their position. Then have a class debate on the topic. Have four students from each team present their arguments. During the debate,

give teams time to formulate counter-arguments after hearing what each speaker from the other team says.

VOCABULARY

A Ask a student to read the words in the box aloud. Have students find them in the **READING** passage.

Have students use the words in the box to complete the paragraph. Check answers.

B As students follow along, read the information in the box aloud.

Have students circle the correct answers. Check answers.

SUPPORT Point out that the expressions in the box can be categorized as noun phrases, verb phrases, or prepositional phrases. (noun phrases: *world record, medical record, permanent record, financial record*; verb phrases: *hold the record, set the record, break the record*; prepositional phrase: *in record time*)

WRITING

Tell students they are going to write a short biography about an athlete who broke a world record. Explain that they will need to do some research to find the information.

A As students follow along, read the example paragraph aloud. Point out the kind of information the writer provides (athlete's name, birth year, sport, and what world record he broke). Tell students that their paragraph should include all of this information.

B Tell students to do some research online and choose an athlete who broke a world record. Tell them to make notes about the athlete's achievement and add any other biographical details they can find.

SUPPORT Tell students to choose a sport they enjoy or one that they have read about in the unit. Tell them to research world records in that sport. Write example search terms on the board (e.g., *world records in skateboarding*).

C Have students write their biographies, using their notes from **B**. You might want to assign the writing as homework, and set a minimum number of sentences students must write (e.g., six).

CONTENT NOTE: LIFE ROLLS ON

Life Rolls On was started by surfer Jesse Billauer in 2001. In 1996, following a surfing accident, Jesse suffered a complete spinal cord injury. As a result, he lost the ability to walk, and had limited movement in his arms and hands. However, Jesse left the hospital determined to surf again and to inspire others. He founded Life Rolls On to help people with paralysis experience the feeling of freedom that comes with surfing and skateboarding. Jesse has since won numerous awards and surfing competitions, and is a two-time World Adaptive Surfing Champion. His story appears in a segment of *Step into Liquid*, a feature-length documentary.

Give students a moment to study the photo Have a student read the caption aloud.

OPTIONAL Ask students to share what they think the person in the wheelchair is doing. Ask them to offer ideas about why the event is called "They Will Skate Again."

Tell students they are going to watch a video called "Life Rolls On." As students follow along in their books, read the sentence about the video aloud.

BEFORE YOU WATCH

Tell students that they are going to take a quiz about spinal cord injury before watching the video. Tell students to circle **T** if they think the statement is true, or **F** if they think it is false. Have a student read the statements aloud.

Have students to do the task. Check answers.

SUPPORT If you brought a picture of human anatomy, show it to the students and point out the spinal cord.

LIFE *ROLLS* ON

Before You Watch

Take a quiz. What do you know about spinal cord injury (SCI)? Circle **T** for true or **F** for false.

1 Traffic accidents are a leading cause of SCI.   (T)   F
2 Over 17,000 new SCI cases occur each year in the United States.   (T)   F
3 Most SCI patients are female.   T   (F)

While You Watch

A ▶2.2 **Watch the video.** How does Life Rolls On help people with disabilities experience the joy of skating? Check (✓) the ways mentioned.

☑ by providing special adaptive equipment   ☐ by building specially designed skate parks

☑ by training volunteers to help disabled skaters   ☑ by getting professional wheelchair skaters to offer guidance

B ▶2.2 **Watch again.** Match each person with their description.

1 Jesse — a 7-year-old participant at Life Rolls On
2 Will — the founder of Life Rolls On
3 David — a professional wheelchair skater

C **Look at these expressions from the video.** Choose the correct meanings of the words in **bold**.

1 "It wants to show people that life **rolls on**."
   (a) continues   b has its ups and downs   c is like a circle

2 "I think we all **killed it**."
   a made a lot of noise   (b) did it very well   c got into an accident

3 "I'm **stoked** to be here."
   a nervous   b surprised   (c) very excited

After You Watch

Talk with a partner. Do you know of organizations similar to Life Rolls On? What do they do? Answers will vary.

Participants at the "They Will Skate Again" event

CONTENT NOTE: SPINAL CORD INJURY

Spinal cord injury (SCI) involves damage to any area of the spine, including the nerves at the tip of the spinal cord. Depending on the severity of the injury, SCI may cause a lack of movement and/or ability to control limb function, and lack of feeling in those limbs. In the most severe cases, the person loses all feeling in the limbs and the ability to control movement of the limbs.

WHILE YOU WATCH

A Tell students they will watch the video and they should check the ways that Life Rolls On helps people with disabilities experience the joy of skating. Have students read the options, before playing the video.

▶ 2.2 Play Video 2.2. Play it again, if necessary.

Check answers.

A Do these sports use a ball? Write **B** (ball) or **NB** (no ball).

NB archery   B basketball

B footgolf   NB taekwondo

B tennis   NB kayaking

B volleyball   B cricket

NB skateboarding   NB rock climbing

B Complete the sentences. Write the correct form of the verbs in parentheses. Then circle *for* or *since*.

1 Luiz _has been waiting_ (**wait**) for you (**for**) / **since** half an hour.

2 Bryan _has been doing_ (**do**) yoga **for** / (**since**) 2015.

3 Mei-ling _has been taking_ (**take**) tennis lessons (**for**) / **since** a month.

4 Erika and Liam _have been working_ (**work**) on their project **for** / (**since**) Monday.

C Complete the sentences. Use the phrases in the box.

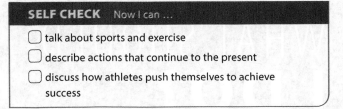

break the record	in record time
financial records	set a record

1 He completed the race _in record time_ .

2 They recently _set a record_ in the relay race.

3 She managed to _break the record_ by 0.5 seconds.

4 If you run your own business, it's important that you keep accurate _financial records_ .

SELF CHECK   Now I can ...

☐ talk about sports and exercise

☐ describe actions that continue to the present

☐ discuss how athletes push themselves to achieve success

B Tell students that they will watch the video again and they should match each person with their description.

▶ 2.2 Play Video 2.2. Play it again, if necessary.

Check answers.

C Point out that many of the speakers in the video are using slang. As students follow along in their books, read the expressions aloud.

Tell students to choose the correct meanings for the words in bold.

Check answers as a class.

AFTER YOU WATCH

Tell students they will get into pairs and talk about any organizations they know of that are similar to Life Rolls On. As students follow along in their books, read the questions aloud. Ask students to think about organizations that focus on sports or that work with people who have various disabilities.

Have students do the task.

CHALLENGE Have students do research online to learn more about organizations like Life Rolls On. Have pairs choose one organization to focus on, and then share their findings with the class in the next lesson.

REVIEW

Explain to students that they are going to review the material from the unit and this will help them remember what they have studied.

A Explain that activity **A** reviews vocabulary from the unit. Tell students they should write **B** for sports that use a ball and **NB** for sports that don't use a ball.

Have students do the task. Check answers as a class.

B Explain that activity **B** reviews the grammar from the unit. Tell students they should write the correct form of the verbs in parentheses, then circle *for* or *since* to complete the sentences.

Have students do the task. Check answers.

C Point out that activity **C** reviews words from **VOCABULARY** activity **B**.

Have students use the phrases in the box to complete the sentences. Check answers.

SELF CHECK

These *I can* statements provide vital feedback on students' perceived ability to use the language from the unit. If you find students are reluctant to check they can do the skills, consider asking them to rate themselves from 1 (not very confident) to 3 (very confident).

OPTIONAL Have students complete the **SELF CHECK** before doing the **REVIEW** activities. After reviewing the unit, have students once again check their confidence for each statement.

UNIT 3
WHAT SHOULD I DO?

Topic: asking for and giving advice; careers

Vocabulary: be bullied, pursue a career, get poor grades, gradually, organization, ability, role model, realistic, challenge

Grammar: modals

Extra material: a world map

Other useful vocabulary: kinds of disabilities: deafness, cerebral palsy, epilepsy, Alzheimer's, stuttering, autism spectrum disorder (ASD), Down syndrome, multiple sclerosis, dyslexia

END OF UNIT PROJECT Have students make a poster about disabilities, and then take turns presenting their posters in the next lesson.

Remind students that in the **READING** section, they learned about a young woman who slowly became blind from the age of four. Explain that a condition that could stop us from doing everything we want to do is called a *disability*. Explain that some people are born with disabilities, whereas others may be in accidents that result in the disability.

Point out that people with disabilities can learn to overcome them and live amazing lives in spite of their limitations.

Have students name some disabilities. Write them on the board as they are given. Students might need to do some quick research online or use their dictionaries to do this. (See **Other useful vocabulary.**)

Tell students they will choose a topic connected to disabilities and make a poster

WHAT SHOULD I DO?

30

about it. Have students get into small groups and brainstorm possible ideas. Then have groups share their ideas with the class. Write the ideas on the board as they are given. Some possible topics are:

1. A story about a person who overcame a disability, like Molly.

2. An introduction about an organization that helps people with disabilities.

3. A story about a famous person who overcame a disability (e.g., Albert Einstein had dyslexia; Bruce Willis stuttered when he was young; Richard Branson suffered from attention deficit hyperactivity disorder).

4. Advice about how to treat someone with a disability fairly.

Tell students they should choose one topic, do research, and make their poster before the next lesson. Explain that their poster should have a title and should be easy to read even from a short distance away. Point out that although the poster should have written information on it, this information should not be in long paragraphs.

A high school student speaks with a guidance counselor.

PREVIEW

A 🎧 3.1 **Listen.** Match the people with their problems.

1 Carrie ○   ○ has a friend who's being bullied.

2 Tomas ○   ○ doesn't know what career to pursue.

3 Keiko ○   ○ gets poor grades in algebra.

B 🎧 3.2 **Predict what advice the people in A will receive.** One piece of advice below is extra. Then listen and write the number for each person (**1–3**). Were your predictions correct?

___3___ talk to your parents

___1___ talk to your teacher

___2___ talk to other classmates

_____ talk to the principal

C **Talk with a partner.** Do you agree with the advice in **B**? If not, what advice would you give? Answers will vary.

> I don't think Tomas received good advice. I think he should …

> I think Keiko received good advice, but she could also …

PEOPLE AND PLACES

UNIT GOALS

- talk about possible careers
- learn language for asking for and giving advice
- learn about people who have achieved success in their careers

31

what advice Carrie, Tomas, and Keiko will receive. Point out that one piece of advice is extra and will not be used.

After students have made their predictions, explain that they will listen and write the number for each person (**1–3**), this time using a pen.

🎧 3.2 Play Audio Track 3.2. Play it again, if necessary. Check answers.

TEACHING NOTE:
IT CAN'T HURT

The idiom *it can't hurt* in the first conversation is used to suggest that trying something won't have a negative impact, and might actually have a positive one.

C Tell students they are going to get into pairs and discuss whether they agree or disagree with the advice in **B**.

Model the conversation with a student.

Have students do the task.

SUPPORT Have students identify the grammar used in the example conversation for offering advice. Write the expressions on the board:

I think she/he should …

She/he could also…

OPTIONAL Have each pair share what other advice they came up with during their discussion.

UNIT GOALS

Direct students' attention to the **UNIT GOALS** box. Explain that these are some of the things students will learn in this unit. Point out that this unit is about people and places. As students follow along, read each of the unit goals to the class. Explain any words students do not know. Remind students that at the end of the unit there is a self check that allows them to see if they have accomplished each goal.

In the next lesson, have part of the class put up their posters. Have the other students go around the room, reading the posters and asking the authors questions. When they have finished, have students swap roles. Continue until all students have presented their posters.

PREVIEW

Ask students to look at the photo. Have a student read the unit title and photo caption aloud. Explain that in this unit they will learn to talk about possible careers. Tell them they

will also learn how to ask for and give advice and suggestions.

A Tell students that they will hear three short conversations. Ask them to match the people with their problems.

🎧 3.1 Play Audio Track 3.1. Check answers.

B Tell students that the three conversations will continue. Have students write the numbers **1–3** in pencil next to the appropriate piece of advice to predict

LANGUAGE FOCUS

A Tell students they will listen to a conversation between Maya and Nadine.

🎧 **3.3** Play Audio Track 3.3 as students listen and follow along in their books.

As students follow along, read the question, *What advice does Maya give Nadine?* Have students answer.

Have students work in pairs and practice the conversation once. Point out the bold words. Tell students to practice the conversation two more times, changing the bold words each time and swapping roles after the first time.

REAL ENGLISH

Direct students' attention to the expression in the **REAL ENGLISH** box. Explain that *On top of that, . . .* is an expression that means "in addition to what I just said." It is often used when listing negative situations. For example:

I lost my wallet. On top of that, I can't find my phone.

B Ask students to look at the chart. Explain that they will study how to ask for and give advice.

🎧 **3.4** Have students follow along as they listen to Audio Track 3.4.

Tell students that we use modals to give advice. Have students identify the modals in the chart (*should, could, would*).

Read the first problem aloud. Explain that in the question, *should* is used to ask for advice or a suggestion. Read the two responses aloud. Explain that the first suggestion (with *should*) is very direct and more definitive, while *could* (in the second suggestion) implies the speaker is giving one of several options, although the other ideas are not said explicitly.

LANGUAGE FOCUS

A 🎧 **3.3** **Listen and read.** What advice does Maya give Nadine? Then repeat the conversation and replace the words in **bold**. *Call the bus company right away*

Maya:	Hey, Nadine. **Is something wrong**? (**What's wrong / Is everything OK**)
Nadine:	I think I left my phone on the bus.
Maya:	Oh, no! **If I were you, I'd call** the bus company right away. (**You should call / You should try calling**)
Nadine:	I already did that. No one's seen it. Do you think **someone will find it**? (**it'll show up / I'll get it back**)
Maya:	Of course I do.
Nadine:	And on top of that, I forgot to bring today's homework. I left it at home!
Maya:	You know, Nadine, you seem really forgetful these days.
Nadine:	But I **remembered your book**! (**brought the book you lent me / didn't forget your book**)

B 🎧 **3.4** **Look at the chart.** Then circle the correct answers below.

ASKING FOR AND GIVING ADVICE (USING MODALS)	
I left my phone on the bus. **What should I do?**	You **should call** the bus company.
	You **could call** your number.
I don't know what career to pursue. **What do you suggest I do?**	You **could try talking** to a guidance counselor.
	Why don't you do some online research?
I'm not doing very well in my algebra class.	**Have you thought about getting** a tutor?
I'd like to get a new phone, but I can't afford it.	**If I were you, I'd continue** using your current phone.

1 We use the modal *should* to say that it is **necessary** / **a good idea** to do something.

2 After modals *could* and *should*, we use **base verb** / **to + base verb**.

3 When we say *If I were you*, the next clause uses **will** / **would** + base verb.

32 Unit 3

SUPPORT Give students several examples and have them decide whether to use *should* or *could* (e.g., He's going to be late. He *could/ should* hurry up.).

Read the second and third problems and the responses aloud. Explain that the second problem offers a more formal question for asking advice: *What do you suggest I do?*

Tell students that the responses for the second and third problems are more polite. In the first response, adding *try* (*You could try . . .*) makes the advice sound more indirect. Point out that verb + *-ing*, which students learned in **UNIT 1**, follows *try*. The second and third responses are question responses. Tell students that question responses aren't as strong as a statement using *should*

C **Complete the sentences.** Circle the correct answers.

1 I'm having trouble finding a good part-time job. What **could** /(**should**) I do?

2 Fatima wants to improve her English. Maybe she(**could**)/ **would** take some lessons.

3 Talia's having trouble making friends at her new school. I think she **would** /(**should**) join a club.

4 I heard you want to adopt a cat. If I were you, I **could** /(**would**) call the animal shelter.

D 🎧 **3.5 Complete the conversations.** Unscramble the words. Then listen and check your answers.

1 **Joni:** Oh, no! I forgot my friend's birthday yesterday.

   Ahmed: (*her / don't / you / text / a / why / send*) ¹ _____Why don't you send her a text_____ ?
   Wish her a belated happy birthday. I'm sure she'll understand.

2 **Chen:** I got into a big argument with my friend, and now we're not talking.

   Noreen: (*thought / about / have / apologizing / you*)
   ² _____Have you thought about apologizing_____ ?

   Chen: Not really. I don't think I should be the one apologizing.

3 **Matt:** I didn't have time to finish my math homework. (*I / do / suggest / do / what / you*)
   ³ _____What do you suggest I do_____ ?

   Gina: (*teacher / you / try / to / your / could / talking*)
   ⁴ _____You could try talking to your teacher_____ . He might give you an extension.

E **Write an example for each category below.** Then turn to page 150 and follow the
instructions. Answers will vary.

1 a family member (male) _____

2 something you wear (plural) _____

3 another thing you wear (plural) _____

4 a color _____

5 a family member (female) _____

6 a healthy food (plural) _____

7 an unhealthy food (non-count) _____

8 a sport _____

Unit 3 **33**

Draw students' attention to the three
statements under the chart. Have
students circle the correct answers.
Check answers.

C Have students circle the correct answers
to complete the sentences.

Check answers.

D Tell students they should rearrange the
bold words to make sentences and
complete the conversations.

Have students do the task. Explain that
they will then listen and check their
answers.

🎧 **3.5** Play Audio Track 3.5. Play it
again, if necessary.

Check answers by having four students
write their sentences on the board.

OPTIONAL Have students get into pairs
and practice the conversations twice,
swapping roles after the first time.

E Tell students they will get into pairs and
take turns asking for and giving advice
about problems. As students follow
along, read the categories in the list
aloud. Point out that for items 1 and 5,
students should write titles of family
members, such as *brother* or *father*,
instead of individual names.

Have students write an example for each
category.

Then have students turn to page 150 and
follow the instructions for the task.

**TEACHING NOTE:
CONSIDERATION FOR
OTHERS**

Before doing **E**, remind students not to
hurt anyone's feelings or to offend anyone,
even when discussing imaginary problems.
Encourage students to always have
consideration and show respect for one
another.

because the speaker might have different
solutions to the problem. Explain that
this type of question response is common
in English.

Read the final problem and suggestion
aloud. Explain that the response is a
conditional sentence, discussing an
imaginary situation.

CHALLENGE Have students think of
other responses to the last problem. Encourage
them to use all of the grammar forms in the
chart. For example:

You should save up for a new phone.

*You could get a part-time job to earn money for
a new phone.*

*Have you thought about buying a cheaper
phone?*

THE REAL WORLD

Ask students to look at the photo. As students follow along, read the title and the photo caption aloud.

A Tell students that they will watch an interview with National Geographic photographer Annie Griffiths. Tell students to circle **T** if the statement is true or **F** if it is false. Have students read the sentences, before playing the video.

▶ **3.1** Play Video 3.1. Play it again, if necessary.

Check answers.

OPTIONAL Have students correct the false statement. (For **3**, Annie decided she wanted to be a photographer only after taking a photography class in college.)

DO YOU KNOW?

Read the sentence and answer choices aloud, as students follow along in their books. Have students guess the answer before providing it (b). (See **CONTENT NOTE**.)

CONTENT NOTE: SOLAR PANEL INSTALLER

The job of a solar panel installer involves setting up solar panels, mostly on rooftops, and taking care of their maintenance. Solar panel installers are also known as PV installers, as a panel is also called a photovoltaic. The job, which in 2018 paid on average roughly $20 per hour in the United States, requires a high school diploma but not a university degree. A solar panel installer learns how to do the job either at a trade school or through on-the-job training. Over the 10-year period from 2018 to 2028, the availability of positions as a solar panel installer is expected to increase 63 percent, compared to the 5 percent increase for most other jobs.

DREAM JOB

Annie Griffiths is an award-winning National Geographic photographer.

ABOUT THE PHOTO

This photo shows Annie Griffiths, one of the first few women photographers to work for National Geographic. Since joining National Geographic in 1978, Annie has traveled to almost 150 countries, photographing people, their cultures, and the places where they live.

Besides photography, Annie is also highly passionate about humanitarian work. After working with several aid organizations, she founded Ripple Effect Images—a non-profit organization dedicated to telling the stories of women in developing countries through photography. Annie's work often draws attention to the various challenges faced by women in the developing world, such as lack of access to education and healthcare.

A ▶ **3.1** **Watch the video.** Circle **T** for true or **F** for false.

1 Annie takes photos of people in developing countries. (T) F

2 Annie was one of the first female photographers for National Geographic. (T) F

3 Annie wanted to be a photographer ever since she was in high school. T (F)

DO YOU KNOW?

The fastest-growing job in the United States is _____.
a app developer
(b) solar panel installer
c nurse

B ▶ **3.1** **Watch again.** What advice does Annie give to young people? Check (✓).

☑ They should travel to different countries.

☑ They should ask a lot of questions.

☐ They should maintain close relationships with family and friends.

☐ They should start saving money as soon as they can.

☑ They should spend more time developing their creative side.

34 Unit 3

B Tell students they will watch the video again and they should check the advice Annie gives to young people. Have students read the sentences, before playing the video.

▶ **3.1** Play Video 3.1. Play it again, if necessary.

Check answers.

OPTIONAL Have students get into small groups and talk about whether they agree with Annie's advice, giving reasons for their answers.

CHALLENGE Have the class discuss Annie's last piece of advice: to develop their creative side. Ask them what this means to them (e.g., to be able to solve problems in innovative ways; to be able to understand how other people think and communicate). Have students get into groups and brainstorm ways to develop their creative side. When they have finished, have them share their ideas with the class.

C As students follow along, read the activity aloud. Tell students to rank the jobs from 1 (happiest) to 6 (least happy).

C Rank.

C Rank. Below are some of the top dream jobs of American teenagers. How happy would you be doing these jobs? Rank them from **1** (happiest) to **6** (least happy). Then compare with a partner. Answers will vary.

_____ music star   _____ jet pilot

_____ actor/actress   _____ video game tester

_____ professional athlete   _____ CEO of your own company

D CRITICAL THINKING Reflecting Talk with a partner. What is your dream job? What do you think would be the most challenging parts of the job? Answers will vary.

> **PROJECT Talk to two adults.** Ask them what they like and don't like about their jobs. Share their answers with a partner.

PRONUNCIATION weak forms of *could* and *should*

🎧 3.6 **Listen.** Write the words you hear. Then listen again and repeat the sentences.

1 You ____*could talk*____ to your teacher about it.

2 I think you ____*should ask*____ your parents for advice.

3 I think you ____*should call*____ your friend now and apologize.

4 You ____*could get*____ a summer job.

COMMUNICATION

Work in groups. Choose three problems below. Take turns asking for and giving advice.
Answers will vary.

I have no idea what I want to study in college.

I'm not sure if I can afford to go to college.

I want to get a part-time job, but my parents are afraid it will affect my grades.

I've been having trouble sleeping lately.

I find it hard to balance my schoolwork and my after-school activities.

Someone I know is being bullied online.

> I have no idea what I want to study in college. What should I do?

> Have you tried talking to a career counselor?

In the next lesson, have students get into pairs and take turns sharing who they interviewed and what they learned. Encourage them to bring in photos of their interviewees, if possible.

PRONUNCIATION

Tell students they will practice their pronunciation of weak forms of *could* and *should*. Remind students that a weak form is a syllable that is not stressed or not pronounced clearly in connected speech.

Tell students that they will hear four sentences and they should write the words they hear.

🎧 3.6 Play Audio Track 3.6. Play it again, if necessary.

Check answers.

🎧 3.6 Play the audio again, pausing after each sentence so students can repeat.

COMMUNICATION

Tell students they are going to get into groups and take turns asking for and giving advice.

Call on a few students to read the problems aloud. Tell students that as a group, they should choose three problems from the list, and then take turns asking for and giving advice. Encourage students to think of original ideas.

Model the conversation with a student.

Have students do the task.

OPTIONAL After all the groups have finished, have groups share their best advice for one problem. Then have the class vote to decide which group gave the best advice.

Explain that they are ranking according to their own opinions, so there are no right or wrong answers.

After students have finished their ranking, have them get into pairs to compare answers. Encourage students to give reasons for their ranking.

D CRITICAL THINKING

Read the questions aloud. Have students get into pairs and talk about their ideas. Then discuss as a class.

PROJECT As students follow along, read the project instructions aloud. Explain that they will interview two adults to ask about their jobs, and find out what they like or don't like about their jobs.

Have students think of two people they would like to interview. Have them work in pairs to brainstorm the interview questions or have a class discussion to come up with some questions. Assign the interviews as homework. Remind students to take notes during the interviews in order to report back to a partner.

READING

Have students look at the photo, and follow along as you read the title and caption aloud.

A As students follow along in their books, read the question aloud. Have students scan the article to find the answer. Remind students that scanning involves looking quickly for a specific piece of information.

Check answers.

OPTIONAL Ask students to imagine what their life would be like if they couldn't see. Have them talk about things they could no longer do and how they would feel.

B Have students skim the article and underline three of Molly's accomplishments.

Check answers.

C As students follow along, read the questions aloud. Tell students they will get into pairs and discuss whether they would like to join the organization Me to We. Before they begin their discussion, you might want to tell them more about Me to We. (See **CONTENT NOTE**.)

Have students do the task.

After completing the task, give students the opportunity to read the article in more detail so they can answer the **COMPREHENSION** questions.

OPTIONAL The text can also be used as a listening activity. Have students close their books. Tell students they will listen to the passage.

🔊 **3.7** Play Audio Track 3.7. Ask students to get into pairs and discuss what information they heard. Then have them read the article more carefully.

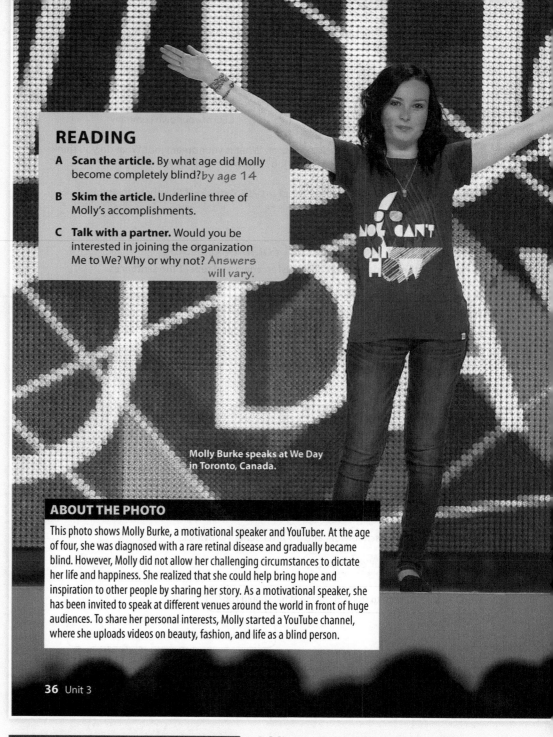

READING

A Scan the article. By what age did Molly become completely blind? by age 14

B Skim the article. Underline three of Molly's accomplishments.

C Talk with a partner. Would you be interested in joining the organization Me to We? Why or why not? Answers will vary.

Molly Burke speaks at We Day in Toronto, Canada.

ABOUT THE PHOTO

This photo shows Molly Burke, a motivational speaker and YouTuber. At the age of four, she was diagnosed with a rare retinal disease and gradually became blind. However, Molly did not allow her challenging circumstances to dictate her life and happiness. She realized that she could help bring hope and inspiration to other people by sharing her story. As a motivational speaker, she has been invited to speak at different venues around the world in front of huge audiences. To share her personal interests, Molly started a YouTube channel, where she uploads videos on beauty, fashion, and life as a blind person.

36 Unit 3

CONTENT NOTE: ME TO WE

Me to We organizes youth volunteer trips that allow young people to travel around the world, to places like the Amazon, Kenya, China, and Nicaragua. The trips are designed with specific purposes: to make a difference (e.g., help build a school), to explore the world (e.g., go on a safari in Africa), and to connect with a community (e.g., go to an Ecuadorian's home and help with the housework).

Additional Activities to Use with the Reading

Summarizing

Encourage students to think critically by summarizing what they read. Writing a summary can help students remember key details as well as put events in the correct order. For example:

VISION OF HOPE

🎧 **3.7** Molly Burke was not born blind. She started losing her sight when she was four years old. Doctors said that she had a rare eye disease that would **gradually** take away her vision. In first grade, she learned to read Braille, although she
5 could still see. Life was pretty normal for the next few years.

However, in seventh grade, things got worse. Black turned to gray. Yellow turned to white. Soon, Molly couldn't see the blackboard. "I just started to cry," remembers Molly. As she began to lose her vision, she started using a cane to help her
10 walk. By age 14, Molly was completely blind. Her classmates soon stopped inviting her to do things. A group of girls— girls who were once her friends—started bullying her. They even accused her of making up her blindness to get attention. Eventually, Molly became depressed. Her high
15 school years were not easy.

After she finished high school, Molly thought about what she wanted to do before college. Her brother was working in a children's home in Africa, and she wanted to do something that would help others, too. Then she found out about Me to
20 We, an **organization** that runs international volunteer trips and leadership camps. She joined the organization on a youth trip to Kenya to help build a school. While there, she spoke at a local girls' school. Molly now knew what she wanted to do next—to help inspire people by being a
25 speaker at Me to We.

Molly began speaking at schools all over the United States and Canada. Her advice? Be strong! During a speech in Toronto, she spoke to about 20,000 people. After her speech, the crowd stood up and clapped. "Molly has a real **ability** to
30 inspire people and to help others," her father says.

In 2014, Molly started her own YouTube channel, uploading things like makeup video blogs, or vlogs. As of 2019, she has close to two million subscribers, some of whom don't even know she's blind. She tries to be a **role model** for young
35 people, but is **realistic** about what she can and can't do. She even makes fun of the **challenges** she faces as a blind person—like tweeting that she once bit into a lemon, thinking it was a potato.

In 2018, Molly moved out of her parents' home and into her
40 own apartment in Los Angeles, where she still lives today. "How can you hold somebody like that back?" says her mother. "She's unstoppable."

Unit 3 **37**

Molly Burke slowly became blind from the age of four. Her friends started bullying her after she became completely blind. After finishing high school, she wasn't sure what she wanted to do, so she went to Africa with a volunteer group. There, she realized she wanted to be a motivational speaker. She decided to help others turn their pain into a positive story like she has. Now, she speaks to thousands of people, inspiring them with her story.

Making Inferences

Guide students in practicing making inferences based on some of the sentences in the passage. For example:

1 *In first grade, she learned to read Braille, although she could still see.* (lines 4 and 5) What can we guess about Braille from this sentence? (Braille is a way for people who can't see to read.)

2 *"I just started to cry," remembers Molly.* (line 8) What does this quote tell us about how Molly felt about losing her ability to see? (She was sad and maybe scared.)

3 *After her speech, the crowd stood up and clapped.* (lines 28 and 29) What does this sentence tell us about how the audience felt about Molly's speech? (They really enjoyed it.)

Developing Reading Speed

Have students read the passage silently to help them develop reading speed. Remind them that as they read, they don't have to stop to look up unknown words right away. Encourage them to keep the flow of their reading pace by continuing on and trying to figure out meaning through context.

🎧 **3.7** Play the audio for the first two paragraphs and have students read along to get an idea of the pace of reading. Point out that this is the speed that they should aim to read at.

Have students read the entire passage silently without the audio.

TEACHING NOTE: DEVELOPING READING SPEED

At this level, students should be developing their reading fluency and speed. Before students read the text, you might want to remind them that they do not need to stop and look up unfamiliar words. Encourage them to think about the context and guess what the meanings are, and then, if necessary, to read the article again and use a dictionary to check the meanings of words they still don't understand.

COMPREHENSION

A Have students read the questions to themselves and circle the correct answers.

After they have finished, check answers as a class.

IDIOM

As students follow along in their books, read the sentence and answer choices aloud. Have them guess the answer before providing it (c). Give an example:

Her smile was a ray of hope that he hadn't lost her trust entirely.

B **EXAM PRACTICE**

A timeline is a graphic representation of events that happen during a period of time. Each event is shown with a mark that is perpendicular to the timeline. An event that happens over a period of time is represented by a horizontal line spanning the period above or below the timeline. Students may find timelines to be helpful in understanding the order of and relationships between a complex group of events.

Although students are not required to make timelines for most standardized tests, the ability to understand the sequence of events is an important skill that is indirectly tested. For instance, multiple-choice questions may require students to accurately assess which event occurred first (e.g., the cause). On the IELTS test Academic Writing Task 1, students have to describe charts, graphs, maps, diagrams (processes), or the sequence of events.

Tell students they should complete the timeline by writing the letters that represent the events. As students follow along in their books, have a student read the events (**a–f**) aloud.

Have students do the task.

Check answers.

C **CRITICAL THINKING**

As students follow along, read the question aloud.

Have students get into pairs and make a list of at least four questions they would ask Molly. Then call on each pair to share two of their questions with the class.

COMPREHENSION

A Answer the questions about *Vision of Hope*.

1 GIST What could be another title for the article?

  a A High School YouTube Star

  ⓑ An Inspiring Role Model

  c How Molly Regained Her Vision

2 INFERENCE Which period of time was probably the most difficult for Molly?

  a elementary school   ⓑ high school   c college

3 CAUSE-EFFECT What led Molly to want to become a motivational speaker?

  a She gave a speech in Toronto.

  b She got positive feedback from her YouTube channel.

  ⓒ She spoke at a girls' school in Kenya.

4 PURPOSE Why does the author mention Molly mistakenly biting into a lemon?

  a to show that people sometimes still play tricks on Molly

  ⓑ to show that Molly has a sense of humor about her daily challenges

  c to show that there are still many things Molly cannot do

5 INFERENCE How does Molly's mother feel about her moving out?

  ⓐ She's supportive of the decision.

  b She's supportive, but feels that Molly is making a mistake.

  c She's not supportive, but knows there is no stopping Molly.

B Complete the timeline below with these events (a–f).

  a started a YouTube channel   d learned to read Braille

  b began to go blind   e became completely blind

  c went on a youth trip to Kenya   f moved to Los Angeles

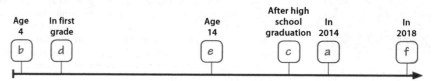

Age 4	In first grade		Age 14	After high school graduation	In 2014	In 2018
b	d		e	c	a	f

C CRITICAL THINKING Reflecting **Talk with a partner.** If you could interview Molly Burke, what questions would you ask her? Make a list. Answers will vary.

IDIOM

Something that provides you with a small amount of hope is called a _____.

 a rock of hope

 b ring of hope

 ⓒ ray of hope

OPTIONAL Have pairs role-play the interview with Molly. First, let them brainstorm possible answers to the questions together. Then have them decide who will be the interviewer and who will be Molly. Have them role-play the interview. If time permits, have them switch roles and do it again.

VOCABULARY

A **Find the words below in the article.** Then complete the paragraph using the words in the box.

> ability challenges gradually organization realistic role model

Molly Burke is a(n) [1] _role model_ for people everywhere. Due to a rare disease, she lost the [2] _ability_ to see at age 14. Her next few years of high school were difficult and full of [3] _challenges_. She was bullied by classmates so badly that she became depressed. But with the support of her family, she [4] _gradually_ recovered. After graduation, she wanted to share her story and help other victims of bullying, so she decided to become a motivational speaker for the [5] _organization_ Me to We. Since then, Molly has worked to educate others about disabilities, both physical and mental. She has even launched her own YouTube channel, where she posts regular vlogs and beauty videos. While she is careful to set [6] _realistic_ goals for herself, Molly doesn't let her disability prevent her from doing the things she loves.

B **Read the information below.** Then circle the correct answers.

> Phrasal verbs are two- or three-word verbs. These phrasal verbs include the verb *make*:
> *make up* = to invent or imagine   *make out* = to see or hear clearly
> *make of* = to understand or judge   *make up for* = to make a bad situation better

1 I hear a woman's voice, but I can't make **up** / **out** what she's saying.

2 He bought her flowers to make **of** / **up for** being late.

3 I don't believe Ian's story. Do you think he made it **up for** / **up**?

4 What do you make **of** / **out** our new classmate?

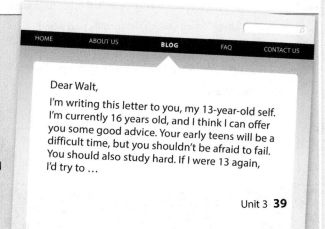

WRITING

A **Read the letter.**

B **Imagine you were 13 years old again.** What would you do differently? What are some things you wish you knew back then? Note your ideas.

C **Write a letter to your 13-year-old self.** Give yourself advice.
Answers will vary.

Dear Walt,

I'm writing this letter to you, my 13-year-old self. I'm currently 16 years old, and I think I can offer you some good advice. Your early teens will be a difficult time, but you shouldn't be afraid to fail. You should also study hard. If I were 13 again, I'd try to …

Unit 3 **39**

TEACHING NOTE: ROLE PLAY

Having students perform a role play of a situation connected to the learning topic can be a fun way to challenge their language skills while letting them be creative. Role plays should be set up keeping in mind a balance between structure and freedom. For example, the structure of the interview format, where pairs already know the interview questions for the interview with Molly, is combined with the freedom of expression from allowing students to decide on the spot what answers they want to give in response to the questions.

VOCABULARY

A Ask a student to read the words in the box aloud. Have students find them in the **READING** passage.

Have students use the words in the box to complete the paragraph. Check answers as a class.

B As students follow along, read the information in the box aloud. Have students circle the correct answers to complete the sentences. Check answers.

WRITING

Tell students they are going to write a letter to their 13-year-old self. Explain that the letter will be one that offers advice.

A As students follow along, read the example letter aloud. Point out that even though it is an imaginary letter, it still has a typical greeting (*Dear Walt,*).

B Read the questions aloud. Ask students to think about what they would do differently or what they wish they had known then that they know now. Have students make notes about their ideas. Tell students to also think about advice they can offer to their 13-year-old self. They can either offer a few pieces of short advice, like in the example, or write a longer piece of advice with a detailed explanation containing example situations.

C Have students write their letters. You might want to assign the writing as homework, and set a minimum number of sentences students must write (e.g., nine).

OPTIONAL Collect the letters and correct them. Pay particular attention to incorrect verb usage. You can correct the verbs, but you might want to just mark them as incorrect, so that students can make the corrections themselves when you return their work.

Have the students revise their writing, correcting the grammar mistakes. Collect the first and second drafts of the writings. If some students still have mistakes, correct the errors. In the next lesson, return the papers. If many students are making the same types of mistakes, review these mistakes in class.

VIDEO

CONTENT NOTE: SANGA MOSES AND ECO-FUEL AFRICA

Before starting Eco-Fuel Africa, Sanga Moses was an accountant for a top bank. However, he quit his job to help find an alternative to wood for fuel in Uganda. He worked with engineering students to make kilns and special machines that now turn food waste into fuel. Not only is this new fuel environmentally friendly, but it has created a positive economic impact, with 2,500 farmers earning about $30 a month each in extra income, and 460 retailers (all women) earning $150 a month each.

Tell students they are going to watch a video called "Eco-Fuel Africa." As students follow along in their books, read the sentence about the video aloud.

SUPPORT Make sure students understand the term *eco-fuel*. Explain that the prefix *eco-* is used in words connected to the ecology or environment, such as *eco-friendly*, *eco-patrol*, and *eco-lodge*. Explain that *fuel* refers to something that is used to make energy, such as gasoline for a car, or kerosene for a lamp.

BEFORE YOU WATCH

Tell students that they will take a quiz to see what they know about Uganda. As students follow along, read the statements aloud. Have students circle what they think are the correct answers.

Check answers.

OPTIONAL Have students find Uganda on a world map. Ask students to talk about what else they know about Uganda.

CONTENT NOTE: UGANDA

Uganda is a tropical, mountainous country in east central Africa with a population of

approximately 41 million. English and Swahili are its official languages. About 71 percent of the country's land is used for farming. The nation's biggest agricultural exports are coffee, tea, and flowers. Of the 41 million people in Uganda, 34 million live without electricity—they depend on wood for fuel. This dependence on wood has led to deforestation in Uganda. The smoky air created by wood burning has also impacted human health by causing respiratory diseases.

ECO-FUEL AFRICA

Before You Watch

Take a quiz. What do you know about Uganda? Circle the correct answers.

1 The capital city of Uganda is **Kira** / **Kampala**
2 Uganda's biggest export is **coffee** / **fuel**.
3 About **40** / **80** percent of the population lives in rural areas.
4 **English** / **French** is one of its national languages.

While You Watch

A ▶ 3.2 **Watch the video.** What could be another title for the video?

a Fuel Shortages in Uganda: Effects and Solutions
b Improving Fuel Storage Sites in Uganda
ⓒ A New Fuel for Cooking

B ▶ 3.2 **Watch again.** What are the advantages of Sanga Moses's eco-fuel? Check (✓) the ones mentioned in the video.

☑ burns cleaner   ☑ saves forests   ☐ creates bigger fires
☑ burns longer   ☑ is cheaper   ☐ can be reused many times

C **Put the events in order (1–6).**

2 Sanga Moses quit his job.
4 Sanga Moses spent all his savings.
5 Sanga Moses created a clean fuel using farm waste.
1 Sanga Moses saw his sister collecting wood.
6 Sanga Moses became CEO of Eco-Fuel Africa.
3 Sanga Moses got some advice from a professor.

After You Watch

Talk with a partner. Sanga Moses's advice to teens is to "follow your heart." What does this mean? Do you think this is good advice? Why or why not?
Answers will vary.

Sanga Moses

ABOUT THE PHOTO

This photo shows Sanga Moses, the founder of Eco-Fuel Africa—an organization working to improve the lives of people in Africa by providing them with a cleaner and cheaper source of fuel. In Uganda, where Sanga is from, wood is a primary source of fuel for many families. However, collecting wood is time-consuming, and the burning of wood causes indoor air pollution. Wanting to increase the quality of life for people, especially women, Sanga set out to create an alternative source of fuel. His solution: converting agricultural waste such as corn waste, coffee husks, and sugarcane waste into environmentally friendly fuel. (See **CONTENT NOTE** for more information.)

WHILE YOU WATCH

A Tell students that they will watch the video and they should circle the alternate title that they think is best. As students follow along in their books, read the options aloud.

▶ 3.2 Play Video 3.2. Check answers.

B Tell students that they will watch the video again and they should check the advantages of the eco-fuel. As students follow along in their books, have a student read the options aloud.

A **Complete the sentences.** Circle the correct answers.

1 If you're sorry, it's a good idea to **apologize** / **get a summer job**.

2 If you aren't sure what to do, it's OK to **pursue a career** / **ask for advice**

3 A **bully** / **role model** is someone who often hurts or frightens other people.

4 Something that is not easy to do is a(n) **challenge** / **ability**.

5 If you're realistic, you're **scared and worried** / **sensible and practical**.

B **Complete the sentences.** Use the words in the box.

could	don't	should	suggest	tried	were

1 Have you ___tried___ telling your friend how you feel?

2 It's getting late. I think you ___should___ call a taxi to get home.

3 I can't find my keys. What do you ___suggest___ I do?

4 There are a lot of ways to earn money. You ___could___ tutor someone in English.

5 If I ___were___ you, I'd tell the teacher the truth.

6 Why ___don't___ you talk to someone about your problem?

C **Complete the phrasal verbs in these sentences.** Use up to two words for each blank.

1 What do you make ___of___ what the principal said this morning?

2 The story he told you wasn't real—he made it all ___up___.

3 Nothing can make ___up for___ his bad behavior.

SELF CHECK   Now I can …

☐ talk about possible careers

☐ ask for and give advice

☐ talk about people who have achieved success in their careers

Unit 3   **41**

▶ 3.2 Play Video 3.2. Play it again, if necessary.

Check answers.

C Tell students to put the events of Sanga Moses's story in order, from 1 to 6. As students follow along in their books, read the events aloud.

Have students do the task.

Check answers.

OPTIONAL To review using a timeline as a graphic organizer, have students work in pairs to create a timeline about Sanga Moses.

AFTER YOU WATCH

Tell students they will get into pairs and talk about the video.

As students follow along in their books, read the questions aloud.

Have students do the task.

SUPPORT Before students begin their discussion, ask students what *follow your heart* means, providing the answer if necessary. (In this case, *your heart* refers to strong feelings you have about something. To follow your heart means to do what you believe is the right thing to do.)

CHALLENGE Have students work in groups to research the latest news connected to the video topic. Have each group give a short presentation to the class, providing an update on Sanga Moses, Eco-Fuel Africa, or the new type of fuel they have created.

REVIEW

Explain to students that they are going to review the material from the unit and this will help them remember what they have studied.

A Explain that activity **A** reviews vocabulary from the unit. Explain that they should circle the correct answers to complete the sentences.

Have students do the task. Check answers as a class.

B Explain that activity **B** reviews the grammar from the unit. Tell students they should use the words in the box to complete the sentences.

Have students do the task. Check answers.

C Point out that activity **C** reviews words from **VOCABULARY** activity **B**.

Have students use up to two words for each blank to complete the phrasal verbs in the sentences. Check answers.

SELF CHECK

These *I can* statements provide vital feedback into students' perceived ability to use the language from the unit. Have students check the things that they can do.

UNIT 4

THE KOALA WAS TAKEN TO A SHELTER

4 THE KOALA WAS **TAKEN TO A SHELTER**

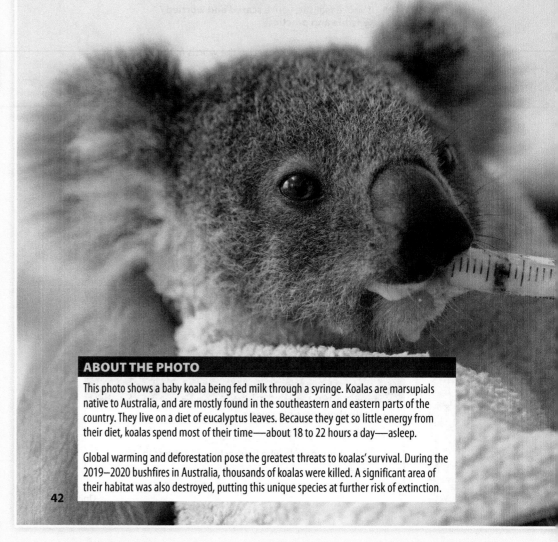

CONTENT AREA: THE NATURAL WORLD

Topic: animal rescue; endangered animals

Vocabulary: actions: weigh, tag, breathe, calm down, feed, check for, release back into, send, wrap, leave, abandon, investigate, hang, cheer; **other words:** blanket, cage, dangerous, suddenly, frightened

Grammar: passive voice

Extra material: a world map, a map of the United States

Other useful vocabulary:
animals: bird, cat, dog, duck, gerbil, goose, guinea pig, hamster, rabbit, swan, turkey, tortoise, iguana

END OF UNIT PROJECT In this unit, students did research on an endangered species for the project in **THE REAL WORLD**. Tell students that for their end of unit project, they will do a presentation about rescue efforts being made to help that endangered species they researched. Explain that they will prepare a short presentation that they will give during the next lesson.

Tell students to do additional research online. Remind them to seek information from reliable websites.

Explain that students should give some basic information about the species in their presentation before talking about what is being done to help them. If necessary, provide ideas for basic information:

ABOUT THE PHOTO

This photo shows a baby koala being fed milk through a syringe. Koalas are marsupials native to Australia, and are mostly found in the southeastern and eastern parts of the country. They live on a diet of eucalyptus leaves. Because they get so little energy from their diet, koalas spend most of their time—about 18 to 22 hours a day—asleep.

Global warming and deforestation pose the greatest threats to koalas' survival. During the 2019–2020 bushfires in Australia, thousands of koalas were killed. A significant area of their habitat was also destroyed, putting this unique species at further risk of extinction.

1 Approximate number of animals in that species left in the world

2 Where the species is (continent, country, etc.)

3 Characteristics of the species (e.g., size, average life span)

4 Threats to the species

Tell them that in addition to this information, they must talk about an organization that is trying to help that species. Ask them to give specific information about the organization, what it does, and how it is helping the species.

Encourage students to use pictures in their presentations.

Assign the presentation preparation as homework.

In the next lesson, have students take turns giving their presentations. If they talk about the location of the organization, have them show this on a world map.

Finish with a class discussion about the different organizations. Ask which organization students think is doing the most interesting work. Encourage them to give reasons why.

PREVIEW

A 🎧 4.1 **Listen.** What happens when an injured koala is found? Check (✓) the actions mentioned.

- ✓ It's wrapped in a blanket.
- ✓ It's placed in a cage.
- ☐ It's weighed.
- ✓ A tag is attached to it.
- ☐ It's paired with another koala.

B 🎧 4.1 **Listen again.** Circle the correct answers.

1 Wrapping the koala in a blanket helps the animal **breathe /** **calm down**.

2 It's easier to **feed /** **check for injuries on** the koala after washing it.

3 Most rescued koalas are eventually **released back into the wild /** sent to a zoo.

C **Talk with a partner.** Have you ever seen, or read a story about, an injured or lost animal? Explain what happened. Answers will vary.

> I found a kitten behind my house once. It was starving.

> How sad. What did you do?

An orphaned baby koala is fed milk in Port Macquarie, Australia.

THE NATURAL WORLD

UNIT GOALS

- talk about animal rescue
- use language to describe things that are/were done
- learn about different ways to save endangered animals

43

CONTENT NOTE: ANIMAL SHELTERS

Animal shelters take in lost and abandoned animals, including some wild creatures, and care for them temporarily. Many shelters function as non-profit organizations, so they rely on donations, gifts, and adoption fees to function. The American Society for the Prevention of Cruelty to Animals (ASPCA) estimates that around 6.5 million animals—mostly dogs and cats—are taken in by animal shelters in the United States every year.

PREVIEW

Have students study the photo for a moment. Read the unit title and the photo caption aloud, as students follow along. Explain that in this unit they will learn to talk about animal rescue. Tell them they will also learn to talk about things that were previously done.

A Tell students that they will listen to a short talk about koalas. Tell them to check the things that are done when an injured koala is found. As students follow along, read the list of actions aloud.

🎧 4.1 Play Audio Track 4.1. Don't check answers yet.

B Tell students that they will listen again, and they should circle the correct answers to complete the sentences.

🎧 4.1 Play Audio Track 4.1. Play it again, if necessary.

Check answers for **A** and **B**.

CHALLENGE Have students do **B** based on their first listening of the audio in **A**. Then play the audio again to have them check answers for **A** and **B**.

C Tell students they are going to get into pairs and take turns sharing a story about an injured or lost animal.

Model the conversation with a student.

Have students do the task.

SUPPORT Before doing the task, review the meaning and pronunciation of words that students heard in the audio that may be helpful in their discussions: *injury, animal shelter, vet, cage, fur, medicine, surgery*.

CHALLENGE Have pairs choose one of their stories and make a storyboard about it. Explain that a storyboard is a like a comic that uses pictures and words to tell the story. Have each pair present their storyboard and use it to explain the story of the rescued animal to the class.

UNIT GOALS

Direct students' attention to the **UNIT GOALS** box. Explain that these are some of the things students will learn in this unit. Point out that this unit is about the natural world. As students follow along, read each of the unit goals to the class. Explain any words students do not know. Remind students that at the end of the unit there is a self check that allows them to see if they have accomplished each goal.

LANGUAGE FOCUS

A Tell students they will listen to a conversation between Stig and Ming.

🎧 **4.2** Play Audio Track 4.2 as students listen and follow along in their books.

As students follow along, read the question, *What does Ming say about all the dogs at the rescue center?* Have students answer. Point out that *rescue center* is a synonym for *animal shelter*.

Have students work in pairs and practice the conversation once. Point out the bold words. Tell students to practice the conversation two more times, changing the bold words each time and swapping roles after the first time.

OPTIONAL Have students repeat the conversation, using another animal. Assign each pair an animal to adopt. (See **Other useful vocabulary**.)

REAL ENGLISH

Direct students' attention to the expression in the **REAL ENGLISH** box. Explain that we use *It's up to you* in informal English when the other person has to make a decision and the speaker doesn't want to make it for him/her. For example:

A: Do you think I should buy this blue dress or the red one?

B: It's up to you. They both look great.

B Ask students to look at the chart. Explain that they will practice how to talk about things that are/were done.

🎧 **4.3** Have students follow along as they listen to Audio Track 4.3.

Direct students' attention to the first three rows in the chart. Explain that the sentences on the left are in the active voice and the sentences on the right are in the passive voice. Tell students that we use the passive voice to describe an

---

A 🎧 **4.2 Listen and read.** What does Ming say about all the dogs at the rescue center? Then repeat the conversation and replace the words in **bold**. *He says they're all so cute.*

> **REAL ENGLISH** It's up to you.

Stig:	I really want to adopt a dog from a rescue center.
Ming:	That's **great**! What kind of dog do you want? (**cool** / **wonderful**)
Stig:	I'm not sure. Do you think I should get a **small dog**? (**little dog** / **puppy**)
Ming:	It's up to you. They're all so cute!
Stig:	Look here. It says this one was brought in **last weekend**. (**a few days ago** / **on Sunday**)
Ming:	Do you think he was abandoned?
Stig:	Yeah, maybe.
Ming:	Hey! **He looks just like you!** (**You two have the same hairstyle** / **You two could be twins**)

B 🎧 **4.3 Look at the chart.** Then circle the correct answers below.

TALKING ABOUT THINGS THAT ARE/WERE DONE (USING PASSIVE VOICE)	
The vet **wraps** the koala in a blanket. →	The koala **is wrapped** in a blanket.
He **is washing** the baby rabbit carefully. →	The baby rabbit **is being washed** carefully.
Someone **left** the dog at the shelter. →	The dog **was left** at the shelter.
Was the dog **abandoned**?	Yes, it was. / No, it wasn't.
How often **are** the animals **fed**?	Every four hours. / Six times a day.

1 We form the passive with the verb *be* + **present participle (e.g., eating)** / **past participle (e.g., eaten)**.

2 We use the passive to focus on the person or thing that **performs** / **experiences** an action.

3 The passive **can** / **cannot** be used when we don't know who performs an action.

---

action when the person who did the action is not the main focus or when we don't know who did the action. Emphasize that the passive voice allows us to focus on the action or the recipient of the action instead of on the person who performs the action.

Read the first sentence on the left aloud. Remind students this sentence is in the active voice. Point out that we know who does the action (*the vet*) and what the action is (*wraps the koala in a blanket*).

Read the first sentence on the right aloud. Point out that what happened and when it happened are the same. Emphasize that in the sentence on the right side, the subject is the animal because the animal is what is important, and it doesn't matter who does the action in this case.

Read the sentences in the second and third rows aloud. Have students use these sentences to identify the form used for passive sentences (*be* + past participle).

C **Complete the conversation.** Use the correct form of the verbs in parentheses.

Max: How was your weekend, Chloe?

Chloe: Very interesting. I volunteered at the animal shelter.

Max: Really? Was it a good experience?

Chloe: It was! On Saturday, a small bird ¹ _was brought_ (**bring**) in. Everyone thought its wings were broken.

Max: Oh, no! Did it survive?

Chloe: Yeah. It ² _was given_ (**give**) some medicine and then its wings ³ _were checked_ (**check**). The vet said they weren't broken.

Max: Well, that's good. ⁴ _Was_ the bird _released_ (**release**) after that?

Chloe: No, it's still too weak. Right now, it ⁵ _'s being treated_ (**treat**) for other minor injuries. It will have to stay at the shelter until it gets stronger.

D 🎧 4.4 **Complete the information.** Use the correct form of the verbs in parentheses. Then listen and check your answers.

If you find a small, injured animal like a bird or squirrel, it probably needs medical attention. Before you ¹ _take_ (**take**) the animal to a shelter, make sure it ² _is covered_ (**cover**) with a towel or blanket. Then try to get it into a box or cage.

Line the box with some paper or old clothes to make the animal more comfortable. ³ _Put_ (**put**) the box somewhere dark and quiet. Once the animal ⁴ _is placed_ (**place**) in a dark environment, it will begin to relax. Then head for the nearest shelter. Don't feed the animal.

If you find a larger animal like a deer or wild boar, you should ⁵ _call_ (**call**) a rescue service for help. Never approach larger wild animals unless you ⁶ _are told_ (**tell**) to do so.

E **Work with a partner. Student A:** Turn to page 151. **Student B:** Turn to page 152.

A volunteer checks on a rescued bird.

C Have students write the correct form of the verbs in parentheses to complete the conversation. Encourage students to use contractions wherever possible, to make the conversation sound more natural.

Check answers.

D Have students write the correct form of the verbs in parentheses to complete the information. Point out that, unlike in **C**, these sentences are considered formal writing, so students should not use contractions.

Tell students that they will listen and check their answers.

🎧 4.4 Play Audio Track 4.4. Check answers as a class.

SUPPORT Remind students that when someone is doing the action, the sentence is in the active voice, whereas when the action is being done upon someone or something, the sentence is in the passive voice.

E Tell students they are going to get into pairs and take turns asking and answering questions to complete a news article about a rescued animal.

Have students get into pairs. Have Student As turn to page 151 and Student Bs turn to page 152. Explain that they have the same news article but with different parts missing, and they need to ask and answer questions to complete the article.

Have students write the questions they need to ask their partner so that they can complete the article. Tell them to use the words in parentheses to help them form questions.

Have students ask and answer questions and complete the article.

Check answers.

SUPPORT Write some active sentences on the board. (e.g., *Volunteers washed the dogs. A nurse gave the cat food.*) Have students turn these active sentences into passive sentences. (*The dogs were washed. The cat was given food.*)

Read the two questions and the responses in the fourth and fifth rows aloud. Explain that both questions use the passive voice, but the first is in the past tense and the second is in the present tense.

OPTIONAL Have students get into pairs and write down five active sentences and their passive equivalents. When they have finished, have each pair get together with another pair. Tell the pairs to take turns reading out one of their active or passive sentences for the other pair to provide the active or passive equivalent.

Draw students' attention to the three statements under the chart. Have students circle the correct answers. Check answers.

THE REAL WORLD

Ask students to look at the photo. As students follow along, read the title and the caption aloud.

A Tell students they are going to watch a video about National Geographic photographer Joel Sartore. Tell them to check the topics that are mentioned. As students follow along, have a student read the topics aloud.

▶ 4.1 Play Video 4.1. Play it again, if necessary.

Check answers.

DO YOU KNOW?

Read the question and answer choices aloud, as students follow along in their books. Have students guess the answer before providing it (b). (See **CONTENT NOTE.**)

CONTENT NOTE: ORANGUTANS

Orangutans are found on the islands of Sumatra and Borneo. Due to heavy deforestation in the jungles where they live, orangutans are facing extinction. Orangutans depend on trees for their survival—they eat fruit, bark, and insects from trees, sleep in trees, and even find the water they drink there. DNA analysis shows that orangutans are closely related to humans.

B Tell students they will watch the video again and they should circle the correct answers to complete the sentences.

▶ 4.1 Play Video 4.1. Play it again, if necessary. Check answers.

C As students follow along, read the task and ways to help save threatened animal species aloud. Tell students to rank the ways according to which ones they are most likely to do, from 1 (most likely) to 4 (least likely).

THE REAL WORLD

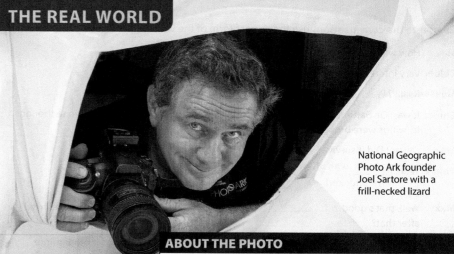

National Geographic Photo Ark founder Joel Sartore with a frill-necked lizard

ANIMAL PORTRAITS

NATIONAL GEOGRAPHIC

PHOTO ARK
JOEL SARTORE

ABOUT THE PHOTO

This photo shows Joel Sartore during a photo shoot. Joel is a wildlife photographer for National Geographic, and one of his biggest projects is the Photo Ark. Joel's goal is to create a comprehensive photo archive of all the animal species living in zoos and sanctuaries around the world. To date, he has photographed more than 9,000 species for the Photo Ark. It isn't always easy to take close-up portraits of animals. To ensure the animals don't get stressed by the shoot, Joel keeps the sessions short. He also has to be careful when taking photos—a crane once tried to blind him. In spite of the challenges, Joel is determined for the project to continue, even after he is gone.

A ▶ 4.1 **Watch the video.** Check (✓) the topics mentioned.

☐ where Joel Sartore lives

☑ when the National Geographic Photo Ark project was founded

☑ the goal of the Photo Ark project

☑ the number of species in the Photo Ark

☐ the countries Joel has traveled to

DO YOU KNOW?

Which of these animals is the most endangered?
a red kangaroo
b orangutan
c giant panda

B ▶ 4.1 **Watch again.** Circle the correct answers.

1 Joel's projects mainly deal with **wildlife conservation** / **the illegal animal trade**.

2 The animals in the Photo Ark are photographed **in the wild** / **against a plain background**.

3 In Joel's photos, small animals and big animals are presented **in the same way** / **differently**.

4 Joel feels that the Photo Ark project **is near completion** / **will continue for a long time**.

46 Unit 4

Have students do the task. Then have students share their rankings with a partner. Encourage them to give reasons for their ranking.

D CRITICAL THINKING

As students follow along, read the task aloud. Have students get into pairs and talk about their ideas. Remind them to support their opinions with reasons. Afterward, call on students to share their opinions (and reasons for their opinions) with the class.

OPTIONAL Give students additional questions to discuss. Remind them to give reasons for their answers.

1 Do you think zoos should try to put animals back into the wild?

2 Do you think Joel Sartore should photograph animals in the wild instead?

PROJECT As students follow along, read the project instructions aloud. If possible, visit the Photo Ark website together.

C Rank. On his website, Joel Sartore suggests the following ways to help save threatened animal species. Which of these are you most likely to do? Rank them from **1** (most likely) to **4** (least likely). Then compare with a partner. Answers will vary.

_____ Donate money to a local conservation group.

_____ Support the Photo Ark by purchasing a photo or book.

_____ Volunteer with a local zoo, aquarium, or wildlife center.

_____ Share photos from the Photo Ark on your social media pages.

D CRITICAL THINKING Justifying an Opinion **Talk with a partner.** Some people think that animals shouldn't be kept in captivity. Others feel that zoos are great places to protect animals and to educate the public. What do you think? Give reasons for your opinion. Answers will vary.

PROJECT Go to the National Geographic Photo Ark website (NatGeoPhotoArk.org) and search for an animal. Where was the photo taken? What is the animal's status? What threats does it face? Make some notes and share with a partner.

PRONUNCIATION intonation in a series

🎧 4.5 **Listen.** Mark each sentence with the intonation pattern ↗ or ↘. Then listen again and repeat the sentences.

1 The shelter was able to save a bird, a raccoon, and a rabbit.

2 The bird was picked up, wrapped in a blanket, and taken to the shelter.

3 The animal was given food, water, and medicine.

COMMUNICATION

Work in groups. Create a headline by matching information from these three columns. Include detailed information to make the story interesting. Then present your group's news story to the class. Answers will vary.

A	B	C
An Angry Monkey		at a Playground
Three Hungry Zebras	Seen	in a High School Cafeteria
Several Snakes	Spotted	outside a Burning Building
Thirty Cats	Found	inside an Ice Cream Shop
A Basket of Puppies	Discovered	near the Zoo Entrance
A Swarm of Bees		on a Cruise Ship

In today's news, several snakes were found inside an ice cream shop.

That's right. The snakes were seen …

When students get to the Photo Ark homepage, they will see photos of animals as they scroll down the page. One way to choose an animal is to scroll through the photos and click on one. Another way is to use the search function at the top of the homepage to type in a specific species name.

Have students make notes about any information they learn about their chosen animal from the page. Remind them to put the information in their own words—they should not copy directly from the site.

Have students get into pairs and share their findings with a partner.

PRONUNCIATION

Tell students they will practice their intonation when reading a series (i.e., a list within a sentence). If necessary, remind students that speakers do not say everything in a flat voice but use intonation to more clearly express meaning.

Have students follow along in their books as you explain that the blue arrows in the first sentence represent the speaker's voice rising or falling. Tell students to listen and mark the second and third sentences with the intonation pattern they hear.

🎧 4.5 Play Audio Track 4.5. Play it again, if necessary.

Check answers.

🎧 4.5 Play the audio again, pausing after each sentence so students can repeat.

COMMUNICATION

Explain to students that they are going to work in groups to create a headline and a news story that they will present to the class. Tell them that they will start by creating a headline for their story. Point out the three columns (A, B, C). Explain that they should choose a phrase from each column to create their headline. Call on a few students to read the phrases in the columns aloud.

Tell students that after they have created their headline, they will create a story to go with it. Explain that they should include detailed information to make the story interesting. Emphasize that students must write the story in such a way that everyone has a speaking part during the presentation.

Model the presentation with a student.

Remind students that the passive voice is useful when explaining events, and that news stories often use the passive voice.

Have students get into small groups to decide their headline and write their story. Encourage students to be creative in their stories.

Walk around the classroom, providing assistance as necessary (e.g., providing new vocabulary). If some groups finish more quickly than others, have them practice their presentations.

Have groups take turns giving their presentations.

READING

CONTENT NOTE: BLACK BEARS

Black bears are the most common bears in North America. They are large, stocky, and have short tails. In spite of their name, their color varies, with some being brown, others having white marks on their chests, and still others having blue-gray or blue-black hues. Black bears are known to be excellent climbers and swimmers. During the winter, they tend to hibernate.

Black bears are extremely adaptive, and if they live near humans they will soon start to look for food in the garbage and at campsites. It doesn't take long for them to start taking food that is being given by tourists. This can lead to conflicts, human injury, and the extermination of bears, so it is better to avoid feeding them.

Ask a student to read the title aloud. Have students look at the photos, and then follow along in their books as you read the captions aloud.

A Read the question aloud. Randomly call on students to share their answers with the class.

Remind students that by thinking about the content before they read, they can understand it more quickly. Tell them this is called *predicting*. Tell students that another technique is called *previewing*. Explain it if necessary. (See **TEACHING NOTE**.)

OPTIONAL Have students find California on a map of the United States.

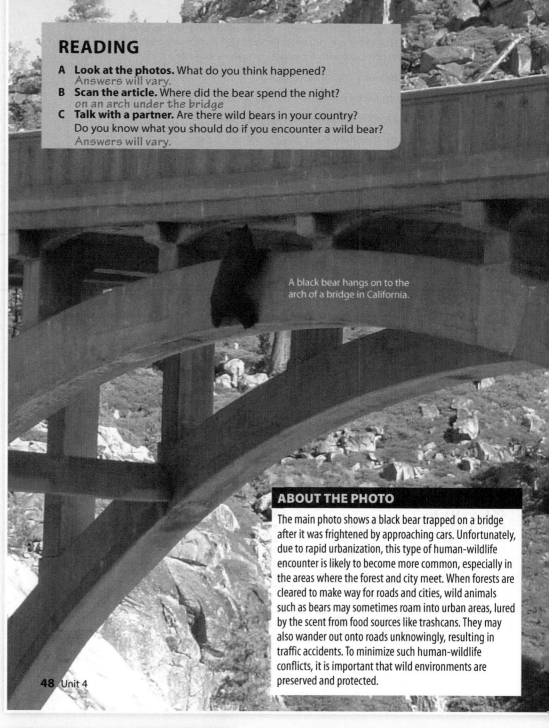

READING

A **Look at the photos.** What do you think happened?
Answers will vary.
B **Scan the article.** Where did the bear spend the night?
on an arch under the bridge
C **Talk with a partner.** Are there wild bears in your country? Do you know what you should do if you encounter a wild bear?
Answers will vary.

A black bear hangs on to the arch of a bridge in California.

ABOUT THE PHOTO

The main photo shows a black bear trapped on a bridge after it was frightened by approaching cars. Unfortunately, due to rapid urbanization, this type of human-wildlife encounter is likely to become more common, especially in the areas where the forest and city meet. When forests are cleared to make way for roads and cities, wild animals such as bears may sometimes roam into urban areas, lured by the scent from food sources like trashcans. They may also wander out onto roads unknowingly, resulting in traffic accidents. To minimize such human-wildlife conflicts, it is important that wild environments are preserved and protected.

48 Unit 4

TEACHING NOTE: PREVIEWING

To preview a text, students should:
1 Read the title.
2 Read the headings, if there are any.
3 Look at the photos, and article/text layout.

These elements will give students clues about what they are going to read.

B As students follow along in their books, read the question aloud. Tell students that they should scan the article to find the answer.

Have students do the task.

Check answers.

C As students follow along in their books, read the questions aloud. Have students get into pairs and discuss their answers.

After completing the task, give students the opportunity to read the article in more detail so they can answer the **COMPREHENSION** questions.

BEAR *RESCUE*

🎧 4.6 A black bear was in a **dangerous** situation when she fell off a 30-meter-high bridge. After a long day in California's Sierra Nevada mountains, the bear probably thought she was taking a shortcut home. She was walking across the bridge when, **suddenly**, two cars entered from both sides. There was nowhere
5 to run, so the **frightened** bear jumped onto the rail and began to fall over the side.

Luckily, the bear pulled herself onto an arch under the bridge, but she was trapped there. A driver at the scene called 911. Robert Brooks, an animal control officer from the nearby town of Truckee, was sent to **investigate**. "I thought it
10 was a joke," he said. But it wasn't a joke, so he called Dave Baker of the BEAR League—an organization that helps bears in trouble. "He thought I was playing a joke on him, too," Brooks said.

Unfortunately, the sky was getting dark, so the rescuers had to wait. Early next morning, the two men returned to the bridge with more volunteers. Amazingly,
15 the bear was still there. They needed to rescue her quickly. Baker had an idea—they should **hang** a net under the bear, push her into it, and then lower her to the ground.

Firefighters volunteered to lower the 100-kilogram bear once she was in the net. Police officers closed the road, and when the net arrived, it was hung under
20 the bridge. Then, an animal control officer shot a dart containing a sleeping drug into the bear's shoulder. Ann Bryant, head of the BEAR League, stood under the bridge. When the bear was sleepy, Bryant yelled, "OK, push!" A volunteer rock climber used his feet to push the bear off the arch, right into the middle of the net.

25 The bear was gently lowered to the ground. When she touched the ground, everyone **cheered**. Bryant and Officer Brooks guided the sleepy bear to a small river, where she could finally get a drink. "She just kind of lay down on her tummy and put her paws under her chin," said Bryant, "like a dog lying on the living room floor … only big!" The rescuers then cleared all the people from the
30 area and left the bear alone so she could sleep. Since then, no one has seen her. "I don't think she's going near that bridge anymore," Brooks said.

Rescuers use a net to carry the bear to safety.

Unit 4 **49**

---

3 Don't make eye contact with the bear.
4 Make loud noises to frighten the bear away.
5 Wave your arms. This will help the bear realize you are human.

Additional Activities to Use with the Reading

Additional Comprehension Questions

1 How did rescuers get the bear into the net? (They shot a dart into the bear from a safe distance away, to make the bear sleepy. Once the bear was sleepy, a volunteer got close to the bear and used his feet to push the bear off the arch and into the net.)

2 Why did everyone cheer (line 26)? (They were happy they could save the bear, without the bear or any people getting hurt.)

3 Why did Brooks say he doesn't think the bear will go near the bridge anymore? (He thinks the bear will remember the danger she was in and won't put herself in the same situation again.)

Listening and Pronunciation

Tell students they will practice intonation in longer sentences. Tell them that they will listen to the first paragraph of the text and should draw arrows to show the intonation (pointing up for rising or down for falling).

🎧 4.6 Play Audio Track 4.6. Have students add arrows as they listen to the first paragraph. Play it again, if necessary.

Check answers. (Falling intonation at: *bridge, home, sides, side*; Rising intonation at: *mountains, when, suddenly, run*)

🎧 4.6 Play the audio again, pausing after each change in intonation in the first paragraph so students can repeat.

OPTIONAL The text can also be used as a listening activity. Have students close their books. Tell them they will listen to the passage.

🎧 4.6 Play Audio Track 4.6. Ask students to get into pairs and discuss what information they heard. Then have them read the article more carefully.

CONTENT NOTE: ENCOUNTER WITH A BEAR

Experts give the following advice for sudden encounters with a bear:
1 Don't panic.
2 Don't run.
  • If the bear isn't coming toward you, walk away slowly.
  • If the bear is running toward you, keep standing there. You cannot outrun it.
  • If the bear is touching you, curl up into a ball or lie on your tummy.

COMPREHENSION

A EXAM PRACTICE

Multiple-choice questions are used on standardized tests around the world. Multiple-choice items can be either questions, or statements with a blank. There are many kinds of items, including detail, purpose, main idea, inference, and reference. Multiple-choice questions usually follow the order of the reading (or listening) passage. Hints for mastering these test items include:

- Students should not spend too much time on one question, particularly when all questions are equally weighted. They can return to a question at the end if they have extra time.
- The students' understanding of meaning is tested. Repetition of words can be deceiving, so they should not choose an answer simply because it has some of the same words as the passage.
- Remember that even though some of the answer choices might be true, they aren't necessarily the correct answer.
- Differentiation of fact, opinion, feeling, and argument may be necessary.
- Pay attention to *don't, always, never, sometimes,* and other words that may change the meaning of the question or answer.
- Make sure you are on the correct number on the answer sheet. It is easy to fill in the circle for the wrong number, potentially affecting more than one answer.

Have students read the questions to themselves and circle the correct answers.

After they have finished, check answers as a class.

COMPREHENSION

A Answer the questions about *Bear Rescue*.

1 **PURPOSE** The purpose of the article is to _____ .

   a teach readers about bears

   ⓑ tell an interesting story

   c persuade readers that wild bears are dangerous

2 **INFERENCE** Baker thought Brooks was joking because _____ .

   ⓐ it was an unbelievable story

   b Brooks often tells jokes

   c it was a very funny story

3 **DETAIL** Why wasn't the bear rescued immediately?

   ⓐ It got too dark.

   b The rescuers couldn't find a net.

   c There were too many cars on the bridge.

4 **INFERENCE** The rescuers had to make the bear sleep first so that she _____ .

   a could rest   b wouldn't feel hungry   ⓒ wouldn't attack people

5 **DETAIL** According to the article, who was NOT involved in the rescue?

   a a firefighter   ⓑ a vet   c a rock climber

B Put the events in order (1–7).

   6 The bear was lowered safely to the ground.

   4 Rescuers hung a net under the bridge.

   3 The bear started to fall and became stuck under the bridge.

   7 The people who were watching were all cleared from the area.

   1 A bear was walking across a tall bridge in the Sierra Nevada mountains.

   5 The bear was shot with a sleeping dart and pushed into the net.

   2 Two cars entered the bridge, and the bear jumped onto the rail.

C **CRITICAL THINKING Evaluating** **Talk with a partner.** Can you think of other ways the bear could have been rescued? Answers will vary.

IDIOM

If you tell someone to "hang in there," you are telling them to _____ .

a cut corners
b forget their problems
ⓒ not give up

IDIOM

As students follow along in their books, read the sentence and answer choices aloud. Have them guess the answer before providing it (c). Give an example:

A: I'm having a rough day. Everything is going wrong.

B: Hang in there. Tomorrow will be a new day!

B Tell students that they will put the events in the order in which they happened in the story. As students follow along in their books, have a few students read the events aloud.

Have students do the task.

Check answers.

OPTIONAL Have students use the events listed in **B** to retell the story in their own words. Ask them to reword the sentences. Then have them get into pairs and take turns retelling the story.

VOCABULARY

A **Find the bold words below in the article.** Then circle the correct answers.

1 Something that is **dangerous** is not (safe) / helpful.

2 An event that happens **suddenly** happens *slowly and expectedly* / (*quickly and unexpectedly*.)

3 A **frightened** animal is (*scared of*) / *unsure about* something.

4 If you **investigate** a situation, you *completely ignore it* / (*try to find out what happened*.)

5 Two things you can **hang** are *a river and a tree* / (*a towel and a painting*.)

6 When people **cheer**, they are probably (happy) / unhappy.

B **Read the information below.** Then look at the verbs in the box. Add them to the correct column in the chart. Use a dictionary to help you.

> A transitive verb requires an object (*He lowered* **the net**.). An intransitive verb does not require an object (*The bear fell*.). Some verbs can be both transitive (*I broke* **the plate**.) and intransitive (*The plate broke*.).

arrive	bring	come	enter	help	rescue

Transitive verbs	Intransitive verbs	Transitive and intransitive verbs
bring, rescue	arrive, come	enter, help

WRITING

A **Look at the photo.** Read the beginning of the news article.

B **Make notes about the photo.** What does it show? What do you think happened next?

C **Write a news article based on the photo.** Use your notes from **B** to help you.
Answers will vary.

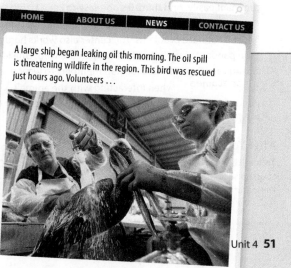

HOME   ABOUT US   NEWS   CONTACT US

A large ship began leaking oil this morning. The oil spill is threatening wildlife in the region. This bird was rescued just hours ago. Volunteers . . .

Unit 4 **51**

CHALLENGE Have students role-play an interview between a rescue worker and a newspaper reporter. Explain that the reporter will ask questions and the rescue worker will describe what happened. Encourage students to use the passive voice when retelling the story.

C CRITICAL THINKING

As students follow along, read the question aloud. Have students get into pairs and discuss their ideas.

VOCABULARY

A Have a student read the bold words aloud. Have students find them in the **READING** passage.

Have students circle the correct words to complete the sentences. Check answers.

B As students follow along, read the information in the box aloud. Then have a student read the verbs in the gray box aloud. Have students add the verbs to the correct column in the chart.

Check answers.

WRITING

Tell students they are going to write a news article about the animal in the photo. Explain that since they don't know exactly what happened, they will need to make up a story.

A Have students look at the photo. Read the example aloud. Point out that this is just the beginning of the article. Tell students that their article should include information about what happened, who was involved, and the end result.

___

OPTIONAL If necessary, remind students about digital literacy. (See **TEACHING NOTE**.) Ask, *Do you think this photo has been altered?* Have students give reasons for their ideas.

TEACHING NOTE: DIGITAL LITERACY

Digital literacy includes the ability to find, use, manipulate, and evaluate information, including images. With the advent of modern technology, it is increasingly important for students to think critically about media, including photos, since they can be digitally altered to appear real.

B Read the questions aloud. Have students look at the photo again and make notes about their ideas. Encourage them to organize their ideas by writing out events in order on a timeline or in a list.

C Have students write their articles, using their notes from **B**. You might want to assign the writing as homework, and set a minimum number of sentences students must write (e.g., nine).

___

OPTIONAL Make a class newspaper with all the articles. Collect the articles and put them together to create a newspaper. Distribute copies for the class to enjoy.

VIDEO

The giant panda can grow up to 1.5 meters tall and weigh up to 136 kilograms. Wild pandas have an average lifespan of 20 years. The giant panda is currently listed as *vulnerable* on the IUCN Red List, which ranks the level of endangerment of species that are under threat of extinction. Giant pandas live in China, in mountainous regions where bamboo is plentiful. They spend about 12 hours a day eating, and their diet consists almost entirely of bamboo. Giant pandas usually live alone in places that are hard to reach, which is why centers like the one featured in the video are useful in not only helping pandas, but also educating us about the species.

Tell students they are going to watch a video called "Raising Pandas." As students follow along in their books, have a student read the sentence about the video aloud.

BEFORE YOU WATCH

Have students look at the photo. As students follow along, read the caption aloud. Then read the questions. Have students get into pairs to share what they know about pandas, as well as use the photo to brainstorm a list of adjectives to describe pandas.

OPTIONAL Randomly call on pairs to share with the class any background knowledge they have about pandas. (See **CONTENT NOTE**.) Then have each pair share at least one adjective to describe pandas.

CHALLENGE Have students work in pairs to do some additional research on pandas and write a short quiz of five questions about the species. Then have each pair get together with another pair, and take turns quizzing the other pair.

RAISING PANDAS

Before You Watch
Talk with a partner. Look at the photo. What do you know about pandas? What adjectives would you use to describe them? Answers will vary.

While You Watch

A ▶4.2 **Watch the video.** Check (✓) all the things you see.

☐ A panda is wrapped in a blanket. ☑ People dress up as pandas.

☑ A man lies down on the grass with pandas. ☑ A panda is released from a cage.

B ▶4.2 **Watch again.** Circle **T** for true or **F** for false.

1 Zhang Hemin's center has successfully bred and released pandas. (T) F

2 Baby pandas are born blind. (T) F

3 Newborn pandas can stand on their own. T (F)

4 At the center, the survival rate for baby pandas has reached 90 percent. (T) F

C **Complete the summary below.** Use the words in the box. Two words are extra.

alive	costumes	cubs	full	mate	predators

It's difficult to breed pandas in captivity. First, it's hard to get them to [1] __mate__ . Second, they don't get pregnant easily. And third, it's not easy to keep baby pandas [2] __alive__ . But Zhang Hemin says that his center has solved these problems. The center also works hard to train pandas to survive on their own in the wild. One idea Zhang came up with was for staff members to wear panda [3] __costumes__ when interacting with the animals. Pandas at the center are also trained to recognize [4] __predators__ .

After You Watch
Talk with a partner. Do you think tourists should be allowed to visit the panda center? Why or why not? Answers will vary.

WHILE YOU WATCH

A Tell students they will watch the video, and they should check the things they see in the video. Have students read the list of things before playing the video.

▶4.2 Play Video 4.2. Play it again, if necessary.

Check answers.

OPTIONAL Ask students what adjectives were used to describe pandas in the video (*cute, cuddly, playful*).

B Tell students that they will watch the video again, and they should circle **T** if the statement is true or **F** if it is false. Have students read the statements before playing the video.

▶4.2 Play Video 4.2. Play it again, if necessary.

Check answers. Have students correct the false statement. (For **3**, newborn pandas cannot stand on their own.)

Twin giant panda cubs

A Write the past participle of these verbs.

1 see   *seen*
2 wrap   *wrapped*
3 put   *put*
4 place   *placed*
5 bring   *brought*

6 feed   *fed*
7 give   *given*
8 treat   *treated*
9 drive   *driven*
10 release   *released*

B Complete the conversation. Circle the correct answers.

Ling: Who (brought) / was brought this raccoon to the shelter?

Jack: No one ² (knows) / is known. It ³ left / (was left) at the door. My guess is that a car ⁴ (hit) / was hit it.

Ling: Oh, no! Do you think it will survive?

Jack: Yeah, I think so. ⁵ It's being examined / (It was examined) about an hour ago. I ⁶ told / (was told) it should make a full recovery.

C Read these sentences. Mark the verbs as **T** (transitive) or **I** (intransitive). If the verb is transitive, underline its object.

1 __T__ He threw the ball a long way.
2 __I__ She arrived late this morning.
3 __T__ Why don't you bring some snacks?
4 __T__ You should enter the building through the side door.
5 __I__ Can you come around 4 p.m. tomorrow?
6 __T__ A brave neighbor rescued the dog from the fire.

SELF CHECK   Now I can …

☐ talk about animal rescue
☐ describe things that are/were done
☐ discuss different ways to save endangered animals

Unit 4 **53**

REVIEW

Explain to students that they are going to review the material from the unit and this will help them remember what they have studied.

A Explain that activity **A** reviews the grammar and vocabulary from the unit.

Have students write the past participle of the verbs. Check answers as a class.

B Explain that activity **B** continues to review the grammar from the unit. Tell students they should circle the correct answers to complete the conversation.

Have students do the task. Check answers.

C Point out that activity **C** reviews words from **VOCABULARY** activity **B**.

Have students read the sentences and mark the verbs as **T** (transitive) or **I** (intransitive). Then have them underline the object if a verb is transitive. Check answers.

SELF CHECK

These *I can* statements provide vital feedback on students' perceived ability to use the language from the unit. If you find students are reluctant to check they can do the skills, consider asking them to rate themselves from 1 (not very confident) to 3 (very confident).

SUPPORT For each skill, have students say sentences demonstrating their ability.

OPTIONAL Have students complete the **SELF CHECK** before doing the **REVIEW** activities. After reviewing the unit, have students once again check their confidence for each statement.

C As students follow along, have a student read the words in the box aloud. Tell students to use the words in the box to complete the summary. Point out that two words are extra and will not be used.

Have students do the task. Check answers.

AFTER YOU WATCH

Tell students they will get into pairs and talk about the video.

As students follow along in their books, read the questions aloud.

Have them do the task. Afterward, have a class discussion by randomly calling on pairs to share their ideas and having the other students comment or ask follow-up questions.

CHALLENGE Have students work in pairs to do more research about the China Conservation and Research Center for the Giant Panda. Ask them to find out any updated information about the center, such as how many pandas the center has released into the wild, and how many pandas are there now.

HOW ARE THEY MADE?

Topic: manufacturing processes and how things are made

Vocabulary: glue, groove(s), lead, assemble, stitch, customize, manufacture, complex, individual, supply, combine, global, variety

Grammar: passive voice + *by*

Extra material: a wooden pencil, a bottle of glue, a screw, a world map, a diagram of a human leg

Other useful vocabulary: everyday items in the classroom: pen, book, paper, scissors, glue, marker, crayon, tack

END OF UNIT PROJECT Tell students they will do research and make a presentation to the class about how something is made.

Remind students that in the unit they learned about various manufacturing processes. Tell students they can choose any kind of item they want to research—an everyday item like a pencil or an iPhone, or something more unique like an artificial eye or prosthetic leg. Encourage them to choose an item they are interested in learning more about. If necessary, as a class, have students brainstorm ideas of both everyday and unique items.

Giving students options for their project helps to promote critical thinking as they analyze what topic to choose.

Explain that their presentation must include:
- a description of what the item is and how it is used.
- a summary of the process of how the item is made.

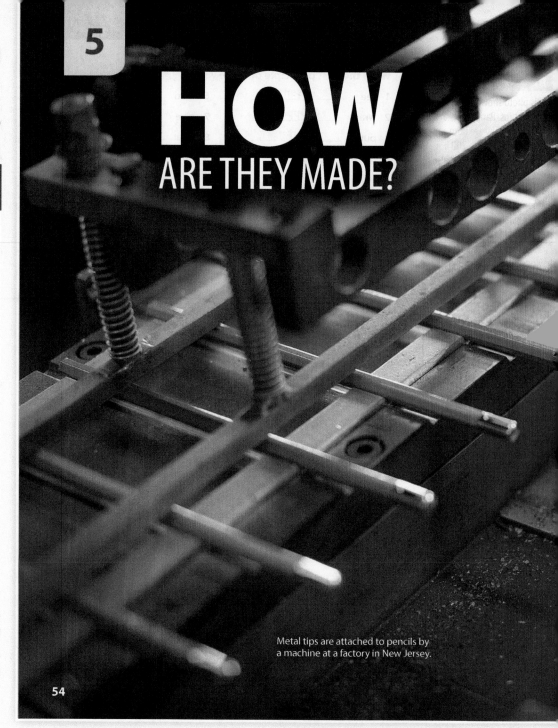

5

HOW
ARE THEY MADE?

Metal tips are attached to pencils by a machine at a factory in New Jersey.

54

- a diagram or graphic organizer to help the other students understand the manufacturing process.
- a statement about why the student chose the item.

Tell students that each person must make a presentation on a different item. Have students tell you what item they have selected, to make sure that all the topics are different.

Have students do their research and prepare their presentations. You might want to assign this as homework.

In the next lesson, have students take turns giving their presentations to the class. You might want to make it a rule that each student must ask at least one follow-up question during the presentations.

PREVIEW

Have students study the photo for a moment. Tell them not to read the caption yet. Read the unit title aloud, as students follow along in their books. Ask students to guess what everyday item is shown in the photo. Then

PREVIEW

A **Read the sentences below.** Match the words in **bold** with their definitions (a–c).

___3___ Another piece of wood is stuck on top using **glue**.

___5___ An eraser is added to each pencil.

___1___ Soft wood is cut into flat pieces.

___2___ **Grooves** are cut into the wood, and **lead** is put in.

___6___ Each pencil is checked by hand.

___4___ The pieces of wood are cut into pencils.

Definitions

a ___grooves___ : deep lines cut into a surface

b ___glue___ : a sticky substance used to join things together

c ___lead___ : the thin, black material in the center of a pencil

B 🎧 5.1 **Listen.** How are pencils made? Put the steps in **A** in order (1–6).

C **Talk with a partner.** Think of another object you use every day. How do you think it is made? *Answers will vary.*

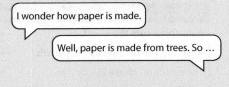

I wonder how paper is made.

Well, paper is made from trees. So …

SCIENCE AND TECHNOLOGY

UNIT GOALS

• talk about manufacturing processes

• use language to describe how things are/were done

• learn about how technology is used in manufacturing

55

ABOUT THE PHOTO

This photo shows metal tips being attached to pencils by a machine. Nowadays, it is common for factories to use machines and computers—instead of people—to do jobs. This is called *automation*. Early automation began during the Industrial Revolution in the late 18th century, when people discovered a way to harness the power of steam engines. This enabled goods to be produced and assembled in a quicker and more precise way. Since then, the manufacturing industry has become increasingly automated. Today, automation is incorporated in nearly all aspects of our lives, from domestic cleaning equipment (robot vacuum cleaners), to personal communications (cell phones), to healthcare (surgical robots).

have students read the caption to check their guesses. Explain that in this unit they will learn to talk about how things are made and learn how technology is used in manufacturing.

A Explain that students have to match the words in bold (*glue*, *grooves*, *lead*) with their definitions (**a–c**). Encourage them to guess meaning from context and to look at clues such as whether the word is singular or plural, etc.

Have students do the task. Check answers.

SUPPORT Show students real-life examples of the three vocabulary items to help with their comprehension of each of the words. Hold up a pencil and point to the lead. Then hold up a bottle of glue. Point to or hold up an item with a groove, such as a screw, or even the lines on your own hand. Say each word as you demonstrate. Have the class repeat the words.

UNIT GOALS

Direct students' attention to the **UNIT GOALS** box. Explain that these are some of the things students will learn in this unit. Point out that this unit is about science and technology. As students follow along, read each of the unit goals to the class. Explain any words students do not know. Remind students that at the end of the unit there is a self check that allows them to see if they have accomplished each goal.

LANGUAGE FOCUS

A Tell students they will listen to a conversation between Ming and Maya.

🎧 **5.2** Play Audio Track 5.2 as students listen and follow along in their books.

As students follow along, read the question, *What is Ming thinking of getting from the store?* Have students answer.

Have students work in pairs and practice the conversation once. Point out the bold words. Tell students to practice the conversation two more times, changing the bold words each time and swapping roles after the first time. Remind students that they are practicing speaking rather than reading, so they should look at each other (have eye contact) and use emotion in their voice as they work with their partner.

SUPPORT To help students understand the situation in the story better, review the meaning of the words *customize, design, stitch,* and *machine*.

REAL ENGLISH

Direct students' attention to the expression in the **REAL ENGLISH** box. Explain that *I don't get it* is a casual way to say *I don't understand.* We use *get* to mean "understand" in informal situations. For example:

A: Do you get this math problem?
B: Yeah, I get it. Let me explain.
...
A: Sorry, I still don't get it.
B: OK, let me try to explain again.

B Ask students to look at the chart. Explain that they will study how to talk about how things are/were done, using the passive voice + *by.*

🎧 **5.3** Have students follow along as they listen to Audio Track 5.3.

LANGUAGE FOCUS

A 🎧 **5.2** **Listen and read.** What is Ming thinking of getting from the store? Then repeat the conversation and replace the words in **bold**. *a white pair of sneakers with a large "M" on the side*

> **REAL ENGLISH** I don't get it.

> **Ming:** Check out this store, Maya. They customize sneakers.
>
> **Maya:** What does that mean?
>
> **Ming:** They can add a design to a pair of sneakers so they're **unique**. (**one of a kind / just for you**)
>
> **Maya:** I don't get it. How exactly **do they do that**? (**does it work / is it done**)
>
> **Ming:** You just buy the sneakers, and your name, design, or picture is **added** by a machine. The store can do whatever you want. (**put on / stitched on**)
>
> **Maya:** So what are you **thinking of getting**? (**getting / going to get**)
>
> **Ming:** I think I'll get a white pair of sneakers with a large "M" on the side. "M" for Ming.
>
> **Maya:** And "M" for Maya! Maybe I'll do the same!

B 🎧 **5.3** **Look at the chart.** Then circle the correct answers below.

TALKING ABOUT HOW THINGS ARE/WERE DONE (USING PASSIVE VOICE + *BY*)	
A machine **cuts** the wood.	→ The wood **is cut by** a machine.
A factory worker **checks** the pencils.	→ The pencils **are checked by** a factory worker.
The customer **chose** the design.	→ The design **was chosen by** the customer.
A logging company **cut down** the trees.	→ The trees **were cut down by** a logging company.
The store **has customized** the shoes.	→ The shoes **have been customized by** the store.
The pencils **are made of** soft wood.	

1 We use the passive to describe what (happens to something or someone) / something or someone does.

2 In passive sentences, the person or thing doing the action follows (by) / in.

3 When describing a manufacturing process, a material such as wood or cotton usually follows by / (made of).

Remind students that the passive voice is used when the receiver of the action or the result is more important than the agent that did the action.

Have a student read the first five sentences on the left side of the chart aloud. Ask students to identify the agent of the actions (*a machine, a factory worker, the customer, a logging company, the store*). Ask students to identify what type of sentences these are (active).

Have a student read the first five sentences on the right side aloud. Explain that in the passive voice example sentences in **UNIT 4**, the agent of the action was left out because the agent was obvious, unknown, or not important. Point out that in the example sentences in this unit, the agent is introduced in the sentence with the word *by*. Explain that in these cases, students should recognize that the main focus of the sentence is whatever is receiving the action, which is why it is placed first and the verb formation becomes passive voice.

C **Rewrite these sentences.**

1 A supervisor checks each item.

Each item _____is checked by a supervisor_____ .

2 Millions of people saw the performance.

The performance _____was seen by millions of people_____ .

3 The teacher answered the students' questions.

The students' questions _____were answered by the teacher_____ .

4 Thousands of tourists have visited the national park.

The national park _____has been visited by thousands of tourists_____ .

5 A machine puts the cookies into boxes.

The cookies _____are put into boxes by a machine_____ .

D 🎧 5.4 **Complete the paragraph.** Use the correct form of the verbs in parentheses. Then listen and check your answers.

In 2018, a tiny house ¹ _was produced_ (**produce**) by ICON, a construction technology company. The house was 350 square feet and took 48 hours to build. It ² _was created_ (**create**) using a 3D printer. A year later, the company ³ _made_ (**make**) an even larger home in about 27 hours. When the company ⁴ _announced_ (**announce**) this, it ⁵ _was considered_ (**consider**) by many people to be a major breakthrough. This means it is now possible to build houses quickly, which could help reduce the number of homeless people around the world.

E **Work with a partner. Student A:** Turn to page 153. **Student B:** Turn to page 154.

An ICON 3D-printed home

Unit 5 57

D Have students complete the paragraph using the correct form of the verbs in parentheses.

Tell students that they will listen and check their answers.

🎧 5.4 Play Audio Track 5.4. Check answers as a class.

E Tell students they will get into pairs and take turns asking and answering questions about how two items are made.

Have students get into pairs. Tell Student As to turn to page 153 and Student Bs to open to page 154.

Explain that Student As should ask their partners questions about how balloons are made and Student Bs should ask their partners questions about how dice are made. Then, as their partner answers their questions, they should fill in the information that is missing in their charts.

Have students do the task. Then check answers as a class.

TEACHING NOTE: FORMING PAIRS

Allowing students to form their own pairs lets them work with a partner they feel comfortable with. On other occasions, it might be better for you to assign partners.

You might want to assign partners in different ways so students have the opportunity to meet more classmates and work with a variety of students. One way to control the assigning of partners is to divide the class in half, group A and group B, and allow students to find their own partner from the opposite group.

Read the last sentence aloud. Tell students that when describing a manufacturing process for an item, they can talk about the material used to make the item, using *made of* + the material.

Draw students' attention to the three statements under the chart. Have students circle the correct answers.

Check answers.

C Have students rewrite the sentences, using the passive voice + *by*.

Check answers.

OPTIONAL Point out how changing the sentence to passive voice shifts the focus of each sentence. Ask students to comment on which sentence they think is more effective. Explain that as writers (or speakers), we frequently have to choose among various grammatical structures to communicate our message most effectively.

THE REAL WORLD

Ask students to look at the photo. As students follow along, read the title aloud.

OPTIONAL Ask students to describe what they see in the photo.

A Tell students they are going to watch a video about making artificial eyes. Have students look at the diagram. Have a student read the words in the box aloud, as the other students follow along in their books. Tell students to label the parts of the eye. Students will likely be guessing and using inference to answer, so encourage them to draw logical conclusions when possible (e.g., the white part of the eye is likely called the *white*).

Have students do the task. Check answers.

DO YOU KNOW?

Read the sentence and answer choices aloud, as students follow along in their books. Have students guess the answer before providing it (b).

CONTENT NOTE: EYE COLORS

Approximately 55 to 79 percent of the world's population have brown eyes. The color appears as dark brown or light brown, depending on the concentration of melanin in the iris. Dark brown eyes are common in East Asia, Southeast Asia, and Africa, whereas light brown eyes are common in Europe, West Asia, and the Americas.

B Tell students they will watch the video and put the steps in the correct order. Have students read the steps silently, before playing the video.

▶ 5.1 Play Video 5.1. Play it again, if necessary. Check answers.

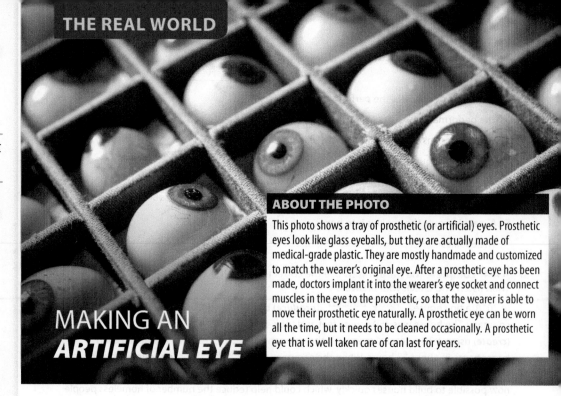

MAKING AN
ARTIFICIAL EYE

ABOUT THE PHOTO

This photo shows a tray of prosthetic (or artificial) eyes. Prosthetic eyes look like glass eyeballs, but they are actually made of medical-grade plastic. They are mostly handmade and customized to match the wearer's original eye. After a prosthetic eye has been made, doctors implant it into the wearer's eye socket and connect muscles in the eye to the prosthetic, so that the wearer is able to move their prosthetic eye naturally. A prosthetic eye can be worn all the time, but it needs to be cleaned occasionally. A prosthetic eye that is well taken care of can last for years.

A Look at the diagram below. Label the parts of the eye.

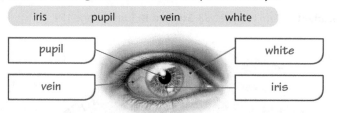

iris   pupil   vein   white

pupil

white

vein

iris

DO YOU KNOW?

The world's most common eye color is _____.
a black
b) brown
c blue

B ▶ 5.1 **Watch the video.** How are artificial eyes made? Put the steps in order (1–6).

- 2 The pupil and the iris are painted.
- 4 The whole mold is heated in an oven.
- 3 The white of the eye is pressed against the iris in the mold.
- 6 The eye is heated again and polished.
- 1 A mold of the eye is created.
- 5 The eye is trimmed, and veins are added using silk.

58 Unit 5

CHALLENGE Ask students to identify any transitional words or phrases that they heard while listening for the process described. For example: *First, ... / Next, ... / then ...*

C Have students read the paragraph silently and circle the correct answers to complete the paragraph.

Check answers by having students take turns reading aloud the sentences in the paragraph.

D **CRITICAL THINKING**

As students follow along, read the question aloud. Emphasize to students that they should come up with as many reasons as possible. Have students get into pairs and talk about their ideas.

CONTENT NOTE: VISIBLE VEINS IN OUR EYES

Each eye has both a main vein and a main artery, both of which spread out and move blood to and within our eyes. So, there are always veins in our eyes. However, some

C **Complete the information.** Circle the correct answers.

An artificial eye ¹ **can** /(**cannot**) restore someone's vision, but it can look very lifelike and move like a real eye. The artificial eye is attached to muscles in the eye socket so that the eye movements match those of the patient's natural eye. It is therefore often ² **easy** /(**difficult**) to tell if a person has an artificial eye. New research using mice is giving scientists hope that they might someday ³(**develop**)/ **discover** an artificial eye that can actually see.

D **CRITICAL THINKING** **Analyzing** **Talk with a partner.** Why do you think it's necessary to add veins to an artificial eye? Answers will vary.

> **PROJECT Look around your home.** Find five things that were made in another country. Examples may include appliances, food items, clothing, etc. Tell a partner where these things were made.

PRONUNCIATION contrastive stress

🎧 5.5 **Underline the word in each response that you think receives the most stress.** Listen and check your answers. Then repeat the questions and responses with a partner.

Question	Response
1 Is the iris painted on by a machine?	No, it's painted by <u>hand</u>.
2 Can an artificial eye see?	No, an artificial eye <u>can't</u> see.
3 Paint is used for the veins.	Actually, <u>silk</u> is used for the veins.
4 Most artificial eyes are made of glass.	Well, they <u>were</u> made of glass, but not anymore.

COMMUNICATION

Find the people below. When you find the person, ask a follow-up question to get additional information. Write their responses in the chart. Answers will vary.

Find someone who ...	Additional information
has been chased by a dog	
has been punished by a teacher	
has been stung by a bee	
has been given flowers by a friend	
has been awarded a prize	

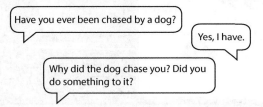

Have you ever been chased by a dog?

Yes, I have.

Why did the dog chase you? Did you do something to it?

---

conditions and situations can cause them to become more visible than usual. Visible red veins can be a sign of discomfort caused by tiny particles (such as dust) getting into our eyes, dryness, allergies, too much sun, or even tiredness. Since these are all quite common conditions, it is natural to have some red veins visible on a regular basis.

PROJECT As students follow along, read the project instructions aloud. Tell students to look around their homes and find five things that were made in another country. Have them make a list of the five items and where each item was made.

In the next lesson, have students get into pairs and take turns talking about where each item was made. Encourage them to use the passive voice in their discussion.

PRONUNCIATION

Tell students that they will practice stress in sentences. Explain that contrastive stress is used to make one word stand out more than another—the stress on one word is in contrast to the stress that is not placed on another. Tell students that we use contrastive stress when we want to emphasize the difference between two things.

Have students read the four questions and responses silently and underline the word in each response that they think receives the most stress. Tell students they will listen and check their answers.

🎧 5.5 Play Audio Track 5.5. Play it again, if necessary. Check answers.

Have students get into pairs and take turns repeating the questions and responses with their partner.

COMMUNICATION

Explain to students that they are going to walk around the classroom and ask their classmates questions to find people with each of the experiences listed in the chart. Point out that they must also ask for additional information about each experience.

As students follow along, read the experiences listed in the chart aloud. Point out that each experience must be turned into a *Have you ever ...?* question.

Model the conversation with a student.

Have students do the task.

SUPPORT Guide students in formulating some follow-up questions that they can use during the activity. Have students make suggestions. Write them on the board. (For example: *Why did the teacher punish you? What did you do? / What kind of prize were you awarded? Why did you get it?*) Display these questions for students to refer to during the activity.

READING

CONTENT NOTE: IPHONE

When Apple's first iPhone was released in 2007, it was hailed as the Invention of the Year by *Time* magazine. The addition of the online Apple App Store in 2008 provided countless options for even more interactive elements to the iPhone. While the iPhone was not the first smartphone to launch, it quickly became popular due to its good looks, ease of use, and numerous apps. The iPhone's staggering commercial success triggered the smartphone revolution that has changed daily life for many people around the world.

Ask students to look at the photo and then follow along as you read the caption aloud.

A As students follow along in their books, read the title aloud. Then read the question. Have students skim the article, look at the map on page 60, and then answer the question.

Check answers.

B Have students scan the article and underline all the countries mentioned.

Check answers. If a world map is available in the classroom, have students point each country out on the map.

SUPPORT Tell students to scan for capital letters because a country name will begin with one.

TEACHING NOTE: HELPING STUDENTS SCAN

Encourage students to scan quickly by saying the time that has elapsed every 10 or 15 seconds. If students are taking too long to find the answer, review how to quickly and efficiently scan a text.

READING

A **Skim the article and look at the map below.** Why is the question in the title difficult to answer?

B **Scan the article.** Underline all the countries mentioned.

C **Talk with a partner.** Do you own an iPhone? Why do you think iPhones are so popular?

A *because manufacturing is done in a variety of countries*

C *Answers will vary.*

WHERE DO IPHONE PARTS COME FROM?

SOUTH KOREA (memory)

GERMANY (movement sensor)

U.S.A. (glass screen, audio chip, Wi-Fi chip)

JAPAN (camera, compass)

CHINA (battery)

SWITZERLAND (positioning system)

60 Unit 5

C As students follow along, read the questions aloud. Have students get into pairs and discuss their ideas.

After completing the task, have students read the article in more detail so they can answer the **COMPREHENSION** questions.

OPTIONAL The text can also be used as a listening activity. Have students close their books. Tell students they will listen to the passage.

🎧 5.6 Play Audio Track 5.6. Ask students to get into pairs and discuss what information they heard. Then have them read the article more carefully.

Tim Cook, CEO of Apple, speaks at an iPhone event in California.

WHERE IS THE IPHONE MADE?

🎧 5.6 Have you ever wondered where Apple's iPhone is made? Apple's headquarters is located in California, where iPhone models are designed by a talented team of engineers and designers. So you might assume that
5 the iPhone is made by workers in the United States. However, the answer to the question is more **complex** than you may expect.

Manufacturing vs. Assembly

To answer the question, we need to understand the
10 difference between manufacturing and assembly. Manufacturing is the process of making the parts that go into the iPhone. Although Apple designs and sells the iPhone, it doesn't manufacture its **individual** parts. Instead, the company uses manufacturers from around
15 the world to **supply** these. And there are hundreds of parts—including wires, batteries, and chips. In total, Apple works with more than 200 different suppliers in over 40 countries. Among the top supplier nations are China, the United States, Japan, and South Korea.

20 Assembly is the process of taking all those individual parts and **combining** them into a finished, working iPhone. The assembly of iPhones takes place in China, which has shown itself to be good at meeting demand quickly. In 2007, for example, just a few weeks before
25 the first iPhone was released, Apple co-founder Steve Jobs decided to replace the iPhone's plastic screen with a glass screen. This new glass screen would be scratch-proof. American companies said this was impossible—they would need several months to
30 create new production lines to make the change. A Chinese factory, however, accepted the work and proved it was possible.

The Bigger Picture

"People just look at where the final product is
35 assembled," says Apple CEO, Tim Cook. According to Cook, we need to look at the bigger picture. In a **global** world, he says, manufacturing needs to be done in a **variety** of countries, so it's not easy to say exactly where a product is made. Thus, making an iPhone is
40 truly a worldwide effort.

Unit 5 **61**

TEACHING NOTE: SENSITIVITY

Note that the iPhone is rather expensive and that issues of money might come up as students discuss the questions in **C**. If your students come from different socioeconomic backgrounds, make sure to be sensitive to the fact that not having an iPhone may be a touchy topic for some students or make them feel inferior. Focus the discussion more on the second question in this case: *Why do you think iPhones are so popular?*

Additional Activities to Use with the Reading

Grammar (Focused)

Have students find examples of passive sentences in the text and reword them to make them active sentences. Ask students to decide which sentence they think is better in each case, passive or active, and why. Give an example from the passage:

(line 3) . . . *iPhone models are designed by a talented team of engineers and designers* → *Talented designers and engineers design iPhone models . . .*

Draw students' attention to this passive sentence in line 2: *Apple's headquarters is located in California . . .* Ask them why it is difficult to make this an active sentence (because we don't know the agent).

Vocabulary Game

Tell students they are going to play a game to guess vocabulary words by discovering, one by one, the letters in each word.

Write the word *HORSE* on the board. Point out that it has five letters. Tell students that when they guess a letter that is *not* in the target vocabulary word you give, you will write one letter in the word *HORSE*. When *HORSE* is written in full on the board, the game is over. If necessary, explain that the objective if the game is to correctly guess the word before the word *HORSE* is completed on the board.

Play the game once as a class. On the board, write one dash for each letter of the word *complex*: _ _ _ _ _ _ _.

Randomly call on one student to say a letter. If the letter is in the word, write it in the correct place(s). If it is not in the word, write it on the board so students will remember not to say it again. Also write the letter *H* for *HORSE*. Have students continue to guess letters until they get the word *complex*, or the word *HORSE* has been spelled out on the board.

Have students get into pairs and play several rounds of the game to review vocabulary from **UNITS 1** to **5**.

COMPREHENSION

A **EXAM PRACTICE**

Multiple-choice items can be either questions, or statements with a blank. There are various kinds of multiple-choice questions.

The answers to **paraphrase** items are not stated in the passage. Instead, students must reword a sentence, quote, or phrase found in the passage. Essentially, they are summarizing or rephrasing written content. In doing so, they show that they understand what was said in the passage. Tests usually ask students to paraphrase:

- a quote by a speaker.
- an idiom or other unusual language.
- a concluding thought by the writer.

Have students read the questions to themselves and circle the correct answers.

After they have finished, check answers as a class.

IDIOM

As students follow along in their books, read the sentence and answer options aloud. Have them guess the answer before providing it (a). Give an example:

The musician didn't play with passion. She was just phoning it in.

Tell students that there is a similar sounding idiom, *dial it in*, that sounds the same but actually means the opposite of *phone it in*. When you *dial something in*, it means you do it with focus and enthusiasm. For example:

That player just had her best game of the season. She really dialed it in.

COMPREHENSION

A Answer the questions about *Where Is the iPhone Made?*

1 **MAIN IDEA** What point is the author trying to make?
   a It's very difficult to manage a global supply chain.
   b Some companies don't want customers to know where their products are made.
   ⓒ It's not always easy to say where a product comes from these days.

2 **DETAIL** Where is the iPhone designed?
   ⓐ in the United States   b in China   c in Japan

3 **REFERENCE** What does *these* in line 15 refer to?
   a manufacturers   ⓑ parts of an iPhone   c finished iPhones

4 **INFERENCE** Apple probably chose to assemble iPhones in China because _____.
   a glass screens are cheaper in China
   ⓑ Chinese factories have proven to be good at meeting last-minute demands
   c more and more skilled workers are moving to China

5 **PARAPHRASE** What does Tim Cook mean when he says we need to *look at the bigger picture* (line 36)?
   a We have to create phones with larger display screens.
   b We have to keep coming up with new ideas and solutions.
   ⓒ We have to take a broad view of an issue, and not focus on small details.

B Read the statements. Circle **T** for true, **F** for false, or **NG** for not given.

1	Apple's main office is in China.	T	Ⓕ	NG
2	The iPhone accounts for nearly half of Apple's sales.	T	F	ⓃⒼ
3	The first iPhones that went on sale had a plastic screen.	T	Ⓕ	NG
4	It takes about 400 steps to assemble an iPhone.	T	F	ⓃⒼ
5	According to the map on page 60, some parts of the iPhone are made in Europe.	Ⓣ	F	NG

C **CRITICAL THINKING Reflecting** **Talk with a partner.** How important is your cell phone to you? At what age do you think children should have cell phones? *Answers will vary.*

IDIOM

If you "phone something in," you do an activity _____.
ⓐ with little effort or interest
b in a very complicated way
c because it's urgent

B As students follow along in their books, have a student read the statements aloud. Tell students to circle **T**, **F**, or **NG** for each statement.

Have students do the task.

Check answers.

OPTIONAL Have students correct the false statements. (**1** Apple's main office is in California; **3** The first iPhones that went on sale had a glass screen.)

C **CRITICAL THINKING**

As students follow along, read the questions aloud. Encourage students to personalize the content. Tell them to support their opinions with reasons.

Have students get into pairs and discuss the questions. Then randomly call on students to share their opinions with the class.

VOCABULARY

A **Find the bold words below in the article.** Then circle the correct answers.

1 Something **complex** is probably *easy /(difficult)*to understand.

2 If you look at a car's **individual** parts, you look at *(each part separately)/ the whole car.*

3 If you **supply** a company with something, you *(provide)/ purchase* it.

4 When you **combine** two or more things, you *(mix them together)/ separate them.*

5 A **global** event is one that *happens only in your country /(affects the whole world.)*

6 If you enjoy eating a **variety** of foods, you like *(many types)/ just one type* of food.

B **Read the information below.** Then complete the sentences (**1–4**) with expressions from the box.

> There are many words that are often used with *global*:
>
> *global awareness*   *global brand*   *global network*   *global warming*

1 The company has an efficient _____*global network*_____ in place so products can reach customers quickly.

2 The organization hopes to increase _____*global awareness*_____ of the benefits of organic products.

3 One effect of _____*global warming*_____ is rising sea levels.

4 Apple is a well-known _____*global brand*_____—everyone recognizes its logo immediately.

WRITING

A **Read the paragraph.**

B **Think of an item you own that was a gift.** Make notes about it. Who gave it to you? Where was it made? What is it made of? Add any other information.

C **Write about the gift.** Use your notes from **B** to help you. Say why this item means a lot to you. Answers will vary.

> A few years ago, I was given a watch by my grandfather. It was made in Germany. He bought it when he went there on vacation. It's made of metal, but the strap is leather. It's not an expensive watch, but it means a lot to me because ...

VOCABULARY

A Have students find the bold words in the **READING** passage.

Have students circle the correct answers to complete the sentences.

Check answers.

B As students follow along, read the information in the box aloud. Have students use the correct expressions to complete the sentences.

Check answers.

WRITING

Tell students they are going to write a paragraph about an item they own that was a gift.

A As students follow along, read the example aloud. Point out that the paragraph starts with how the author got the item. Then the author goes on to describe the item and explain what it is made of. Finally, the author starts to say why the item is important. Tell students that their paragraph should include all of this information.

B Read the questions aloud. Have students think of an item they received as a gift and make notes about it. Encourage them to use a graphic organizer, such as a mind map, to write out their ideas for the paragraph. If necessary, explain how to use mind maps. (See **TEACHING NOTE**.)

Ask students to add more information. Encourage them to add these ideas to the mind map. Tell students that when an idea connects to another, they should show this by connecting a branch between the two ideas.

TEACHING NOTE: MIND MAPS

A mind map is a useful tool to help organize ideas and thoughts before writing. Draw a mind map on the board to demonstrate how students can use it for this writing activity. Use the example paragraph in your demonstration. On the board, write *Watch* and circle it. Draw four different branches from that circle. At the end of each branch, write one of the questions asked in **B** and circle it: *Who gave it to you? When did you get it? Where was it made? What is it made of?* Add one more branch and circle: *Why is it important?* Write notes around each circle according to the information in the paragraph. For example, draw a short line from *Who gave it to you?* and write *grandfather.*

C Have students write their paragraphs, using their notes from **B**. You might want to assign the writing as homework, and set a minimum number of sentences students must write (e.g., nine). Collect students' paragraphs and correct them.

OPTIONAL In the next lesson, have students read their paragraphs aloud to the class and show the item they received or a photo of it. After each student reads and displays the item, encourage others to ask questions.

VIDEO

Tell students they are going to watch a video called "Prosthetic Legs." As students follow along in their books, read the sentence about the video aloud.

BEFORE YOU WATCH

Tell students that they will label the parts of the prosthetic leg in the diagram on the right. As students follow along, have a student read the words in the box aloud.

Have students do the task. Check answers. If you brought in a diagram of a human leg, use the diagram and point out each part of the leg.

WHILE YOU WATCH

A   Tell students they will watch the video, and they should number the parts of the prosthetic leg in the order they are made.

▶ **5.2** Play Video 5.2. Play it again, if necessary. Check answers.

OPTIONAL Before playing the video, have students use the diagram from **BEFORE YOU WATCH** to predict what order they think the leg is made in. Tell students to write down their predictions in pencil and check their predictions while they watch.

TEACHING NOTE: MAKING PREDICTIONS

Having students make predictions about content ahead of time helps keep them engaged and interested while watching (or reading). Encouraging students to predict also leads them to preview and think about the content ahead of time, which can help improve their comprehension while watching (or reading).

B   Explain to students that they will watch the video again and they should match each body part with the material it is made from. As students follow along in their books, have a student read the words in the right column aloud.

PROSTHETIC *LEGS*

Before You Watch

Look at the diagram on the right. Label the parts of the prosthetic leg.

| ankle | foot | knee | shin | socket |

While You Watch

A ▶ **5.2** **Watch the video.** Number the parts of the prosthetic leg in the order they are made (1–6).

_4_ knee   _2_ shin   _5_ socket

_1_ foot   _6_ skin   _3_ ankle

B ▶ **5.2** **Watch again.** Match each body part with what it's made from.

1 foot   aluminum
2 shin   carbon fiber
3 ankle   silicon
4 skin   rubber

C **Complete the information below.** Use the words in the box. One word is extra.

| assemble | average | cost | materials | patient |

All prosthetic limbs are customized according to the needs of each individual [1] _patient_ . A doctor takes several factors into consideration, such as the person's weight, age, and lifestyle. A new prosthetic limb can [2] _cost_ anywhere from $5,000 to $50,000, depending on the [3] _materials_ used. But even the most expensive limbs will need to be replaced after a few years. A prosthetic limb usually lasts a(n) [4] _average_ of three to five years.

After You Watch

Talk with a partner. Do you think athletes with prosthetic limbs should be allowed to compete against regular athletes? Why or why not? Answers will vary.

64 Unit 5

socket

knee

shin

ankle

foot

▶ **5.2** Play Video 5.2. Play it again, if necessary. Check answers.

CONTENT NOTE: MATERIALS USED IN PROSTHETICS

Four materials are mentioned in the video for making prosthetic legs.

Some of these materials are chosen for their strength, such as the aluminum for the ankle joint. Others are chosen for their flexibility, such as the silicon for the skin. The rubber used to make the foot is a combination of two elements: isocyanate and polyol. The carbon fiber in the shin is lightweight but strong. It is also commonly used in race cars.

C As students follow along in their books, read the words in the box aloud.

Have students use the words in the box to complete the paragraph. Point out that one word is extra and will not be used.

Check answers.

A Match the words with their definitions.

1 assemble   to produce something on a large scale

2 stitch   to make something unique

3 customize   to provide

4 manufacture   to put the parts of an object together

5 supply   to join or decorate using a needle and thread

B Complete the sentences. Use the correct form of the verbs in the box.

| choose | design | leave | make |

1 This building _____was designed_____ by a team of three architects. They won an award for their creation.

2 This shirt _____is made_____ of Egyptian cotton. Feel how soft it is.

3 Last week, our city _____was chosen_____ as the host city for the conference.

4 These books _____were left_____ here a week ago. Can you please put them away?

C Complete the sentences. Circle the correct answers.

1 Coca-Cola is a global (**brand**) / **awareness**.

2 Scientists worldwide agree that global (**warming**) / **brand** is happening and that human activity is the main cause.

3 The company has built up a global **warming** / (**network**) with a presence in more than 80 countries.

SELF CHECK   Now I can …

☐ talk about manufacturing processes

☐ describe how things are/were done

☐ discuss how technology is used in manufacturing

Unit 5 **65**

CHALLENGE As a critical thinking exercise, have students review connected content from the unit in a discussion. Present them with the following discussion question: *Would you prefer to work in a factory that makes prosthetic legs, artificial eyes, or parts of an iPhone? Why?* Give students time to think or write their ideas and responses first. Then have them get into small groups and take turns sharing their answers and reasons why.

REVIEW

Explain to students that they are going to review the material from the unit and this will help them remember what they have studied.

A Explain that activity **A** reviews vocabulary from the unit. Explain that they should match the words on the left with their definitions on the right.

    Have students do the task. Check answers.

B Explain that activity **B** reviews the grammar from the unit. Tell students they should use the correct form of the verbs in the box to complete the sentences.

    Have students do the task. Check answers.

C Point out that activity **C** reviews words from **VOCABULARY** activity **B**.

    Have students circle the correct answers to complete the sentences. Check answers.

SELF CHECK

These *I can* statements provide vital feedback on students' perceived ability to use the language from the unit. If you find students are reluctant to check they can do the skills, consider asking them to rate themselves from 1 (not very confident) to 3 (very confident).

OPTIONAL Ask students to share in their own words any additional information they learned from the paragraph that was not mentioned in the video.

AFTER YOU WATCH

Tell students they will get into pairs and talk about the video. As students follow along in their books, read the questions aloud.

Have them do the task.

OPTIONAL Have students use what they have learned in the unit to write five sentences about making either prosthetic legs or artificial eyes. Encourage them to use the passive voice. Collect their papers and correct any grammatical mistakes before returning them to students in the next lesson. Have students rewrite the sentences as "quiz" sentences, inserting blank lines for some grammatical structures. When they have finished making their quiz sentences, have them get into pairs and complete their partner's sentences. Have partners check answers.

UNIT 6
LOOK AT THOSE NARWHALS!

CONTENT AREA:
THE NATURAL WORLD

Topic: oceans, marine life, and coral reefs

Vocabulary: parts of animals: flipper, shell, tusk, tail; **ocean names:** Atlantic, Pacific, Indian, Arctic; **marine animals:** dugong, king crab, narwhal, seahorse, hermit crab, sea cucumber, humpback whale, coral polyp; **other words:** coral reef, shallow, remains, popular, attract, warn, damage

Grammar: non-defining relative clauses

Extra material: photos of sea creatures mentioned in **PREVIEW** and **Other useful vocabulary**, a world map

Other useful vocabulary:
other sea creatures: anemone, sea star, clownfish, shrimp, angelfish, Christmas tree worm, parrotfish, squid, shark

END OF UNIT PROJECT Tell students they will do research and then make a presentation to the class. Explain to students that they will do research about:
  • a marine animal that they didn't study in the unit (e.g., its habitat and characteristics).
  • a coral reef other than the Great Barrier Reef (e.g., its location, size, and importance to the surrounding environment).

Explain that in the next lesson, they will take turns sharing their information.

Emphasize that they will need to talk about their research, not give a speech or read a written report. Have students choose their topic and assign the research as homework.

In the next lesson, have students take turns talking about their research. Encourage the other students who are listening to ask at least three follow-up questions.

CONTENT NOTE:
MARINE ANIMALS

Dugongs are marine mammals that are similar to American manatees, but that live in the warm waters of the Indian Ocean and Pacific Ocean. The largest populations are found near Australia.

King crabs are some of the largest crabs in the world. A full-grown king crab can weigh up to five kilograms or more. King crabs are found near Japan, Alaska, and in the Bering Sea.

Narwhals are small whales that live along the coasts and in the rivers of the Arctic. They are mammals, meaning they are warm-blooded so their bodies maintain the same temperature in any climate. Like all other mammals, the females produce milk to feed their young.

Narwhals are often called the "unicorns of the sea."

PREVIEW

A 🎧 6.1 **Listen.** Check (✓) the ocean(s) each animal lives in: Atlantic (**At**), Pacific (**P**), Indian (**I**), or Arctic (**Ar**).

	At	P	I	Ar
dugong		✓	✓	
king crab		✓		✓
narwhal				✓
seahorse	✓	✓	✓	

B 🎧 6.1 **Listen again.** Complete the sentences with words from the box.

| flippers | shells | tail | tusk |

1 The dugong, which is a kind of mammal, uses its ___flippers___ for steering while swimming.

2 King crabs, which have red, blue, or brown ___shells___, are caught for food.

3 The narwhal, which has a long, straight ___tusk___, is a type of whale.

4 The seahorse, which is a type of fish, uses its ___tail___ to move forward.

C **Talk with a partner.** Make a list of all the sea creatures you know about. Which ones have you seen? *Answers will vary.*

THE NATURAL WORLD

UNIT GOALS

- talk about marine animals and their habitats
- use language to add information about things and people
- learn about the importance of coral reefs

67

SUPPORT Before students listen, familiarize them with the pronunciation of each ocean name. Read each aloud and have students repeat together as you point each out on a world map.

B Tell students that they will listen again and they should use the words from the box to complete the sentences.

🎧 6.1 Play Audio Track 6.1. Play it again, if necessary. Check answers.

SUPPORT Use photos of the animals mentioned in the audio to point out each body part. Ask students to say what other animals have the same body parts (e.g., tusk—elephant; flippers—dolphin and whale; shell—snail and turtle; tail—dog and cat).

C Tell students they are going to get into pairs and make a list of all the sea creatures they know about, and talk about which ones they have seen.

Have students do the task.

OPTIONAL Have pairs take turns sharing sea creature names with the class. Make a list on the board as each pair contributes. Go around the class until all students have shared all the animals they know about. Have students copy the list into their notebooks to refer to as they study the unit.

UNIT GOALS

Direct students' attention to the **UNIT GOALS** box. Explain that these are some of the things students will learn in this unit. Point out that this unit is about the natural world. As students follow along, read each of the unit goals to the class. Explain any words students do not know. Remind students that at the end of the unit there is a self check that allows them to see if they have accomplished each goal.

Seahorses are a type of marine fish that live in places like coral reefs, mangroves, and seagrass beds. They remain vertical while swimming. They tend to move little, and when they do, they swim slowly. However, because they blend in well with their habitats, seahorses are good predators.

PREVIEW

Have students study the photo for a moment. Read the unit title and the photo caption aloud, as students follow along. Explain that in this unit they will learn to talk about marine life. Tell them they will also learn to give additional information about people and things.

A Tell students that they will listen to four short talks about marine animals. Tell them to check the ocean(s) each animal lives in.

🎧 6.1 Play Audio Track 6.1. Play it again, if necessary. Check answers.

LANGUAGE FOCUS

A Tell students they will listen to a conversation between Nadine and Ming.

🎧**6.2** Play Audio Track 6.2 as students listen and follow along in their books.

As students follow along, read the question, *What kind of shells do hermit crabs usually live in?* Have students answer.

Have students work in pairs and practice the conversation once. Point out the bold words. Tell students to practice the conversation two more times, changing the bold words each time and swapping roles after the first time.

CHALLENGE Have students use the conversation as a model to talk about another marine animal and its habitat. Have pairs pick an animal they know about. (See **Other useful vocabulary**.)

REAL ENGLISH

Direct students' attention to the expression in the **REAL ENGLISH** box. Explain that *You're telling me …* is used in informal English to restate or confirm what the other person just said. The phrase can be a good speaking strategy when you aren't certain you understood what was said. For example:

A: I spent 13 hours on my computer yesterday.
B: You're telling me that you spent the whole day indoors?

Note that there is another use of *You're telling me* that is similar to the **REAL ENGLISH** phrase students learned in **UNIT 1**: *Tell me about it.* Here the speaker is communicating that they relate to whatever is being said. For example:

A: I'm so tired. I was up till 2 a.m. studying for the test.
B: You're telling me. I went to bed at 3!

A 🎧**6.2** **Listen and read.** What kind of shells do hermit crabs usually live in? Then repeat the conversation and replace the words in **bold**. *abandoned snail shells*

> **REAL ENGLISH** You're telling me …

Nadine:	Look! **That shell is moving**! (**That shell has something in it** / **There's something inside that shell**)
Ming:	Oh, that's just a hermit crab.
Nadine:	I've never seen one before.
Ming:	They usually live in abandoned snail shells, which **provide** protection. (**they use for** / **they need for**)
Nadine:	Really? Do they live in the same shell all their lives?
Ming:	No, they change shells. It's **incredible** to watch. If they don't like their new shell, they go back to their old one. (**amazing** / **fascinating**)
Nadine:	So, you're telling me they want the **most fashionable** shell-ter! (**most stylish** / **coolest-looking**)

B 🎧**6.3** **Look at the chart.** Then circle the correct answers below.

ADDING INFORMATION TO A SENTENCE (USING NON-DEFINING RELATIVE CLAUSES)
The narwhal, **which is a type of whale**, has a long tusk.
The dugong, **which is a kind of mammal**, is sometimes called a sea cow.
Last weekend we went to the aquarium, **which now has a collection of seahorses**.
My uncle, **who visits us every summer**, is a marine biologist.
My cousin Lisa, **who is a scuba diving instructor**, knows a lot about coral reefs.
If you have questions, ask the tour guide, **who is an expert on ocean conservation**.

1 A clause that adds extra information about a person begins with **which** / **who**

2 A clause that adds extra information about a thing begins with **which** / **who**.

3 We use **commas** / **semicolons** to separate a non-defining relative clause from the rest of the sentence.

B Ask students to look at the chart. Explain that they will study how to add information to a sentence by using either *which* or *who*.

🎧**6.3** Have students follow along as they listen to Audio Track 6.3.

Have a student read the sentences in the top half of the chart aloud. On the board, write *The narwhal has a long tusk.* Ask students if this is a complete sentence (yes) and what the subject is (the narwhal).

On the board, write *is a type of whale.* Ask students if this is a complete sentence. (No. It doesn't have a subject.)

Write *which* in front of *is a type of whale.* Explain that *which* is a relative pronoun, and it replaces *the narwhal* when the two sentences are combined.

Explain that the verb after *which* must agree with the noun it replaces. Point out in the chart that *The narwhal*, a singular subject, takes a singular verb, *has*.

C 🎧 6.4 **Complete the paragraph.** Use the phrases in the box (**a–d**). Then listen and check your answers.

> **a** which is where they find all their food
> **b** which they gather with their tentacle-like feet
> **c** which means they're active at night
> **d** which are related to starfish and sea urchins

Sea cucumbers, ¹ __d__, are one of the ocean's most interesting creatures. There are over 1,200 known species, and they come in a variety of colors. They are typically 10 to 30 centimeters long, although the largest species can reach 3 meters. Most sea cucumbers live on the ocean floor, ² __a__. They eat algae, tiny sea creatures, and even waste materials, ³ __b__. When threatened, some sea cucumbers shoot sticky threads out of their bottoms to trap their enemies. Sea cucumbers are nocturnal creatures, ⁴ __c__.

A sea cucumber

D **Rewrite these sentences.** Use *which* or *who*.

1 Alice is writing a research paper on narwhals. She's a marine biologist.
   Alice, who's a marine biologist, is writing a research paper on narwhals.

2 The *Titanic* is now an underwater shelter for marine life. It sank in 1912.
   The Titanic, which sank in 1912, is now an underwater shelter for marine life.

3 My friend Jada is coming to visit this weekend. She's studying medicine in Toronto.
   My friend Jada, who's studying medicine in Toronto, is coming to visit this weekend.

4 Rio de Janeiro is an interesting place to live. It has a population of more than six million.
   Rio de Janeiro, which has a population of more than six million, is an interesting place to live.

5 My science teacher is very patient and friendly. He's from Australia.
   My science teacher, who's from Australia, is very patient and friendly.

E **Play a chain game.** Work in groups of three. One student says a sentence. The other two students add more information to the sentence using *which* or *who*. Answers will vary.

Jun is from Seoul.

Jun, who is our classmate, is from Seoul.

Jun, who is our classmate, is from Seoul, which is …

C Have students use the phrases in the box (**a–d**) to complete the paragraph.

Tell students they will listen and check their answers.

🎧 6.4 Play Audio Track 6.4. Check answers as a class.

OPTIONAL Have students work in pairs to summarize the information in the paragraph about the sea cucumber in their own words.

D Have students combine the two sentences into one, using *which* or *who*.

Note that answers might vary depending on which sentence becomes the non-defining relative clause in the new sentences. For example, for item **1**, the answer could also be *Alice, who's writing a research paper on narwhals, is a marine biologist*.

Check answers.

SUPPORT Ask students:

1 Did you use *which* or *who* correctly?

2 Is the verb after *who/which* correct?

3 Did you use one or two commas?

4 Is the most important information in the main clause?

E Tell students they are going to play a chain game in groups of three. Explain that it involves adding on to a sentence with *which* or *who* to give more information.

Model the game with two students. Tell groups to make sentences about each other or about another topic that everyone knows, such as school, so that everyone can easily add information.

Have students play the game.

Read the entire sentence again and, if necessary, remind students that they can remove the relative clause and the author's main idea will still be understood.

Draw students' attention to the third sentence and explain that when the relative clause is at the end of the sentence, we only use one comma.

Have a student read the sentences in the bottom half of the chart aloud. Explain that we use *who* with people, and the rules are the same as with *which*.

SUPPORT Have students look at the sentences and decide which the writer thinks is more important: (1) the information in the base sentence (called the *main clause*) or (2) the information in the *which/who* clause (called the *relative clause*). (the information in the main clause)

Draw students' attention to the three statements under the chart. Have students circle the correct answers. Check answers.

THE REAL WORLD

Ask students to look at the photo. Have a student read the title and the caption aloud.

A Tell students they are going to watch a video about humpback whales and how they have inspired better technology. Explain that students should circle the correct answer to the question as they watch. Before they watch the video, have students read the question and answer choices silently.

▶ **6.1** Play Video 6.1. Play it again, if necessary.

Check answers.

DO YOU KNOW?

Read the sentence and answer choices aloud, as students follow along in their books. Have students guess the answer before providing it (a).

CONTENT NOTE: THE BIRDWATCHING TRAIN ENGINEER

It is thanks to a hobby of one of the engineers of the Shinkansen that Japan's famous bullet trains got their kingfisher nose. Avid birdwatcher Eiji Nakatsu realized that the shape of the kingfisher's beak was the reason the bird was able to dive through water so smoothly at fast speeds, and so his team set out to mimic the beak's design in order to make the train's movement smoother and quieter.

B Tell students they will watch the video again, and they should circle the correct answers to complete the sentences.

▶ **6.1** Play Video 6.1. Play it again, if necessary. Check answers.

C Read the definition aloud, as students follow along. Tell students to check the options that are examples of biomimicry. Read the options aloud.

LEARNING FROM HUMPBACKS

Humpback whales have inspired new wind turbine technology (inset).

A ▶ **6.1** **Watch the video.** What characteristic of humpback whales has inspired scientists to create more efficient wind turbines?

  a the blowholes on the top of a humpback's head

  ⓑ the structure of a humpback's flippers

  c the shape of a humpback's head

B ▶ **6.1** **Watch again.** Circle the correct answers.

  1 The drag on something makes it move more ⟨**slowly**⟩ / **quickly**.

  2 Wind turbines with tubercles experience **more** / ⟨**less**⟩ drag.

  3 Researchers are considering adding tubercles to **the bottom of ships** / ⟨**airplane wings**⟩ to increase speed and improve safety.

70 Unit 6

DO YOU KNOW?

The nose of Japan's Shinkansen bullet trains is modeled after _____.
ⓐ a kingfisher's beak
b a narwhal's tusk
c the head of a fish

Have students do the task. Check answers.

D **CRITICAL THINKING**

As students follow along, read the questions aloud. Give students time to think about or write down their ideas first. Then have students get into pairs and share their ideas. Encourage them to continue to brainstorm ideas as they discuss. Afterward, discuss as a class.

PROJECT As students follow along, read the project instructions aloud. Explain that they will do research about another example of biomimicry. Give students time to search the internet and make notes. If necessary, suggest the search term *examples of biomimicry*.

You might want to assign the research as homework. Then in the next lesson, have students get into pairs and share what they learned.

C **Read the definition of biomimicry below.** Then check (✓) the options that are examples of biomimicry.

> **biomimicry** (*n.*): the science of copying designs from nature in human engineering and invention

☐ putting bird feathers in a jacket to stay warm in cold weather

☑ inventing a multilegged robot that can move through tight spaces like a spider

☐ sticking pieces of shark skin onto swimwear to help people swim faster

☑ developing a bat-inspired drone that can fly around in the dark by itself

☑ designing a prosthetic arm that looks and functions like an octopus tentacle

D **CRITICAL THINKING** **Applying** **Talk with a partner.** What other traits or abilities of animals or plants do you think would be useful to copy? In what situations might these traits or abilities be useful to humans? Answers will vary.

> **PROJECT Go online.** Find another example of biomimicry. Make some notes about it and share with a partner.

PRONUNCIATION pausing in relative clauses

🎧6.5 **Listen.** Mark the pauses in these sentences with a slash (/). Then listen again and repeat the sentences.

1 My friend Maria/who runs the aquarium/is interested in marine conservation.

2 Saltwater crocodiles/which are very dangerous/are the largest living reptiles.

3 The scientists/who work for WhalePower/are studying humpback whales.

4 Sea otters/which live in the Pacific Ocean/are very playful animals.

COMMUNICATION

Play a guessing game. Work in groups. **Group A:** Turn to page 155. **Group B:** Turn to page 156. Follow the instructions on the page. Answers will vary.

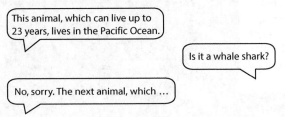

This animal, which can live up to 23 years, lives in the Pacific Ocean.

Is it a whale shark?

No, sorry. The next animal, which …

PRONUNCIATION

Tell students they will practice pausing in relative clauses. Explain that using pauses correctly makes it easier for the listener to understand what the speaker is saying.

Tell students that they will hear four sentences, and they should mark the pauses they hear in the sentences with a slash (/).

🎧6.5 Play Audio Track 6.5. Play it again, if necessary. Check answers.

🎧6.5 Play Audio Track 6.5 again, pausing after each sentence so students can repeat.

COMMUNICATION

Explain to students that they are going to play a guessing game about marine animals. Tell them that they will play in groups, and each group will make clues for the other group. Explain that the group with the higher number of correct guesses is the winner.

Have students get into groups of three or four. Assign each group as A or B. Have Group As turn to page 155 and Group Bs turn to page 156. Explain that each group will combine two facts about each animal using a relative clause. Tell them that these will be the clues they give the other group. Remind students not to say the name of the animal.

Model the conversation with a student.

Have students get into groups to write their clues. Then have each Group A get together with a Group B and play the game.

Whenever a combined group of A and B finish, ask which group (A or B) was the winner.

TEACHING NOTE: DOING INTERNET RESEARCH

Tell students that they must evaluate information they find online and judge whether it is true and legitimate. For example, explain that a blog written by *F* may not be as trustworthy as, for example, one by National Geographic, which is known for its scientific research. Give students questions to consider as they evaluate a source:

- Is the information what I need? (Have I gotten distracted and strayed from the topic?)
- Who wrote the information? What is their motive for writing it?
- What are the author's qualifications? (Is the author an expert or authority?)
- Does the author have bias?
- When was the information written? (Is it out of date?)
- Does the author support his or her assertions with evidence and proof?

READING

Ask students to look at the photo. As students follow along, have a student read the caption aloud. Then have another student read the title aloud.

A Tell students they will read paragraph A to find out what polyps are. As students follow along, read the answer choices aloud.

Have students do the task.

Check answers.

OPTIONAL Have students find the Great Barrier Reef on a world map. Ask students to tell you things that they already know about the Great Barrier Reef (e.g., it is famous because it has many kinds of beautiful fish; it is a popular place to visit to go snorkeling or scuba diving).

B Tell students that they will skim the article and add headings (**1–4**) to the correct places. Point out the blanks next to paragraphs B, D, F, and I. As students follow along in their books, have a student read the headings aloud. Remind students that skimming involves reading quickly.

Have students do the task.

Check answers.

C Ask students to scan the article and underline all the things that are threatening the health of coral reefs.

After completing the task, have students read the article in more detail so they can answer the **COMPREHENSION** questions.

OPTIONAL The text can also be used as a listening activity. Have students close their books. Tell students they will listen to the passage.

🎧 **6.6** Play Audio Track 6.6. Ask students to get into pairs and discuss what information they heard. Then have them read the article more carefully.

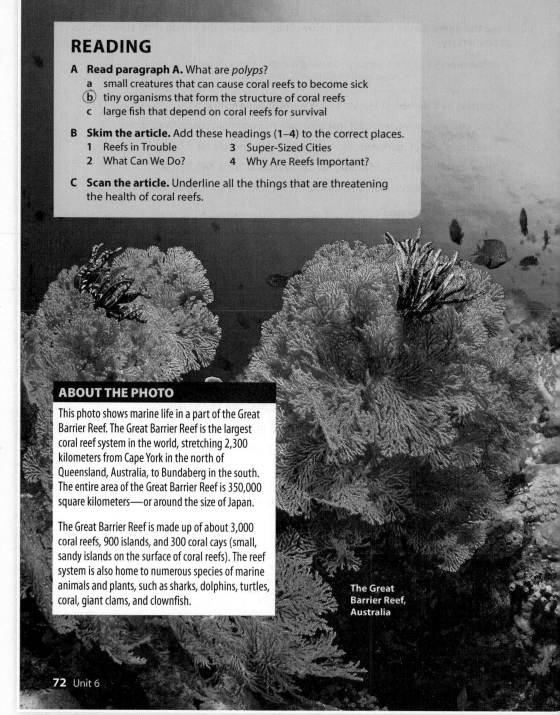

READING

A **Read paragraph A.** What are *polyps*?
   a   small creatures that can cause coral reefs to become sick
   ⓑ   tiny organisms that form the structure of coral reefs
   c   large fish that depend on coral reefs for survival

B **Skim the article.** Add these headings (1–4) to the correct places.
   1   Reefs in Trouble   3   Super-Sized Cities
   2   What Can We Do?   4   Why Are Reefs Important?

C **Scan the article.** Underline all the things that are threatening the health of coral reefs.

ABOUT THE PHOTO

This photo shows marine life in a part of the Great Barrier Reef. The Great Barrier Reef is the largest coral reef system in the world, stretching 2,300 kilometers from Cape York in the north of Queensland, Australia, to Bundaberg in the south. The entire area of the Great Barrier Reef is 350,000 square kilometers—or around the size of Japan.

The Great Barrier Reef is made up of about 3,000 coral reefs, 900 islands, and 300 coral cays (small, sandy islands on the surface of coral reefs). The reef system is also home to numerous species of marine animals and plants, such as sharks, dolphins, turtles, coral, giant clams, and clownfish.

The Great Barrier Reef, Australia

Additional Activities to Use with the Reading

Additional Comprehension Questions

1   What are coral polyps made of? (calcium)

2   How many different ways do humans benefit from coral reefs? (six—jobs, food, coasts protected, entertainment [diving], tourism [helps economies of those countries], new medicines)

3   According to experts, what percentage of the world's reefs could be gone by 2050? (100 percent)

Identifying the Main Idea

Ask students what the main idea of the article is (e.g., coral reefs are important but are endangered, and humans need to act to protect them). If students have difficulty identifying the main idea, remind them that a topic sentence, which is usually the first sentence of the paragraph, often states what they are going to read about. Have students

CITIES IN THE SEA

A 🎧 6.6 They may be small, but they build big things! Coral polyps, which live in the warm, **shallow** parts of the ocean, are probably the biggest builders on the planet. Each polyp uses calcium from seawater to build itself a hard limestone skeleton. When a polyp dies, its skeleton **remains**. Young polyps attach themselves to the old skeletons and make new skeletons. Over time, strange and wonderful shapes are slowly built up into amazing coral reefs.

B ___3___ Some coral reefs are huge, and the Great Barrier Reef in Australia is the largest of them all. It covers nearly 350,000 square kilometers.

C Scientists sometimes think of coral reefs as underwater cities. A quarter of all known ocean species live in and on reefs—there are nearly a thousand coral species. Reefs are also home to millions of sea creatures, like fish, crabs, turtles, and sharks.

D ___4___ Humans don't live in coral reef cities, but we benefit from them. Reefs create jobs for people in the fishing industry and other related businesses. They also supply us with food. Reefs protect our coasts—the coral slows down waves and protects beaches from erosion.

E Coral reefs are also **popular** with divers—many countries benefit from the tourists they **attract**. Finally, chemicals from reef creatures are used to create new medicines, which help doctors treat different illnesses.

F ___1___ Coral reefs are important, yet we don't take good care of them. About 20 percent of the world's reefs are already dead. Some experts **warn** that all reefs may be gone by 2050.

G Why are reefs in such trouble? For one thing, people catch too many reef fish and often **damage** the reefs—divers sometimes break off pieces of coral. Many people make and sell coral jewelry, too.

H Polluted water also causes problems because a certain type of algae grows in dirty water. This type of algae harms the reefs. Another type of algae is good for the reefs. But global warming is causing warmer ocean temperatures, which can cause polyps to lose this helpful algae. Without it, coral turns white. This is called "coral bleaching."

I ___2___ Can we save coral reefs? Experts say yes—if we make hard choices. More than 100 countries have created marine protected areas, where fishing is limited or banned. Another important step is fighting pollution.

J Humans and coral polyps are very different, but both build amazing cities. All of us will benefit if we protect our beautiful oceans.

Unit 6 **73**

Developing Critical Thinking

Encourage students to think critically by asking them to verify information in the article. If necessary, have students identify the facts they can confirm (e.g., The Great Barrier Reef covers nearly 350,000 square kilometers). Tell them to check reliable sources online to see if the information and statistics match with what is in the article.

Have students do research and talk about their findings in the next lesson.

Developing Fluency

Tell students they have one minute to read as much of the text as they can. Make it a fun "race" by using a stopwatch or saying *Ready? Go!*

After one minute, tell students to stop and see how far they have read. If a few students are significantly slower than the other students, discuss how to read more quickly.

Share tips for becoming a faster reader. (See **TEACHING NOTE**.)

TEACHING NOTE: TIPS FOR READING FASTER

Encourage students to do the following:
1 Read in "chunks" (phrases and sentences) rather than reading one word at a time.

2 Practice reading more quickly by timing themselves at home.

3 Use the reading strategies they have already learned, such as skimming and scanning.

Remind students that understanding the content is more important than the speed at which they can read it, so they should not sacrifice understanding for speed, but that it is helpful to try to develop faster reading skills over time. This skill can be especially helpful when they are taking exams and have a time limit.

---

identify the topic sentence after each heading: *Some coral reefs are huge, . . . / Humans don't live in coral reef cities, but we benefit from them. / Coral reefs are important, yet we don't take good care of them. / Experts say yes (we can save the reefs if we make hard choices).*

Remind students that the next part of each section explains the main idea by giving details, examples, evidence (e.g., facts, statistics), and reasons. Ask students to identify one or more facts or pieces of evidence in each section (e.g., paragraphs B and C: *350,000 square kilometers, a quarter of all known ocean species, nearly a thousand coral species, millions of sea creatures*; paragraphs D and E: *jobs, food, protect our coasts, tourists, new medicines*; paragraphs F, G, and H: *20 percent of the world's reefs are already dead, people catch too many reef fish, divers, coral jewelry, polluted water, global warming*; paragraphs I and J: *marine protected areas, fighting pollution*).

COMPREHENSION

A Have students read the questions to themselves and circle the correct answers.

After they have finished, check answers as a class.

IDIOM

As students follow along in their books, read the sentence and answer choices aloud. Have them guess the answer before providing it (c). Give an example:

I don't believe what he said. Something's fishy about his story.

SUPPORT Explain that when a fish rots, it smells bad, and if students form a mental image of this, it will be easier to remember they should use *fishy* when something about a situation feels wrong or suspicious to them.

B   EXAM PRACTICE

A word web, also known as a concept map or relationship chart, is a type of graphic organizer. Word webs can be used to classify and describe. They are also effective for demonstrating cause and effect.

In class, word webs can be used to brainstorm new ideas, but on tests, students must be certain they do not include ideas that are not in the passage. Using a word web, students must reduce the reading passage into an easy-to-understand visual representation. To do this, students must determine which information is most important. As a result, students analyze information to establish relationships between ideas.

Tell students that they will use words or phrases from the article to complete the word web. Ask a few students to read

different parts of the word web aloud. Start with the question in the middle box. Then move to the information on the left side before reading the right side.

Have students do the task.

Check answers.

SUPPORT Point out that the information needed for the word web can be found in the second half of the article from paragraph F onward.

COMPREHENSION

A **Answer the questions about *Cities in the Sea*.**

1 PURPOSE The main purpose of the article is to _____ .

 a identify the plants and animals that live in coral reefs

 (b) explain why coral reefs are important

 c tell readers about the Great Barrier Reef

2 DETAIL Coral reefs help protect coasts by _____ .

 (a) slowing down waves

 b releasing important chemicals

 c absorbing pollution

3 DETAIL What does the author say about the chemicals from reef creatures?

 a They damage the coral reefs.

 b They affect the algae growing near reefs.

 (c) They help scientists create new medicines.

4 COHESION The following sentence would best be placed at the end of which paragraph?

 If this process continues, the coral dies.

 a paragraph D   b paragraph F   **(c)** paragraph H

5 INFERENCE The helpful type of algae gives corals their _____ .

 (a) color   b hardness   c shape

B **Complete the word web.** Use words or phrases from the article.

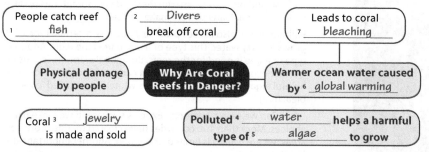

C CRITICAL THINKING Reflecting **Talk with a partner.** What kinds of "hard choices" do you think we need to make in order to save coral reefs? Answers will vary.

IDIOM

If you think something is "fishy," you think it's _____ .

a amazing

b funny

(c) suspicious

C   CRITICAL THINKING

As students follow along, read the question aloud. Have students get into pairs and discuss their ideas.

OPTIONAL Have pairs select their best ideas and share one with the class. Then have students talk about how realistic their ideas are and how willing they are to implement these ideas.

VOCABULARY

A **Find the bold words below in the article.** Then circle the correct answers.

1 A lake that is **shallow** is *very big* / (*not deep*).

2 If something **remains**, it (*continues to exist*) / *disappears*.

3 Things that are **popular** are enjoyed by *very few* / (*many*) people.

4 If something **attracts** people, it has features that cause people to (*come to it*) / *go away*.

5 When you **warn** someone about something, you tell them that something *good* / (*bad*) may happen.

6 When you **damage** an object, you (*break or destroy*) / *fix or improve* it.

B **Read the information below.** Then draw an arrow from the **bold** word or phrase to where it should go in each sentence (1–5).

> When we don't know the exact number or wish to be vague, we can use expressions to give approximate numbers:
>
> *about …*   *around …*   *more than …*   *nearly …*   *… or so*

1 The Great Barrier Reef covers an area of 350,000 square kilometers. **nearly**

2 It contributes 70,000 jobs to the Australian economy. **around**

3 It consists of 3,000 individual coral reefs. **about**

4 It's home to 1,500 species of fish. **more than**

5 The reef grows a centimeter each year. **or so**

WRITING

A **Read the email.**

B **What can the government do to help protect coral reefs?** Note some ideas.

C **Write a formal email using your notes from B.** Persuade a government official to help protect coral reefs in your country. Answers will vary.

New message

To   governmentofficial@mail.com

Subject   Help protect coral reefs

Dear Sir or Madam,

I am writing about the state of our country's coral reefs. There are beautiful reefs near our beaches, which many tourists currently enjoy, but these reefs have suffered a lot of damage recently from fishermen and divers. I feel that we can protect our coral reefs by …

Unit 6 **75**

WRITING

Tell students they are going to write a formal email to a government official to try to persuade the official to help protect coral reefs.

A As students follow along, read the email aloud. Point out that the email starts with the greeting, *Dear Sir or Madam.* Explain that if possible, students should find out the name of the official and address their email to the official. Ask students what this greeting would be, providing the answer if necessary (e.g., *Dear Ms./Mr. Moore,*).

Point out that the first sentence gives the reason for the email. Emphasize that this is important so the official will continue reading the email. Ask students what is written next (information about the problem and reasons why the reefs should be protected).

B Read the question aloud.

Have students make notes.

C Have students write their emails, using their notes from **B**. You might want to assign the writing as homework, and set a minimum number of sentences students must write (e.g., 10).

CHALLENGE Have students write a longer email of three paragraphs. Tell students that if they are going to write a longer email, they need a clear structure. Provide the following outline and have students use it:

Paragraph 1: Introduce yourself and give your reason(s) for writing.

Paragraph 2: Give facts about the coral reefs in your country and give reasons why protecting them is important. Point out that students must convince the government official, so they should try to provide reasons why the people in the area will benefit.

Paragraph 3: Suggest how the official can help. Encourage students to be specific.

VOCABULARY

A Have students find the bold words in the **READING** passage.

Have students circle the correct answers to complete the sentences. Check answers.

B As students follow along, read the information in the box aloud. Tell students to draw an arrow from the bold word or phrase to where it should go in each sentence.

Have students do the task. Check answers.

CONTENT NOTE: GREAT BARRIER REEF

The Great Barrier Reef was added to UNESCO's (United Nations Educational, Scientific and Cultural Organization) list of World Heritage Sites in 1981. Because of its massive size (which covers nearly 350,000 square kilometers), it can be seen from outer space. It has more than 300 types of hard coral and a great variety of fish, birds, and marine life.

VIDEO

Tell students they are going to watch a video called "Boneless Beauties." As students follow along in their books, have a student read the sentence about the video aloud.

OPTIONAL Teach students the meaning of the suffix *-less* by going over the meaning of *boneless*. If necessary, remind students that *-less* means "without."

BEFORE YOU WATCH

Tell students that they will take a quiz to see what they know about jellyfish. As students follow along, have a few students read the statements aloud. Have students circle **T** if the statement is true or **F** if it is false.

WHILE YOU WATCH

A Tell students they will watch the video to check their answers to the quiz in **BEFORE YOU WATCH**.

▶ 6.2 Play Video 6.2. Play it again, if necessary. Check answers.

OPTIONAL Have students talk about what else they know about jellyfish. Encourage them to also share personal stories if they have seen or encountered jellyfish.

B Tell students that they will watch the video again and they should circle the correct answers to complete the sentences. Have students read the sentences silently, before playing the video.

▶ 6.2 Play Video 6.2. Play it again, if necessary. Check answers.

OPTIONAL Ask students if they know what to do if they get stung by a jellyfish at the beach. (See **CONTENT NOTE**.)

BONELESS **BEAUTIES**

Before You Watch

Take a quiz. What do you know about jellyfish? Circle **T** for true or **F** for false.

1	Jellyfish appeared on the Earth before dinosaurs.	(T)	F
2	Jellyfish are a type of fish.	T	(F)
3	Some jellyfish stings can kill a human.	(T)	F
4	Jellyfish have no hearts, blood, or brains.	(T)	F
5	A group of jellyfish can cover hundreds of square kilometers.	(T)	F

While You Watch

A ▶ 6.2 **Watch the video.** Check your answers to the quiz above. Is any of the information surprising?

B ▶ 6.2 **Watch again.** Circle the correct answers.

1 Another name for jellyfish is (sea jellies) / **jelly bells**.

2 The Australian box jellyfish is considered to be the **longest** / (**most venomous**) marine animal in the world.

3 Jellyfish are **60** / (**95**) percent water.

4 Groups of jellyfish—called **schools** / (**blooms**)—have been known to damage (**ships**) / **coral reefs**.

C **Look at these possible impacts of jellyfish.** Are they positive or negative? Or could they be both? Write **P** (positive), **N** (negative), or **B** (both). Then compare with a partner and discuss reasons for your answers.

1 Jellyfish use up much of the oxygen that farmed fish require. __N__

2 Jellyfish provide shelter for younger fish that live within their tentacles. __P__

3 Jellyfish are an additional food source for certain communities. __P__

4 Jellyfish discourage tourism because beachgoers avoid going into the water. __B__

5 Large groups of jellyfish block the water pipes of seaside power plants. __B__

After You Watch

Talk with a partner. Look back at all the marine animals you have learned about in this unit. Which animal do you find most interesting? Why? Answers will vary.

CONTENT NOTE: WHAT TO DO IF A JELLYFISH STINGS YOU

While it is true that some jellyfish stings can be deadly, the common kinds of jellyfish that are found on most beaches simply deliver some discomfort and slight pain with their stings. If you are stung by a jellyfish while swimming at the beach, doctors recommend these steps for treatment:

1 Use tweezers to remove any tentacles still in your skin.

2 Put whatever body part was stung into warm water. The water must not be too hot, but around 43 to 45°C. Soak the affected area for 20 to 45 minutes.

C Tell students to read the statements about the possible impacts of jellyfish and decide if each impact is positive (**P**), negative (**N**), or both (**B**). If necessary, clarify that *both* means it can be seen as both positive and negative, depending on the viewpoint they have.

A Complete the sentences. Use the words in the box. Two words are extra.

| feathers | flippers | shells | tails | tusks |

1 Oysters, mussels, and snails all live inside __shells__ .

2 Cats, dogs, and mice all have ___tails___ .

3 An elephant has two ___tusks___ , but a narwhal has just one.

B Rewrite these sentences. Use *which* or *who*.

1 The sea otter lives along the Pacific coast. It uses rocks to break open shellfish.

The sea otter, which uses rocks to break open shellfish,

lives along the Pacific coast.

2 My teacher loves diving. She has a degree in oceanography.

My teacher, who has a degree in oceanography, loves

diving.

3 Fur seals have large eyes. These allow them to see well underwater.

Fur seals have large eyes, which allow them to see well

underwater.

C Correct the error in each sentence.

1 We spent ~~six about~~ *about six* weeks at the research center.

2 He's 40 years ~~around~~ *around 40 years* old.

3 We saw ~~or so~~ 30 *30 or so* fish while snorkeling.

4 There ~~nearly are~~ *are nearly* 20 people in the queue.

SELF CHECK   Now I can …

☐ talk about marine animals and their habitats

☐ add information about things and people

☐ discuss the importance of coral reefs

Unit 6 **77**

Sea nettle jellyfish

ABOUT THE PHOTO

This photo shows two Pacific sea nettles, a type of jellyfish found in the eastern Pacific Ocean. They generally have a round body (bell) with long tentacles extending from it. These tentacles, which are covered in stinging cells, are the sea nettles' hunting weapon. When a prey comes into contact with the tentacles, the stinging cells inject toxins into the prey, paralyzing it. The prey is then slowly moved to the mouth of the sea nettle for ingestion. Pacific sea nettles are carnivores, feeding on fish, comb jellies, and other jellyfish. Although their sting can be very painful, sea nettles aren't usually dangerous to humans.

REVIEW

Explain to students that they are going to review the material from the unit and this will help them remember what they have studied.

A Explain that activity **A** reviews vocabulary from the unit. Have students use the words in the box to complete the sentences. Point out that two words are extra and will not be used. Check answers as a class.

B Explain that activity **B** reviews the grammar from the unit. Tell students they should combine the two sentences by using *which* or *who*.

Have students do the task. Check answers. Note that, as in **LANGUAGE FOCUS** activity **D**, answers might vary depending on which sentence becomes the non-defining relative clause in students' rewritten sentences.

C Point out that activity **C** reviews words from **VOCABULARY** activity **B**.

Have students read the sentences and correct the error in each sentence. Tell them to draw a line through the error and write the correct expression above it. Have students do the task. Check answers.

SELF CHECK

These *I can* statements provide vital feedback on students' perceived ability to use the language from the unit. If you find students are reluctant to check they can do the skills, consider asking them to rate themselves from 1 (not very confident) to 3 (very confident).

SUPPORT For each skill, have students say sentences demonstrating their ability.

OPTIONAL Have students complete the **SELF CHECK** before doing the **REVIEW** activities. After reviewing the unit, have students once again check their confidence for each statement.

Have students read the sentences silently and do the task. Then have them get into pairs and compare answers with a partner. Encourage them to give reasons for their answers.

AFTER YOU WATCH

Tell students they will get into pairs and talk about the marine animal they learned about in the unit that they find the most interesting. Elicit the names of the animals for a quick review (*dugong, narwhal, seahorse, king crab, hermit crab, sea cucumber, humpback whale, coral polyp, jellyfish*).

Have students do the task. Remind them to explain why they find the animal the most interesting.

CHALLENGE As a critical thinking exercise, ask students to make their own discussion questions about the video (e.g., How many new species of jellyfish do you think scientists will find this year? / Have you ever been stung by a jellyfish? What did you do?). Give students time to write their questions and then have them get into pairs and take turns asking and answering them.

UNIT 7

IT MIGHT HAVE BEEN A TEMPLE

IT MIGHT HAVE BEEN A TEMPLE

CONTENT AREA: HISTORY AND CULTURE

Topic: ruins, lost civilizations, and mysteries

Vocabulary: ancient, discover, legend, religion, treasure, temple, ruins, peak, abandon, population, lack of, collapse, imagine

Grammar: modals of probability

Extra material: a map of the U.S., an enlarged (blown-up) photo of an object and something (such as sticky notes) to cover most of it, examples of treasure maps, photos of the mysterious crop circles in England

Other useful vocabulary: civilization, tribe, folklore, myth, fable, ceremony, invader, raid, pillage, plunder, ravage, conquer, crush, overpower

END OF UNIT PROJECT Have students do research about an ancient civilization and get into small groups to share their information.

Remind students that in this unit, they learned about ancient civilizations and places. Explain that they will research a different civilization or ruins—with a mystery, if possible—and talk about their research in a small group.

Tell students that during their discussion, they should explain the civilization or the ruins and its significance. Explain that if they talk about a mystery, they should give enough background for the other students to understand the mystery, and then talk about two or more theories about what happened.

Ruins of an ancient temple in Turkey

78

If necessary, have students brainstorm ancient civilizations or empires (e.g., Ottoman, Babylonian, Roman, Persian, Byzantine, Han Dynasty, Mongolian, Greek, Aztec, Macedonian) and mysteries (e.g., the Hanging Gardens of Babylon, the Temple of Artemis, the Amber Room).

Assign the research as homework.

In the next lesson, have students get into small groups. Ask them to take turns talking about their research. Explain that group members should ask questions to clarify anything they don't understand after each presentation. Encourage them to also decide, as a group, which theory (in the case of mysteries) is most likely, providing reasons for their ideas.

When the groups are finished with their discussions, ask students to write one or two sentences about each of the other students' presentations, demonstrating what they learned. (This also encourages them to be active listeners.)

PREVIEW

A 🎧 **7.1** **Listen.** Number these titles in order (1–3). One title is extra.

<u>2</u> Empty Homes

_____ Mysterious Bones Discovered

<u>1</u> The Legend of the Lost Gold

<u>3</u> Religion in the Ancient World

B 🎧 **7.1** **Listen again.** What is the mystery in each story? Circle **a** or **b**.

1 a Where is the Inca king buried?

b Where is the lost treasure of the Inca?

2 a Why did the Anasazi suddenly leave their homes?

b How did the Anasazi build their multi-story homes?

3 a How old are the temple ruins?

b Which came first—religion or cities?

C **Talk with a partner.** Of the stories above, which do you find most interesting? Why?

Answers will vary.

> I find the story about the Anasazi most interesting because …

> I think the most interesting story is …

HISTORY AND CULTURE

UNIT GOALS

• talk about ancient and modern-day mysteries

• learn language for describing probability

• learn about ancient civilizations

79

CHALLENGE Have students do **B** based on their first listening of the audio in **A**. Then play the audio again to have them check answers for **A** and **B**.

C Tell students they are going to get into pairs and take turns sharing their opinions about which story they find most interesting, out of the stories they heard in **A** and **B**. Remind them to offer reasons for their opinions.

Model the conversation with a student.

Have students do the task.

SUPPORT Before doing the task, review the meaning and pronunciation of words that students heard in the audio that may be helpful in their discussions (e.g., *the Inca, invaders, treasure, the Anasazi, mud structures, climate, temple, discovery, religion*).

CHALLENGE Have students find out more about one of the stories. Assign this as homework or give students time in class to research online to find any new theories about the lost treasure of the Inca, the disappearance of the Anasazi, or the 12,000-year-old temple in Turkey. Have students share any additional information they learn with the class.

UNIT GOALS

Direct students' attention to the **UNIT GOALS** box. Explain that these are some of the things students will learn in this unit. Point out that this unit is about history and culture. As students follow along, read each of the unit goals to the class. Explain any words students do not know. Remind students that at the end of the unit there is a self check that allows them to see if they have accomplished each goal.

PREVIEW

Have students study the photo for a moment. Read the unit title and the photo caption aloud, as students follow along. Explain that in this unit they will learn to talk about ancient and modern-day mysteries, and how to describe probability. Tell them they will also learn about ancient civilizations.

A Tell students that they will hear three stories about three ancient civilizations. Tell them to choose the best title for each story and number the titles in order, from one to three. As students follow along, have a student read the titles aloud. Point out that there is one extra title that will not be used.

🎧 **7.1** Play Audio Track 7.1. Check answers.

B Tell students that they will listen again and they should circle the correct mystery in each story. As students follow along, read the mysteries aloud.

🎧 **7.1** Play Audio Track 7.1. Play it again, if necessary. Check answers.

LANGUAGE FOCUS

A Tell students they will listen to a conversation between Maya, Nadine, and Stig.

 🔊 **7.2** Play Audio Track 7.2 as students listen and follow along in their books.

As students follow along, read the question, *What does Nadine think the item is?* Have students answer. If necessary, elicit or explain the meaning of *ancient* (very old).

Have students work in threes and practice the conversation once. Point out the bold words. Tell students to practice the conversation two more times, changing the bold words each time and swapping roles after the first time.

OPTIONAL Have students brainstorm some other ways that an ancient arrowhead could have been used. Encourage students to use their creativity. Write their ideas in a mind map on the board.

REAL ENGLISH

Direct students' attention to the expression in the **REAL ENGLISH** box. Explain that we use *What on earth . . . ?* when we are shocked, surprised, or puzzled about something that almost seems unbelievable or confusing.

> **A:** Look at that strange object in the sky!
> **B:** What on earth is that?

Note the expression is interchangeable with the idiom *What in the world . . . ?* Both expressions can also be used to express annoyance or anger at something someone said. For example:

> **A:** I didn't realize that the meeting was this afternoon.
> **B:** What on earth are you talking about? I reminded you about it yesterday!

B Ask students to look at the chart. Explain that they will study how to talk about things that we are not certain about.

LANGUAGE FOCUS

A 🔊 **7.2** **Listen and read.** What does Nadine think the item is? Then repeat the conversation and replace the words in **bold**. *an ancient arrowhead*

Maya:	Look what I found **behind the school**. (**near the playground / on the soccer field**)
Nadine:	What on earth is that?
Maya:	I'm not sure. I think it's made of stone.
Nadine:	It **could** be an ancient arrowhead. (**might / may**)
Maya:	Cool! It must have been used **to hunt wild animals**. (**to fight other tribes / in fierce battles**)
Nadine:	We should **take it to** the history museum. (**show it to people at / hand it over to**)
Maya:	Hey, Stig! Check this out!
Stig:	Hey! I've been looking everywhere for that! I made it in my jewelry-making class.

B 🔊 **7.3** **Look at the chart.** Then circle the correct answers below.

DESCRIBING PROBABILITY (USING MODALS OF PROBABILITY)		
	Less Sure	**More Sure**
Present	The lost treasure **could/might** be in a cave. But the treasure **might not** even exist.	The jewels **can't** be in that cave—it's too high. This gold necklace **must** be valuable. No one's ever found the treasure. It **must not** exist.
Past	This house **could/might** have belonged to the royal family. However, it **might not** have belonged to an important person.	The house is huge, so it **must** have belonged to the royal family. There are bedrooms in the building, so it **couldn't** have been a school.

1 If we use modal + *be*, we are referring to the **past** / **present**.

2 If we use modal + *have been*, we are referring to the **past** / **present**.

3 We use *could* or *might* when we are **less** / **more** sure of something, and *must* or *can't* when we are **less** / **more** sure.

 🔊 **7.3** Have students follow along as they listen to Audio Track 7.3. Tell students that the bold words in the chart are called *modal verbs*, and in these sentences they are used with another verb to express the probability of something. Point out that the other verb in each sentence shows the tense (past or present). Have students identify these verbs (*be, exist, belonged, been*) and all of the modal verbs (*can, could, might, must*). Explain that with the present tense usage of these modal verbs, the main verbs that are used with the modal are always in their base form, so instead of *is* we use *be*, and instead of *exists* we use *exist*. The past tense will always take the form of modal verb + *have* + past participle.

Read the sentences in the *Less Sure* column aloud. Explain that the speaker is less certain about the fact or is just guessing. Explain that in these sentences, *could* and *might* are interchangeable. Tell students that *The lost treasure could be in a cave* means the treasure could be there, but it could be somewhere else, so we're not sure where it is.

C 🎧 **7.4 Complete the conversations.** Circle the correct words. Then listen and check your answers.

1 Mary: This building is very old. What do you think it was used for?

Greg: I'm not sure. It ¹(**might**) / **must** have been a temple. What do you think?

Mary: No, it ²(**couldn't**) / **might not** have been a temple because there's already one right next to it. They wouldn't have built two temples so close together.

2 Yasmin: Whose notebook is this?

Karl: I have no idea. It ³(**might**) / **must** be Jessie's.

Yasmin: Oh, wait—here's a photo of a puppy. It ⁴ **must have belonged** / (**must belong**) to Laura. She just got a puppy last month.

D Rewrite these sentences. Use the words in parentheses.

1 It's possible that the treasure is at the bottom of the lake. (**could**)

The treasure _could be at the bottom of the lake_.

2 I'm certain that this item is thousands of years old. (**must**)

This item _must be thousands of years old_.

3 It's possible that he didn't call his parents. (**might not**)

He _might not have called his parents_.

4 She definitely got home before midnight. (**must**)

She _must have gotten home before midnight_.

5 We're certain that the teacher isn't over 40 years old. (**can't**)

The teacher _can't be over 40 years old_.

E Work with a partner. Student A: Turn to page 150. **Student B:** Turn to page 153. Take turns reading each mystery. Discuss what you think happened. Answers will vary.

A stone ball from Costa Rica

The stone balls might have been part of a religious ceremony.

Maybe. Or they could have been used in games.

Unit 7 **81**

Read the sentences in the *More Sure* column aloud. Explain that the speaker has much more confidence in what is being said.

SUPPORT Cover with sticky notes most of an enlarged photo of an object. Show it to the students and have them speculate on what the object is. Show a little more of the photo and have students guess again using *could, might, couldn't,* and *must.* Continue until students guess what is in the photo.

OPTIONAL Say, *I will go to a movie tonight.* Ask how certain the speaker is (100 percent). Say, *I can't go to a movie tonight.* Ask about certainty again (100 percent). Say, *I might go to a movie tonight.* Ask again (perhaps 50 percent certain). Say, *I could go to a movie tonight.* Explain that the person is debating between the movie and another (unnamed) option. Say, *I must go to a movie tonight.* Explain that the person will go (100 percent certainty), but the implication is that the person is being forced to go. Have students get into pairs and practice using the modals to change the meaning of a sentence.

Draw students' attention to the three statements under the chart. Have students circle the correct answers.

Check answers.

C Have students circle the correct words to complete the conversations.

🎧 **7.4** Play Audio Track 7.4. Check answers as a class.

OPTIONAL Have students get into pairs and practice the conversations twice, swapping roles after the first time.

D Have students rewrite the sentences using the modals in parentheses.

Check answers as a class.

E Tell students they are going to get into pairs, take turns to read their mystery to their partner, and discuss what they think happened. Have Student As turn to page 150 and Student Bs turn to page 153.

Model the conversation with a student. Point out that the speakers in the example use modals of probability to express levels of certainty.

CONTENT NOTE: THE STONE BALLS OF COSTA RICA

While the original use of the stone balls, also called the Diquís Spheres, is still unknown, almost all of the 300 balls found have been moved from the site where they were discovered. Many are now used as ornaments outside people's homes in Costa Rica. However, some stone balls have been carefully preserved and are displayed at Costa Rica's National Museum in San José.

THE REAL WORLD

Ask students to look at the photo. As students follow along, read the title and the caption aloud.

A Tell students they are going to watch a video about Rapa Nui (Easter Island). Tell students to check the topics that are discussed. As students follow along, have a student read the topics aloud.

▶ **7.1** Play Video 7.1. Play it again, if necessary.

Check answers.

DO YOU KNOW?

Read the sentence and answer choices aloud, as students follow along in their books. Have students guess the answer before providing it (a).

CONTENT NOTE: THE STATUE OF UNITY

The Statue of Unity, which stands 182 meters tall, is located near the Narmada River in Kevadia in Gujarat, India. It is a statue of Sardar Vallabhbhai Patel, who is famous for his nonviolent protests during the struggle for independence in India. There is a viewing area at 153 meters above ground that is open to visitors.

B Tell students they will watch the video again and they should circle the correct answers to complete the sentences.

▶ **7.1** Play Video 7.1. Play it again, if necessary. Check answers.

C As students follow along, read the task aloud. Tell students that they will work in groups to list the pros (good points) and cons (bad points) of an increase in tourism on Rapa Nui.

Have students get into groups and complete the chart.

When all the groups have finished, call on students to share their group's ideas with the class.

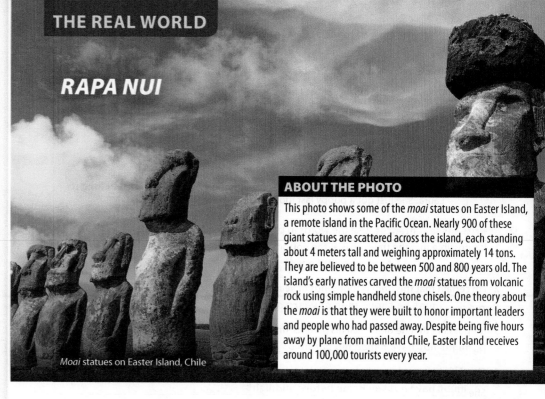

RAPA NUI

Moai statues on Easter Island, Chile

ABOUT THE PHOTO

This photo shows some of the *moai* statues on Easter Island, a remote island in the Pacific Ocean. Nearly 900 of these giant statues are scattered across the island, each standing about 4 meters tall and weighing approximately 14 tons. They are believed to be between 500 and 800 years old. The island's early natives carved the *moai* statues from volcanic rock using simple handheld stone chisels. One theory about the *moai* is that they were built to honor important leaders and people who had passed away. Despite being five hours away by plane from mainland Chile, Easter Island receives around 100,000 tourists every year.

A ▶ **7.1** **Watch the video.** Check (✓) the topics discussed.

- ☐ when the island of Rapa Nui was discovered
- ☑ the height and weight of the *moai* statues
- ☑ how the *moai* may have been moved around the island
- ☐ where to get the best view of the *moai*
- ☑ theories about the purpose of the *moai*

B ▶ **7.1** **Watch again.** Circle the correct answers.

1 There are nearly **500** / **900** *moai* on Rapa Nui.

2 The early Rapa Nui people probably used **ropes** / **animals** to move the statues.

3 Most *moai* **face inland** / **look out to sea**.

4 One theory about the *moai* is that they **helped scare away enemies** / **represented political leaders**.

DO YOU KNOW?

The Statue of Unity, which is the tallest statue in the world, is located in _____.

a India
b Japan
c Dubai

82 Unit 7

D CRITICAL THINKING

As students follow along, read the questions aloud. Have students get into pairs and talk about their ideas. Encourage them to support their opinions with reasons.

OPTIONAL Give students additional questions to discuss. Remind them to give reasons for their answers.

1 Do you think tourists should be allowed to get close to the *moai* statues?

2 Do you know any places where you think tourism should be limited?

PROJECT As students follow along, read the project instructions aloud. Give students basic background information on each mystery to help them choose. (See **CONTENT NOTE**.) Give students time to do their research and make notes about what they learned. Remind them to put the information in their own words—they should not copy directly from the internet. Have students get into pairs with a partner who chose a different topic and share their findings.

C **Work in groups.** Rapa Nui has seen a big increase in tourism in the past few years, as many people come to see the *moai*. What are some pros and cons of this? Complete the chart.

Pros	Cons
Answers will vary.	

D CRITICAL THINKING Reflecting **Talk with a partner.** Based on your notes in **C**, would you want to visit Rapa Nui? Does the mystery of the *moai* make you want to see the statues for yourself?
Answers will vary.

PROJECT Go online. Choose one of these ancient structures and learn about the mystery surrounding it. Share your findings with a partner.
- Stonehenge
- Machu Picchu
- The Yonaguni Monument

PRONUNCIATION review: reduction of *have*

🎧 7.5 **Listen.** Write the words you hear. Then listen again and repeat the sentences.

1 The effort to construct the statues ___must have been___ considerable.

2 The heavy statues ___couldn't have been___ easy to move.

3 The Rapa Nui people ___might have used___ the statues for religious purposes.

COMMUNICATION

Solve a puzzle. Work in groups. You are on a quest to find treasure from different civilizations. There are three chests, each containing an item from a certain culture. Each chest is in a different place. Use the clues to complete the chart below.

CULTURES
Aztec, Inca, Maya

ITEMS
mask, cup, bowl

PLACES
mountain, cave, jungle

CLUES
The Maya chest is one number smaller than the Inca chest.

The Aztec chest can't be Chest 1, but it must contain the cup.

Chest 2 is in a cave.

Chest 1 contains the bowl, but it isn't in the jungle.

CHEST	CULTURE	ITEM	PLACE
1	Maya	bowl	mountain
2	Inca	mask	cave
3	Aztec	cup	jungle

The Maya chest could be Chest 1 or 2.

---

looks like an underwater pyramid. Some scientists think it is what remains of what was once a city that became submerged after an earthquake. Others argue it was created by nature.

PRONUNCIATION

Tell students they will practice saying the reduction of *have* naturally. Explain that even though some native English speakers may sound like they are saying the word *of*, they are actually saying *have*.

Tell students to listen and write the words they hear to complete the sentences.

🎧 7.5 Play Audio Track 7.5. Play it again, if necessary. Check answers.

🎧 7.5 Play the audio again, pausing after each sentence so students can repeat.

COMMUNICATION

Explain to students that they are going to work in groups to solve a puzzle. Tell them their goal is to find treasure from different civilizations. Point out that there are three chests. Explain that each is in a different place and has an item from a different culture. As students follow along, have a few students read the information (*CULTURES, ITEMS, PLACES,* and *CLUES*) aloud. Tell students they should use the clues to complete the chart.

Model the example.

Have groups do the task, then check answers as a class.

OPTIONAL Have groups draw a treasure map for each chest. If you brought in examples of treasure maps, show them to the students so they can use the examples as a reference. When all the groups have finished drawing their maps, have them take turns to share their treasure maps with the class.

CONTENT NOTE: STONEHENGE, MACHU PICCHU, THE YONAGUNI MONUMENT

Stonehenge is located near Salisbury, England. Scientists know that the circular stone structure was built between 3000 B.C. and 1520 B.C., but the reason it was built is still a mystery. Researchers have presented a range of theories about what its function was, such as a Druid temple, a tool to read astronomical events, a cemetery, a place of healing, or a place where people from different tribes got together.

The ruins of the ancient Inca site Machu Picchu are in the Andes Mountains in Peru. Scholars are not sure what Machu Picchu actually was. Some theories are: a home for a leader, a temple, a place for a special tribe, or a vacation place for the royal family.

The Yonaguni Monument is an underwater structure made of rocks found off the coast of Japan. No one is certain what it is. It

READING

CONTENT NOTE: THE MAYA

Long before the Spanish invaded Mexico and Central America, the Maya were there. As early as 1500 B.C., they lived in villages and farmed corn, beans, and squash; and by A.D. 200, they were cutting limestone with harder stones and building cities that had temples, pyramids, and palaces. They had also developed hieroglyphics, advanced calendars, and astronomical systems, and they wrote in books made from paper (from the bark of trees).

Have students look at the photo and then follow along in their books as you read the title and the caption aloud.

A Read the questions aloud. Randomly call on students to share their answers with the class. Remind students that by reviewing any background information they have before they read, they can understand the content more quickly.

OPTIONAL Before students read the article, have them brainstorm words they might come across in the text, writing their ideas on the board as they are given. Come back to this list after students have read to check their predictions.

B Have students scan the article and underline the two cities mentioned.

Check answers.

C As students follow along in their books have a student read the questions aloud. Have students skim the article to find the answers. Check answers.

After completing the task, have students read the article in more detail so they can answer the **COMPREHENSION** questions.

READING

A Look at the title and the photo. What do you know about the Maya? When and where did they live? Answers will vary.

B Scan the article. Underline the two cities mentioned.

C Skim the article. What did archeologists use to think happened to the Maya? What do they think now?

Archeologists used to think that a disaster or disease hit the Maya. They now think the Maya had a lot of different problems.

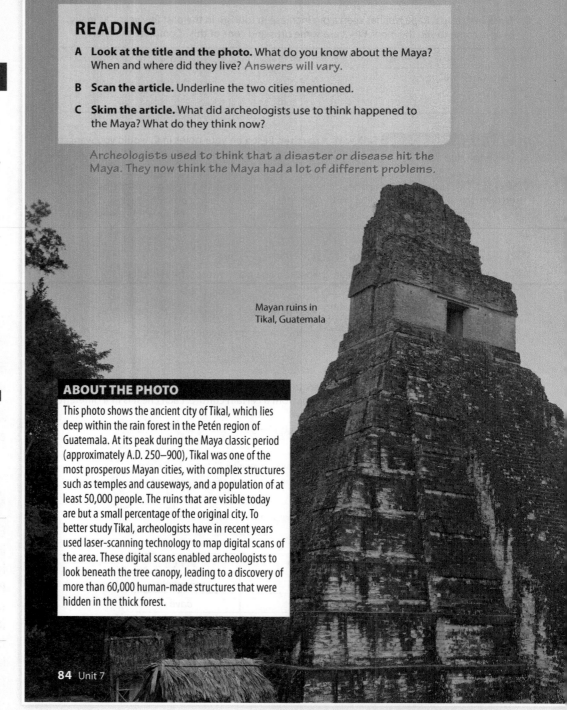

Mayan ruins in Tikal, Guatemala

ABOUT THE PHOTO

This photo shows the ancient city of Tikal, which lies deep within the rain forest in the Petén region of Guatemala. At its peak during the Maya classic period (approximately A.D. 250–900), Tikal was one of the most prosperous Mayan cities, with complex structures such as temples and causeways, and a population of at least 50,000 people. The ruins that are visible today are but a small percentage of the original city. To better study Tikal, archeologists have in recent years used laser-scanning technology to map digital scans of the area. These digital scans enabled archeologists to look beneath the tree canopy, leading to a discovery of more than 60,000 human-made structures that were hidden in the thick forest.

84 Unit 7

OPTIONAL The text can also be used as a listening activity. Have students close their books. Tell students they will listen to the passage.

7.6 Play Audio Track 7.6. Ask students to get into pairs and discuss what information they heard. Then have them read the article more carefully.

TEACHING NOTE: READING SPEEDS

If some students finish reading the text much more quickly than others, use one of the following two approaches:

1 Give the students who finish first an additional task (e.g., have them write comprehension questions that can later be used in a quiz).

2 Give the class a time limit so the students who read more slowly will try to read more quickly.

MAYA **MYSTERY**

By Guy Gugliotta, writing for *National Geographic*

A 🎧 7.6 A lost world is hidden in the rain forests of Central America. There, the ancient Maya built huge, incredible cities. The Maya civilization was at its **peak** for 650 years, but about a thousand years ago, the cities were suddenly **abandoned**. Today, trees and plants cover the buildings, and many temples are now ruins. What happened? Why did the Maya leave their cities?

B For years, archeologists thought that a disaster, like a volcano or an earthquake, must have hit the Maya. Diseases, which were brought by invaders, might have spread quickly through the **population**. However, researchers now think the Maya had a lot of different problems, leading to their disappearance.

C To understand what happened to the Maya, *National Geographic* sent me to Central America. I visited Mayan cities and talked to archeologists who are studying them.

D One hot day, I stood next to a river near the ruins of <u>Cancuén</u>. It used to be a great city, but everything changed 1,200 years ago. Invaders came suddenly—probably by boat. I pictured them as I looked at the river. In my mind, I saw the invaders fighting the soldiers—first at the river, and then in the town.

E I followed the path that the invaders must have taken, which led to the ruins of a large pool. The pool once provided drinking water for the city. The invaders killed the city's leaders and threw their bodies into the water. They killed the king and queen, too, and buried them nearby.

F The invaders then left, taking nothing of value. No one knows who they were, what they wanted, or where they went. Experts think that the city's remaining population escaped into the rain forest.

G I learned a different story in <u>Tikal</u>, one of the greatest Mayan cities. Thirteen hundred years ago, over 50,000 people lived there. The city had about 3,000 major buildings. But, like Cancuén, its people left.

H Archeologists think Tikal might have had a drought. The **lack of** rain would have made it hard to grow food. War with neighboring cities might also have made Tikal weak. The Maya believed that their leaders were gods, so when the king couldn't bring rain or protect them, people started to question his power. Their community might then have **collapsed**.

I Walking among the temples at Tikal, I **imagined** the people living there in the city's last days. I could picture them hungry, tired, and scared. Like the Maya in Cancuén, they left behind a great city and a great mystery.

Unit 7 **85**

Additional Activities to Use with the Reading

Additional Comprehension Questions

1 For how many centuries were the Maya strong? (six and a half)

2 When did the Maya culture start to decline? (It started to decline about 1,000 years ago.)

3 In the first sentence of paragraph C, who is *me*? (Guy Gugliotta, the author of the article)

4 Why did the community fall apart when the king couldn't protect the people? (They thought he was a god so they thought he could do anything. When they realized that he couldn't bring rain or protect them, they began to question his power.)

Vocabulary

To help students remember new vocabulary from the second half of the Student's Book, make a vocabulary box that you can use for the rest of the term. Hand out small pieces of paper to the students. Have students write the new words on them. Put them into the box. Whenever you complete a lesson a few minutes early, take a word from the box and have students explain it or use it in a sentence.

If you will be using the box for several months, every time students review the word, write the date on the piece of paper and then place it back in the box. If you draw the same word within a week or two of the previous review, put it back in the box and take out a different word.

Content Expansion

Remind students that one way to develop their critical thinking is by making their own discussion questions about the reading. Emphasize that the questions should not be factual but should instead ask about opinions, feelings, and reactions. Give an example, if necessary. (Factual question: *Where are the Tikal ruins? [In Guatemala.]* Discussion question: *If you had been in Cancuén when the king and queen were killed, how would you have felt? Would you have been scared?*)

Give students time to write their discussion questions.

After they have made their questions, have them get into pairs and take turns asking and answering them.

TEACHING NOTE: CONTENT WORDS

Remind students that as they read, it is helpful to focus on content words. These are not structural words like *the*, *a*, or *of*, but the words that give key information about the article (e.g., *hidden*, *rain forest*, *Central America*). These words can help students to understand the text more quickly.

COMPREHENSION

A EXAM PRACTICE

On some standardized multiple-choice tests, for example, the MET Go! exam, students must choose the best response from three choices. On many other exams, including TOEFL, TOEFL Jr., and IELTS, four choices are provided.

For all tests, students must determine how each option is different so they do not inadvertently mark the wrong answer. Many students find it helpful to quickly read the multiple-choice questions before reading the passage. This allows them to identify the key points to look for, but they should not spend too much time previewing the questions.

Have students read the questions to themselves and circle the correct answers.

After they have finished, check answers as a class.

IDIOM

As students follow along in their books, read the sentence and answer choices aloud. Have them guess the answer before providing it (b). Explain that we use this expression when someone is trying to find the main reason for or truth about something. For example, in a news report, we might hear:

Investigators haven't gotten to the bottom of what caused the 12-car collision, but some experts believe bad weather and increased traffic because of the holiday weekend were contributing factors.

B

Tell students to read the sentences silently, then circle **Fa** if the sentence is a fact or **Th** if it is a theory.

Have students do the task. Check answers.

COMPREHENSION

A Answer the questions about *Maya Mystery*.

1 MAIN IDEA What is the mystery in the title?

   (a) Why did the Maya civilization disappear?

   b Who were the Maya people?

   c Where did the Maya hide their treasure?

2 INFERENCE The archeologists thought the Maya probably died from a natural disaster or a disease because _____.

   (a) they disappeared so suddenly

   b the Maya had a lot of enemies

   c they were bad at farming

3 COHESION Where is the best place for this sentence in paragraph E?

   Then it became a tomb for the local leaders.

   a after sentence 1   (b) after sentence 2   c after sentence 4

4 DETAIL Why did invaders attack Cancuén?

   a to take their treasure   **b** to take over the city   (c) no one knows

5 DETAIL What is known to be true about Cancuén but not Tikal?

   a Its people left the city.

   b Its people believed in gods.

   (c) Its rulers were killed by invaders.

B Read the sentences below. Circle **Fa** for fact or **Th** for theory.

1 The ancient Maya built huge cities in Central America.	(Fa)	Th
2 The Maya population was affected by a natural disaster.	Fa	(Th)
3 There is a river near the ruins of Cancuén.	(Fa)	Th
4 The people who invaded Cancuén came by boat.	Fa	(Th)
5 Tikal experienced a drought, which made it hard to grow food.	Fa	(Th)

C CRITICAL THINKING Ranking **Which of these ancient civilizations would you like to go back and live in?** Rank them from **1** (most like to live in) to **4** (least like to live in). Then share your ranking and reasons with a partner. Answers will vary.

_____ Maya   _____ Rapa Nui   _____ Egypt   _____ China

86 Unit 7

IDIOM

To "get to the bottom of" a mystery is to _____.

a leave it unsolved

(b) find out the truth

c tell people about it

OPTIONAL Tell students that we often use modals of probability when theorizing, but we don't use them when stating facts. Have students look more closely at the modals used in the article and determine how they are used. Have them find *couldn't* in paragraph H (*the king couldn't bring rain*). Ask students if *couldn't* shows the writer's degree of certainty (no). Have students explain this usage of *couldn't* (an inability to do something). Follow the same procedure for *could* in paragraph I (which also shows ability, not degree of certainty).

C CRITICAL THINKING

As students follow along, read the task aloud. Have students rank the ancient civilizations from 1 (most like to live in) to 4 (least like to live in). Then have them get into pairs and discuss their ideas. Remind students to provide reasons for their ranking.

VOCABULARY

A Find the bold words below in the article. Then circle the correct answers.

1 A civilization at its **peak** is at its *weakest /* (*strongest.*)

2 If people **abandon** a city, they *invade /* (*leave*) it.

3 A country's **population** is the number of (*people*) */ buildings* there.

4 A **lack of** water means there's (*not enough*) */ too much* water.

5 When a civilization **collapses**, it *continues to be successful /* (*is unable to continue.*)

6 If you **imagine** something, you *try to forget about it /* (*form a picture of it in your mind.*)

B Read the information below. Then add the examples to the correct column in the chart. What other natural disasters can you name? Which occur in your country?

> Below are some examples of natural disasters. Use a dictionary to check their meanings.
>
> avalanche   blizzard   flood   hurricane   tsunami

They involve water	They involve snow
flood	avalanche
hurricane	blizzard
tsunami	

CROP FORMATIONS

Every year, mysterious crop circles or formations appear in fields in England. Some people think aliens might have made them. Others think that people made them as a prank …

WRITING

A Read the paragraph.

B What mysteries do you know of? Choose one and make notes about it.

C Write a short essay. Describe the mystery. Use your notes from **B** to help you.
Answers will vary.

A Have students look at the photo. If you brought in photos of the mysterious crop circles in England, show them to the students. Then, as students follow along, have a student read the example aloud. Point out that it starts with a title, introduces the mystery, and provides several theories about what causes the formations.

B Tell students to think about mysteries they know of and choose one to write about. Give them time to make notes about it. Encourage them to use a graphic organizer, such as a mind map, to organize their ideas.

C Have students write their essays, using their notes from **B**. You might want to assign the writing as homework, and set a minimum number of sentences students must write (e.g., 10).

OPTIONAL Make a *Mysteries of the World* magazine. Collect the short essays and put them together to create a magazine. Encourage students to find pictures to go with their essays. Distribute copies to the class so students can read each other's essays.

CONTENT NOTE: CROP FORMATIONS

Crop circles have been reported globally since the 1970s. Many have proven to be man-made creations, made with the intention to trick people into believing that aliens made the intricate designs. In a candid interview, an admitted crop-circle designer pointed out that spreading the belief that aliens created the crop formations is a good way for people to make money through mystery tours and books about the formations. Nevertheless, there are still some researchers who believe that crop circles may be extraterrestrial.

VOCABULARY

A Have students find the bold words in the **READING** passage.

Have students circle the correct answers to complete the sentences. Check answers.

B As students follow along, read the information in the box aloud. Have students add the examples from the box to the correct column in the chart.

Check answers. Then ask students what other natural disasters they can name and which ones occur in their country.

WRITING

Tell students they are going to write a short essay about a mystery that they know of. Encourage them to use information they already have, but explain that if they don't know of any mysteries, they can do some research on the internet and find one.

VIDEO

Tell students they are going to watch a video called "The Lost Colony." As students follow along in their books, have a student read the sentence about the video aloud.

BEFORE YOU WATCH

Have students look at the photo. As students follow along, read the caption aloud. Then read the question. Have students get into pairs to discuss their ideas. If a map of the U.S. is available, point out the island of Roanoke off the coast of North Carolina.

SUPPORT Before students watch the video, tell them about English settlements in the Americas. For example: Within 100 years of Roanoke, there would be almost 12 more English settlements in the Americas—more than any other European country. People left England to escape from poverty as well as to have religious freedom.

WHILE YOU WATCH

A Tell students they will watch the first part of the video, and they should match each statement to the correct expedition(s) by checking the correct columns. As students follow along in their books, have a student read the statements aloud.

▶ **7.2** Play Video 7.2. Play it again, if necessary. Check answers.

CHALLENGE Tell students that the governor was delayed in returning to Roanoke. Have them guess why he was delayed. (See **CONTENT NOTE**.)

CONTENT NOTE: DELAYED RETURN TO ROANOKE

When John White, the governor of Roanoke, left the colony to get supplies in England, he was supposed to be away from the colony for only a short time. Instead, three whole years passed. The delay in his return was due to Spain invading England in 1588.

THE *LOST COLONY*

Before You Watch

Talk with a partner. What challenges do you think the early English settlers in the New World (i.e., the Americas) faced? Answers will vary.

While You Watch

A ▶ 7.2 **Watch Part 1 of the video.** Which expedition(s) do the statements below relate to? Check (✓) the correct columns.

	Expedition 1	Expedition 2	Expedition 3
It returned to England.	✓	✓	
The colonists disappeared.			✓
A map of Roanoke was created.	✓		
It arrived at Roanoke in 1587.			✓
A child was born in the colony.			✓

B ▶ 7.3 **Watch Part 2 of the video.** What theories about the colonists' disappearance are mentioned? Circle the correct answers.

1 The colonists moved to (Croatoan Island) / an island near Croatoan.

2 The colonists **tried to return to England** / (moved farther inland).

3 The colonists died from disease or **an earthquake** / (drought).

4 The colonists were killed by (Native Americans) / wild animals.

C **Work with a partner.** Of the theories in **B**, which do you think is most likely? Which is least likely? Can you think of any other possible explanations?
Answers will vary.

After You Watch

Talk with a partner. The mystery of the Roanoke colony has been adapted into a TV show. Would you like to watch it? Why or why not? Answers will vary.

An actress portraying Eleanor Dare, the governor's daughter

B Tell students that they will watch the second part of the video, and they should circle the correct answers to complete the sentences. As students follow along, read the sentences aloud.

▶ **7.3** Play Video 7.3. Play it again, if necessary.

Check answers.

CONTENT NOTE: NATIVE AMERICANS ON ROANOKE

The Native American people who lived on Roanoke were Carolina Algonquian speakers. Various Native American tribes who spoke Algonquian lived along the east coast of what is now the United States, in addition to Canada. The tribe that the settlers met had the same name as the island mentioned in the video: the Croatoan.

A Complete the sentences. Use the words in parentheses. In each set, one word is extra.

1 In many early ___civilizations___ , people ___farmed___ the land and practiced ___religion___ . (**civilizations, collapsed, farmed, religion**)

2 When the ___invaders___ finally ___captured___ the king, they took all his ___treasure___ . (**built, captured, invaders, treasure**)

3 Written ___records___ have helped ___archeologists___ solve the ___mystery___ . (**archeologists, mystery, records, ruins**)

B Complete the conversations. Circle the correct answers.

1 **A:** Do you think the early Rapa Nui people died from disease?
B: Definitely. Disease **must play** / (**must have played**) a big part.

2 **A:** Do you know where my jacket is?
B: It (**could**) / **mustn't** be in the dining room. Have you looked there?

3 **A:** Whose backpack is this? Is it Ken's?
B: It **might** / (**can't**) be his. His is blue—this one is black.

C Complete the sentences. Use the words in the box. One word is extra.

avalanche	flood	hurricane	tsunami

1 After a week of rain, the river overflowed and caused a(n) ___flood___ .

2 We fear that the sudden ___avalanche___ may have buried the skiers in the mountains.

3 A huge earthquake caused ___tsunami___ warnings across the Pacific.

SELF CHECK Now I can …

☐ talk about ancient and modern-day mysteries

☐ use language for describing probability

☐ talk about ancient civilizations

Unit 7 **89**

Explain that they will present their storyboards to the class. Tell them to draw pictures for six scenes that show what happens and to prepare an explanation for each scene. In the next lesson, have students present their storyboards to the class.

REVIEW

Explain to students that they are going to review the material from the unit and this will help them remember what they have studied.

A Explain that activity **A** reviews vocabulary from the unit. Have students use the words in parentheses to complete the sentences. Point out that in each set, one word is extra and will not be used. Check answers as a class.

B Explain that activity **B** reviews the grammar from the unit. Have students circle the correct answers to complete the conversations. Check answers.

C Point out that activity **C** reviews words from **VOCABULARY** activity **B**.

Have students use the words in the box to complete the sentences. Point out that one word is extra and will not be used. Check answers.

SELF CHECK

These *I can* statements provide vital feedback on students' perceived ability to use the language from the unit. If you find students are reluctant to check they can do the skills, consider asking them to rate themselves from 1 (not very confident) to 3 (very confident).

OPTIONAL Have students complete the **SELF CHECK** before doing the **REVIEW** activities. After reviewing the unit, have students once again check their confidence for each statement.

C As students follow along, read the questions aloud. Have students get into pairs and use the information in **B** to discuss which theories they find most likely. Remind them to use modals for talking about probability as they discuss. Encourage them to also come up with at least one new theory.

CHALLENGE Have pairs present their new theories to the class. Then have the class vote on which theory they find the most believable.

AFTER YOU WATCH

Tell students they will get into pairs and talk about the video.

As students follow along in their books, read the questions aloud.

Have them do the task.

CHALLENGE Tell students that they are going to come up with a story idea for one episode of the TV show about Roanoke. Ask students to work in pairs or small groups to make a storyboard of one episode of the show.

IT'S TALLER THAN THE EIFFEL TOWER!

CONTENT AREA: PEOPLE AND PLACES

Topic: human-made structures

Vocabulary: adjectives: deep, interesting, long, old, tall, expensive, hungry, slow, wide; **other words:** elevator, clock tower, castle, tourist attraction, board, export, transport, region, rely on, goods

Grammar: using *too, enough,* comparative/superlative adjectives

Extra material: a world map

Other useful vocabulary: subway station, underground rail, undersea tunnel, escalator, suspension bridge, green museum

END OF UNIT PROJECT Tell students that they are going to write a short report. Remind them that they wrote a paragraph about an interesting human-made structure for **WRITING**. Explain that they are going to expand this paragraph into a short report comparing that structure with one they learned about in the unit or the attraction they wrote about for the **REAL WORLD** project.

Tell students that in their report, they should briefly introduce both places before making the comparisons. Remind students to include a list of references at the end of their report.

Assign the report as homework.

In the next lesson, have students get into small groups and take turns reading their reports. Encourage group members to ask questions to clarify anything they don't understand.

8

IT'S TALLER THAN THE EIFFEL TOWER!

90

After students have completed reading their reports, have them write a short self-evaluation about what they did well and what they could have improved on. (See **TEACHING NOTE**.)

TEACHING NOTE: SELF-EVALUATION

In order to develop critical thinking and a sense of personal responsibility for learning outcomes, periodically encourage learners to think critically about their preparation before class and their performance in class.

Ask students to complete the statement: *In my report, I did well with . . ., but I could have done better with . . .*

CONTENT NOTE: EXTREME BUILDINGS

Arsenalna Station, opened in 1960, is the deepest subway station in the world. It was built far below the surface because of the city's geography. Although the station's entrance is at the top of a deep valley, the station had to be built at the same level as

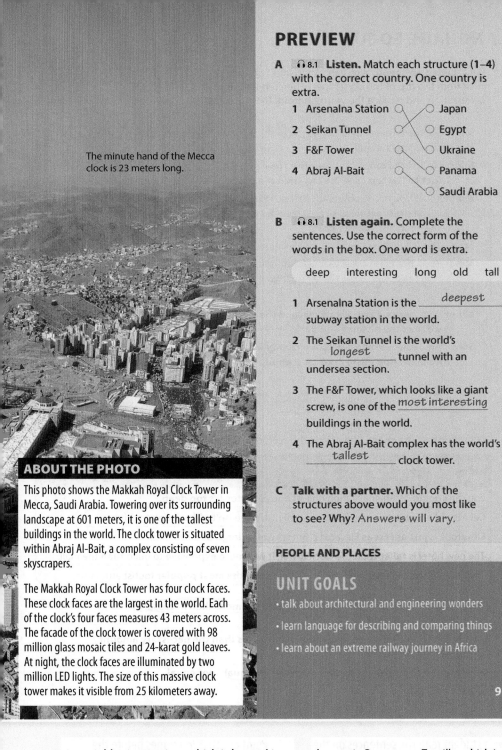

The minute hand of the Mecca clock is 23 meters long.

ABOUT THE PHOTO

This photo shows the Makkah Royal Clock Tower in Mecca, Saudi Arabia. Towering over its surrounding landscape at 601 meters, it is one of the tallest buildings in the world. The clock tower is situated within Abraj Al-Bait, a complex consisting of seven skyscrapers.

The Makkah Royal Clock Tower has four clock faces. These clock faces are the largest in the world. Each of the clock's four faces measures 43 meters across. The facade of the clock tower is covered with 98 million glass mosaic tiles and 24-karat gold leaves. At night, the clock faces are illuminated by two million LED lights. The size of this massive clock tower makes it visible from 25 kilometers away.

PREVIEW

A 🎧 8.1 **Listen.** Match each structure (1–4) with the correct country. One country is extra.

1 Arsenalna Station — Japan
2 Seikan Tunnel — Egypt
3 F&F Tower — Ukraine
4 Abraj Al-Bait — Panama
— Saudi Arabia

B 🎧 8.1 **Listen again.** Complete the sentences. Use the correct form of the words in the box. One word is extra.

deep   interesting   long   old   tall

1 Arsenalna Station is the _deepest_ subway station in the world.

2 The Seikan Tunnel is the world's _longest_ tunnel with an undersea section.

3 The F&F Tower, which looks like a giant screw, is one of the _most interesting_ buildings in the world.

4 The Abraj Al-Bait complex has the world's _tallest_ clock tower.

C **Talk with a partner.** Which of the structures above would you most like to see? Why? *Answers will vary.*

PEOPLE AND PLACES

UNIT GOALS

- talk about architectural and engineering wonders
- learn language for describing and comparing things
- learn about an extreme railway journey in Africa

91

A Tell students that they will listen to four short talks about four structures. Have students match each structure with the correct country. Point out that one country is extra and will not be used.

🎧 8.1 Play Audio Track 8.1. Don't check answers yet.

B Tell students that they will listen again, and they should complete the sentences using the correct form of the words in the box. Have a student read the words aloud. Point out that one word is extra and will not be used.

🎧 8.1 Play Audio Track 8.1. Play it again, if necessary.

Check answers for **A** and **B**.

CHALLENGE Have students do **B** based on their first listening of the audio in **A**. Then play the audio again to have them check answers for **A** and **B**.

C Tell students they are going to get into pairs and take turns talking about which of the four buildings they would most like to visit. Explain that they should give reasons for their opinions.

Have students do the task.

CHALLENGE Tell students to also discuss how likely it is that they might visit one of these places. Have them use the modals of probability that they learned in **UNIT 7**.

UNIT GOALS

Direct students' attention to the **UNIT GOALS** box. Explain that these are some of the things students will learn in this unit. Point out that this unit is about people and places. As students follow along, read each of the unit goals to the class. Explain any words students do not know. Remind students that at the end of the unit, there is a self check that allows them to see if they have accomplished each goal.

its neighboring station, which is located just above ground level.

The decision to construct the Seikan Tunnel was made after a ferry, the primary means of transportation between the main island of Honshu and the northern Japanese island of Hokkaido, sank in 1954, killing more than 1,400 people. The tunnel took 24 years to complete, with up to 3,000 people digging at times.

The F&F Tower, named after F&F Properties, the developer that built it, is commonly known in Panama as *Tornillo*, which is the Spanish word for "screw." The building , located in the financial district, has 52 floors above ground and 4 floors below ground.

PREVIEW

Have students look at the photo. Read the unit title and the photo caption aloud, as students follow along. Explain that in this unit they will learn to talk about buildings and interesting feats of engineering, as well as how to describe and compare things.

LANGUAGE FOCUS

A Tell students they will listen to a conversation between Ming and Stig.

🎧 **8.2** Play Audio Track 8.2 as students listen and follow along in their books.

As students follow along, read the question, *Why can't Ming and Stig see much from the top of the skyscraper?* If necessary, explain that a *skyscraper* is a very tall building. Have students answer.

Have students work in pairs and practice the conversation once. Point out the bold words. Tell students to practice the conversation two more times, changing the bold words each time and swapping roles after the first time.

OPTIONAL Have students repeat the conversation but change the situation so instead the weather is good and the view is clear. Ask them to change the last line that Stig says to fit the new circumstances.

REAL ENGLISH

Direct students' attention to the expression in the **REAL ENGLISH** box. Explain that we use *What a shame!* to express disappointment. For example:

A: I'm sorry, I can't come over because I still have a lot of homework.

B: What a shame! I was really looking forward to seeing you.

B Ask students to look at the chart. Explain that they will study how to describe and compare things.

🎧 **8.3** Have students follow along as they listen to Audio Track 8.3.

Read the first line in the chart aloud. Remind students that we use *too* + adjective to mean "more (or less) than the necessary amount." Give an example: *I have too much homework, so I can't go to the movies tonight.* Ask, *What will the person do tonight?* (homework)

LANGUAGE FOCUS

A 🎧 **8.2** **Listen and read.** Why can't Ming and Stig see much from the top of the skyscraper? Then repeat the conversation and replace the words in **bold**. It's *too cloudy*.

> **REAL ENGLISH** What a shame!

Ming: So, you've never been to the top of this skyscraper before?

Stig: No, never. I can't wait to **see the view**! (**get to the top / see the city from the top**)

Ming: You'll love it. The observation deck has one of the **prettiest** views of the city. You can see for miles! (**nicest / best**)

Stig: This is the tallest building in the city, isn't it?

Ming: Yeah. But it has a really fast elevator, so it won't take long to go up. Let's get going.

Ming: Well, **here we are**. (**we've reached the top / we're at the observation deck**)

Stig: Aw, I can't see a thing! It's **too cloudy**. What a shame! (**too misty / not clear enough**)

B 🎧 **8.3** **Look at the chart.** Then circle the correct answers below.

DESCRIBING AND COMPARING THINGS (USING *TOO*, *ENOUGH*, COMPARATIVE/ SUPERLATIVE ADJECTIVES)
You can't get to Arsenalna Station on just one escalator. It's **too deep**.
Celia is **old enough** to drive. But Max is only 14, so he is**n't old enough** to drive.
Elevator 1 is just **as fast as** Elevator 2. But it's **not as large as** Elevator 2.
The new hotel is **taller than** the clock tower. It was **more expensive** to build **than** the mall.
The castle is **the oldest** building in the city. It's also **the most popular** tourist attraction.

1 We use *too* + adjective to say something is (less or more than necessary) / **the necessary amount**.

2 We use adjective + *enough* to say something is **less than the necessary amount** / (the necessary amount).

3 We use *as* + adjective + *as* to say two things are (equal) / **not equal**.

Have a student read the sentences on the next line aloud. Tell students that we use adjective + *enough* in positive sentences when we have the necessary amount. Give an example: *Amy is tall enough to go on the roller coaster.* Ask, *Can Amy go on the roller coaster?* (Yes, she can.)

Explain that we use *enough* in negative sentences to express the idea that the amount is less than necessary. If needed, give an example: *Amy's little brother isn't tall enough to go on the roller coaster.*

Point out that *too* comes before the adjective but *enough* comes after it.

Have a student read the third line in the chart aloud. Explain that *as* + adjective + *as* is used when two things are the same, and *not as* + adjective + *as* when they are not the same.

Have a student read the fourth line aloud. Remind students we use adjective + *-er* and *more* + adjective to compare two things. Have students identify what word we must use when making a comparison between two things (*than*).

C **Complete the sentences.** Use the words in the box. Add *too* or *enough*.

expensive	hungry	slow	tall	wide

1 I can't afford the ticket price to the observation deck. It's _____*too expensive*_____ .

2 Six cars can't drive side by side on that bridge. It's not _____*wide enough*_____ .

3 This train is _____*too slow*_____ . We'll never get to the theater in time.

4 I'm not _____*tall enough*_____ to reach the top shelf. Can you help me?

5 Sorry, but I already ate. I was _____*too hungry*_____ to wait!

D 🎧 8.4 **Complete the information.** Use the correct form of the adjectives in parentheses. Add *the* or *as* if necessary. Then listen and check your answers.

1 *The most memorable* (**memorable**) way to see New York City is from one of its many skyscrapers. 2 *The most famous* (**famous**) is surely the Empire State Building. But some visitors who have gone to Top of the Rock at Rockefeller Center say the view from there is just 3 *as good as* (**good**) the view from the Empire State Building. Others even claim that the view is actually 4 *the best* (**good**) in the whole city. Tickets, however, are just 5 *as expensive as* (**expensive**) those for the Empire State Building, so you don't save any money. But Top of the Rock's lines are 6 *shorter* (**short**), and its elevator is 7 *faster* (**fast**). So while Top of the Rock is not 8 *as famous as* (**famous**) the Empire State Building, it's attracting more and more tourists.

E **Work in pairs.** Complete the questions below. Use the correct form of the adjectives in parentheses, and add *the* or *than* if necessary. Then take turns asking and answering the questions with your partner. Ask follow-up questions to get additional information.

1 What's _____*the hottest*_____ (**hot**) place you've ever been to?

2 Who's _____*the most interesting*_____ (**interesting**) person you know?

3 Which animal is _____*more intelligent*_____ (**intelligent**)—a dolphin or a dog?

4 Is it better to have a sibling who's _____*older*_____ (**old**) or _____*younger than*_____ (**young**) you?

5 What's _____*the best*_____ (**good**) present you've ever received?

6 What's _____*the scariest*_____ (**scary**) movie you've ever seen?

SUPPORT Go over each answer individually, pointing to the information in the **LANGUAGE FOCUS** chart that is relevant for each answer.

CONTENT NOTE: NEW YORK CITY'S SKYSCRAPERS

When New York City's Empire State Building was being constructed, it was in a fierce competition with the Chrysler Building, another iconic New York City skyscraper, to be the tallest human-made structure in the world. At 319 meters, the Chrysler Building held the title for 11 months, until the Empire State Building was completed in 1931 at 381 meters.

Top of the Rock consists of three viewing decks on 30 Rock, one of the 14 buildings of Rockefeller Center that were constructed between 1931 and 1940.

E Tell students they are going to get into pairs and complete the questions together before taking turns to ask and answer the questions.

Have pairs complete the questions using the correct form of the adjectives in parentheses, adding *the* or *than* if necessary.

Check answers. Give students time to correct any mistakes.

Then have pairs take turns to ask and answer the questions. Encourage them to ask and answer follow-up questions.

OPTIONAL Randomly call on pairs to share their answers with the class. Have one partner answer one of the questions, and have the other partner provide the additional information he/she found out.

Have a student read the last line in the chart aloud. If necessary, remind students that we use *the* adjective + *-est* and *the most* + adjective to make a comparison between three or more things.

Draw students' attention to the three statements under the chart. Have students circle the correct answers. Check answers.

C Tell students to complete the sentences using the words in the box, adding *too* or *enough*. As students follow along, have a student read the words in the box aloud.

Have them do the task. Check answers.

D Have students write the correct form of the adjectives in parentheses to complete the paragraph, adding *the* or *as* if necessary.

Tell students that they will listen and check their answers.

THE REAL WORLD

Ask students to look at the photo. As students follow along, read the title and the caption aloud.

A Tell students they are going to watch a video about the world's longest footbridge, and they should circle **T** if the statement is true or **F** if it is false. As students follow along, have a student read the statements aloud.

▶ 8.1 Play Video 8.1. Play it again, if necessary.

Check answers.

DO YOU KNOW?

Read the sentence and answer choices aloud, as students follow along in their books. Have students guess the answer before providing it (b).

CONTENT NOTE: NUTTY NARROWS BRIDGE

The unusual and popular Nutty Narrows Bridge was built in Longview, Washington, U.S.A., in 1963 by a construction company whose offices were near a busy road where squirrels were often hit by cars. The bridge, which is a well-loved local attraction, was renovated and moved to a more central location near a park in 2007.

B Tell students they will watch the video again, and they should complete the notes using the numbers in the box. Point out that two numbers are extra and will not be used.

▶ 8.1 Play Video 8.1. Play it again, if necessary. Check answers.

C Tell students to circle the correct answers to complete the paragraph.

Have students do the task. Check answers.

THE WORLD'S LONGEST FOOTBRIDGE

ABOUT THE PHOTO

This photo shows the Charles Kuonen Suspension Bridge, located along the Europaweg—a popular two-day hiking trail between Grächen and Zermatt in the Swiss Alps. Completed in 2017, the 494-meter-long bridge rises 85 meters above the Grabengufer ravine. Access to the bridge is free of charge. From the bridge, hikers can enjoy spectacular views of the Matterhorn, the Weisshorn, and the Bernese Alps. The bridge is not for those with a fear of heights, though, as the design is completely open, with see-through grating on the footpath.

Charles Kuonen Suspension Bridge, Switzerland

A ▶ 8.1 **Watch the video.** Circle **T** for true or **F** for false.

1 It takes an hour to cross the bridge.　　　　　　　　　T　**(F)**

2 The bridge replaced an older bridge.　　　　　　**(T)**　F

3 The bridge was designed so it would not swing.　**(T)**　F

4 The bridge is open all year long.　　　　　　　　　T　**(F)**

B ▶ 8.1 **Watch again.** Complete the notes about the bridge with numbers from the box. Two numbers are extra.

10	28	65	85	250	494	2017

1 Length: _____494_____ meters

2 Highest point: _____85_____ meters above ground

3 Time it took to build: _____10_____ weeks

4 Width: _____65_____ centimeters

5 Maximum number of hikers on the bridge: _____250_____

94 Unit 8

Nutty Narrows Bridge, the world's narrowest bridge, allows _____ to cross above the road.
a koalas
(b) squirrels
c monkeys

D CRITICAL THINKING

As students follow along, read the questions aloud. Have students get into pairs and talk about their ideas. Remind them to support their opinions with reasons. Tell them to use language for making comparisons as they talk about both attractions.

OPTIONAL Give students additional questions to discuss. Remind them to give reasons for their answers.

1 Which do you think is scarier—a suspension bridge or a zipline? Why?

2 What kind of people do you think want to cross the world's longest footbridge? Why?

C **Complete the information below.** Circle the correct answers.

The United Arab Emirates is the proud holder of many world records. For example, Dubai is home to the world's ¹ **taller** /(**tallest**) building, the Burj Khalifa. A mosque in Abu Dhabi has the ²(**largest**) / **most large** hand-woven carpet in the world. And in Ras al-Khaimah—about 45 minutes from Dubai—people can take a ride on the world's ³ **long enough** /(**longest**) zipline. Riders zoom down from a mountaintop 1,680 meters above sea level, reaching speeds of up to 150 kilometers per hour. The zipline is 2.83 kilometers long—that's ⁴(**longer than**) / **too long** 28 soccer fields! Would you be ⁵ **as brave as** /(**brave enough**) to take a ride on this zipline?

D CRITICAL THINKING Comparing **Talk with a partner.** Would you rather walk across the Charles Kuonen Suspension Bridge or ride the zipline in Ras al-Khaimah? Why? Answers will vary.

> **PROJECT Go online.** Find another example of a famous tourist attraction. Make some notes about it and share with a partner.

PRONUNCIATION emphatic stress

🎧 8.5 **Listen.** Underline the word in each sentence that receives the most stress. Then listen again and repeat the sentences.

1 The bridge is <u>only</u> 65 centimeters wide.

2 The walk across the bridge is <u>way</u> too scary for me.

3 We didn't spend <u>nearly</u> enough time in the Alps.

4 The views were <u>much</u> more beautiful than I expected.

COMMUNICATION

Create a quiz. Work with a partner. Complete these sentences to create a true/false quiz. Then test your quiz on another pair. Answers will vary.

1 _____ is the biggest _____ in the world.

2 _____ is taller than _____ .

3 _____ is not as long as _____ .

4 _____ is faster than _____ .

5 _____ has a smaller population than _____ .

6 _____ is the oldest _____ .

> Dubai International Airport is the biggest airport in the world. True or false?

Unit 8 **95**

Tell students to listen and underline the word in each sentence that receives the most stress.

🎧 8.5 Play Audio Track 8.5. Play it again, if necessary. Check answers.

🎧 8.5 Play the audio again, pausing after each sentence so students can repeat.

COMMUNICATION

Explain to students that they are going to work in pairs to create a true/false quiz. Have students get into pairs and complete the sentences with their own ideas. Point out that they should use real information as far as possible. If phones or other electronic devices are allowed in your class, give students time to do some research online. Walk around the classroom as students are writing, to quickly check their sentences and offer help if needed.

Tell students that now that they have created their sentences, they will get together with another pair to test them. Model the example in a fun way that sounds like a game-show host. Encourage students to enjoy the activity.

Have pairs take turns quizzing each other.

When they have finished, randomly call on a few pairs and ask them how well they did on the quiz.

OPTIONAL Collect students' sentences and make a giant game show for the class to participate in.

PROJECT As students follow along, read the project instructions aloud. Encourage students to choose a famous attraction near their hometowns (if students in the class come from different regions or countries) or a place that they have visited, so students can learn more about their classmates through the project. Give students time to research online to learn more about the attraction and make notes about any information they want to share.

In the next lesson, have students get into pairs and share with a partner. Afterward, randomly call on students to tell the class about the attraction they researched.

PRONUNCIATION

Tell students they will practice using emphatic stress. Explain that we use emphatic stress to emphasize an adjective or intensifier (e.g., *so*, *too*) rather than the main content words. Remind students that individual words have stress, but when we combine the words together in a sentence, the speaker decides which words are important so they should be stressed.

TEACHING NOTE: MAKING ACTIVITIES INTO GAMES

To make the activity more like a game, create a festive game show atmosphere in the classroom where you or a volunteer plays the host. Divide students into teams and have a friendly competition, using the sentences created by the students.

READING

CONTENT NOTE: MAURITANIA

A large coastal country in western Africa, Mauritania is home to an expansive stretch of the Sahara Desert. The country's population is around 4.1 million, and its official language is Arabic. Iron ore, along with the minerals copper and gypsum, are mined there.

As students follow along, read the title aloud. Have students look at the photo. Ask a student to read the photo caption aloud.

A Read the questions aloud. Tell students to scan the article to find the answers.

Check answers by randomly calling on students to share their answers with the class.

OPTIONAL Have students find Mauritania on a world map.

TEACHING NOTE: HELPING STUDENTS SCAN

Encourage students to scan quickly by saying the time that has elapsed every 10 or 15 seconds. If students are taking too long to find the answer, review how to quickly and efficiently scan a text.

B Have students skim the article and underline all the adjectives that describe the train journey.

Check answers.

OPTIONAL Ask students if they think the writer has a positive or negative view of the train journey. Encourage them to give reasons for their answers.

TEACHING NOTE: USING ADJECTIVES TO COMMUNICATE OPINION

Explain to students that writers often use adjectives as a way to communicate their feelings or opinions without directly stating them. In the article, the writer uses only adjectives with negative meanings to describe the journey: *extreme, dirty, uncomfortable, hot, cold, bumpy*. Students should be able to infer that the writer did not enjoy the train ride very much.

READING

A **Scan the article.** In which country does the Iron Ore Train operate? What is the main purpose of this train?
Mauritania; to bring iron ore from the mines

B **Skim the article.** Underline all the adjectives that describe the train journey.

C **Talk with a partner.** The Iron Ore Train doesn't charge people who ride on it. Why do you think this is?
Answers will vary.

THE IRON ORE *TRAIN*

A 🎧 8.6 As the sun starts to set, a group of people stand by the rail track near the village of Choum, deep in the Sahara Desert. They pass around water and move into position. Suddenly, bright lights appear in the distance and a train comes into view. When it arrives for a five-minute stop, people pull themselves up to the top of the train cars. They have just **boarded** what has been called "the world's most <u>extreme</u> railway."

B Here, in a remote corner of the West African country of Mauritania, is the Iron Ore Train. Opened in 1963, the train runs every day from the mining town of Zouérat to the port of Nouadhibou, then back again. Its main purpose is to bring iron ore—the country's biggest **export**—from the mines. Consisting of more than 200 cars, the train is about 2.5 kilometers in length and can **transport** 17,000 tons of iron ore. It's one of the longest trains in the world.

C As students follow along in their books, read the sentence and question aloud. Have students get into pairs and discuss their ideas.

After completing the task, have students read the article in more detail so they can answer the **COMPREHENSION** questions.

OPTIONAL The text can also be used as a listening activity. Have students close their books. Tell students they will listen to the passage.

Passengers on the Iron Ore Train
(photographed by Daniel Rodrigues)

Have students find the phrasal verb in the second sentence of paragraph A (*pass around*) and ask them to separate it with an appropriate noun or noun phrase (e.g., *pass water around*). Explain that when a pronoun is used with a separable phrasal verb, it must be placed within the phrasal verb (e.g., *passing it around*).

Have students identify the phrasal verbs in paragraph C (*get across, rely on, search for*). Tell students that inseparable phrasal verbs cannot be separated by a noun, noun phrase, or pronoun. Ask them to identify which of the phrasal verbs in paragraph C are inseparable (all).

Developing Reading Fluency

Introduce the idea of extensive reading to your students, and encourage them to begin reading English books that they are interested in. (See **TEACHING NOTE**.)

TEACHING NOTE: EXTENSIVE READING

Extensive reading (ER) is a language teaching/learning procedure, the aim of which is to get students to read as much as possible. Reading, in this sense, becomes an enjoyable pastime and its own reward, much like reading a novel in one's first language.

As the reading is primarily for pleasure, it is not necessary for students to understand every word, and, in fact, students should be encouraged not to use a dictionary. The primary goal should be reading, so there should be few, if any, tasks that students must complete after finishing the text.

Through ER, students are exposed to a variety of materials that they can choose from. Because students work independently, there is no obligation to finish materials that they find uninteresting.

Graded readers, such as National Geographic's *Footprint Reading Library*, are often used in ER programs because students can choose a text that is at approximately the correct grammatical level and length for them, and that has vocabulary they will be familiar with.

C There are few roads in this **region** of the Sahara, so the railway is one of the few ways to get across the desert. For many Mauritanians, it is the only way to reach places deep in the Sahara. They **rely on** the train for many things: to see family, to sell their **goods**, and to search for work. They pass the time by chatting and sipping tea.

D It is by no means an easy ride. The journey—which can take anywhere from 16 to 21 hours traveling one-way—is dirty and uncomfortable. Passengers wrap their faces in scarves to protect themselves from the hot desert winds and the iron ore dust. Temperatures can exceed 40°C

during the day, and it gets very cold at night. Sandstorms are frequent, the ride is bumpy, and death from falling is not uncommon.

E But for some tourists, a trip on the Iron Ore Train is the adventure of a lifetime. It requires no reservations, no tickets, and no cash. There is little to do but enjoy the incredible landscape and make friends with the locals.

F For photographer Daniel Rodrigues, who made the trip and took photographs of his experience, it was the night sky that he remembers the most. "Only in the desert can you see this," he said. "Millions and millions of stars."

Unit 8 **97**

🔊 8.6 Play Audio Track 8.6. Ask students to get into pairs and discuss what information they heard. Then have them read the article more carefully.

Additional Activities to Use with the Reading

Additional Comprehension Questions

Ask students the following reference-type questions:

1 Who does *They* refer to in the second sentence of paragraph A? (a group of people)

2 What does *It* refer to in the first sentence of paragraph D? (the journey on the train)

3 What does *this* refer to in the second sentence of paragraph F? (the millions of stars in the night sky)

Identifying Phrasal Verbs

Explain that there are two kinds of phrasal verbs: separable and inseparable.

Explain that with some separable verbs, the phrasal verb can be separated by a noun or a noun phrase.

COMPREHENSION

A Have students read the questions to themselves and circle the correct answers.

After they have finished, check answers as a class.

IDIOM

As students follow along in their books, have a student read the sentence and answer choices aloud. Have students guess the answer before providing it (b). Give an example:

A: I've been studying hard to get into a good college.

B: You're on the right track with your great grades.

B **EXAM PRACTICE**

Students consider the organization of a passage when they match specific information to the passage's paragraphs. This type of practice is beneficial for at least two reasons. First, it develops students' ability to quickly find specific information in a passage. By locating the paragraph that contains the information, they can then search for specific information. Second, this type of practice helps students prepare for exams such as the IELTS Reading Module, on which they must, among other things, complete summaries and answer questions.

Have students match each paragraph with the information it contains. Check answers.

CHALLENGE Have students find specific examples of the information listed for each paragraph in **B**. Give them time to go back through the article and make notes. Then have them compare answers in pairs or check answers as a class.

COMPREHENSION

A **Answer the questions about** *The Iron Ore Train*.

1 DETAIL Which statement about the Iron Ore Train is true?

   a It has been operating since the 1940s.

   (b) A round-trip journey could take about 40 hours.

   c No one has ever fallen off the train and died.

2 INFERENCE What kind of traveler would probably be most interested in taking a trip on this train?

   a someone who is most comfortable traveling in cities

   (b) someone who likes to go on adventure trips

   c someone who enjoys taking group tour packages

3 PURPOSE What is the purpose of paragraph C?

   a to make the train ride sound enjoyable to the reader

   b to describe what life would be like without the train

   (c) to explain why the train is important to local people

4 VOCABULARY The phrase *by no means* in paragraph D can be replaced with _____.

   (a) not at all   b expected to be   c in some ways

5 DETAIL What should a tourist do if they want to ride the train?

   a make a reservation

   b ask a local to help them buy a ticket

   (c) just jump on when it stops

B **Match each paragraph with the information it contains.**

1 Paragraph A ○——○ statistics about the train

2 Paragraph B ○——○ a quote from a photographer who took the train

3 Paragraph C ○——○ reasons why the train journey can be unpleasant

4 Paragraph D ○——○ reasons why some tourists take the train

5 Paragraph E ○——○ reasons why locals take the train

6 Paragraph F ○——○ a description of how people get on the train

C CRITICAL THINKING Reflecting **Talk with a partner.** Would you be interested in taking a trip on the Iron Ore Train? Why or why not? Answers will vary.

IDIOM

If everything is going well in your life, you are _____.

a off the rails

(b) on the right track

C CRITICAL THINKING

As students follow along, read the questions aloud. Have students get into pairs and discuss their ideas. Encourage students to give examples to clarify, support, and expand on their ideas and opinions about the train. (See **TEACHING NOTE**.)

Afterward, find out how many students in the class would be interested in taking a trip on the Iron Ore Train and how many would not. Have students provide reasons for their answers.

TEACHING NOTE: GIVING EXAMPLES

There are several reasons we give examples. First, examples help clarify our ideas for the listener/reader. Second, examples extend and expand on our ideas. If our first statement is broad, an example can help provide a more specific context. Third, examples support and provide proof that helps substantiate our arguments.

VOCABULARY

A Find the bold words below in the article. Then circle the correct answers.

1 If you **board** a train, you get (on) / off it.

2 **Exports** are things that are *bought from* / (sold to) another country.

3 (Cars and trucks) / *Phones and laptops* are used to **transport** people and things.

4 A particular **region** of a country refers to *its official language* / (an area of land).

5 If you **rely on** something, you (need) / *don't need* it.

6 **Goods** refer to (physical items) / *people's feelings*.

B Read the information below. Then complete the word web about travel using the words in the box. Can you think of other examples to add to the word web? Tell a partner.

> A word web is one way to organize vocabulary around a topic. You can add more words to it as you learn them.

car	first-class	journey	luggage	passengers
passport	plane	round-trip	tourists	trip

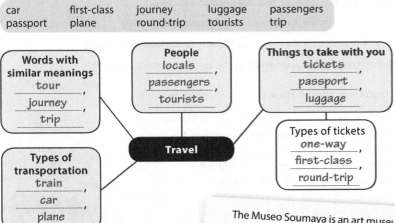

Words with similar meanings
tour, journey, trip

People
locals, passengers, tourists

Things to take with you
tickets, passport, luggage

Types of tickets
one-way, first-class, round-trip

Types of transportation
train, car, plane

Travel

WRITING

A Read the paragraph.

B Choose an interesting human-made structure. Make notes about it.

C Write about the structure. Say why it's impressive. Answers will vary.

The Museo Soumaya is an art museum in Mexico City. It's one of the most famous buildings in Mexico. Opened in 2011, it was designed by the architect Fernando Romero. The outside of the building is covered in tiles …

Unit 8 **99**

VOCABULARY

A Have students find the bold words in the **READING** passage.

Have students circle the correct answers to complete the sentences.

Check answers.

B As students follow along, read the information in the box aloud. Then have a student read the words in the gray box aloud. Ask another student to read the categories in the word web aloud. Have students use the words in the box to complete the word web.

Check answers. Then ask students to think of other examples to add to the word web. Have them get into pairs and share their ideas.

WRITING

Tell students they are going to write a paragraph about a human-made structure. Explain that they can choose one they know or research one.

A Have students look at the photo. Then read the example aloud, as students follow along. Point out that this is just the beginning of the paragraph. Tell students that the paragraph should have a topic sentence and supporting details, such as statistics and examples. Explain that they should write about why the structure is interesting or impressive.

CONTENT NOTE: MUSEO SOUMAYA

The Museo Soumaya in Mexico City was developed by one of the world's wealthiest people, telecommunications businessman Carlos Slim. Slim's son-in-law, architect Fernando Romero, designed the six-story structure which has no windows. The museum contains over 65,000 items from Slim's own collection, which includes pieces by renowned artists such as Van Gogh, Matisse, Degas, and Picasso.

B Tell students to choose an interesting human-made structure to write about. Give students time to research and make notes. Encourage them to use a graphic organizer, such as a word web, to make notes about the structure.

C Have students write their paragraphs, using their notes from **B**. You might want to assign the writing as homework, and set a minimum number of sentences students must write (e.g., eight).

OPTIONAL Have students get into pairs and take turns reading their paragraphs.

CHALLENGE Have students turn their paragraphs into posters (with photos included) to share with the class. Put their posters up around the classroom, then give students time to go around the classroom and read about all the structures. Have students find all the countries where the structures are located on a world map. After this, have students get into pairs and talk about which ones they would like to visit and which are the most amazing, providing reasons for their answers.

VIDEO

The California Academy of Sciences, which is located in San Francisco's Golden Gate Park, was opened to the public in 2008. The building was designed by architect Renzo Piano, who wanted to create a home for the academy that was camouflaged within the surrounding nature. The building's many offerings include a rainforest, an aquarium, a planetarium, a natural history museum, and an expansive roof garden.

Tell students they are going to watch a video called "The Green Museum." As students follow along in their books, have a student read the sentence about the video aloud.

BEFORE YOU WATCH

Have students look at the photo. As students follow along, read the caption aloud. Then read the question. Have students get into pairs and share their ideas.

SUPPORT Encourage students to use a dictionary or thesaurus to look up the word *green*. This will enable them to get a clear idea of the word's meaning and use in this case.

Give students opportunities to practice how to use an English dictionary. Even for words that students think they know, it can be helpful to encourage them to use a dictionary to gain a deeper understanding of the word's meaning and use, especially in cases where there is more than one definition for a word. Although students should not rely too much on dictionaries, being able to use them effectively is an important skill.

THE *GREEN* MUSEUM

Before You Watch

Talk with a partner. Look at the photo. What do you think makes this museum "green"?
Answers will vary.

While You Watch

A   ▶ 8.2   **Watch the video.** Check (✓) four things you can find at the California Academy of Sciences.

- ✓ a research center
- ✓ a rain forest
- ☐ a playground
- ☐ a flower market
- ✓ an aquarium
- ✓ a coral reef

B   ▶ 8.2   **Watch again.** Circle the correct answers.

1 The California Academy of Sciences has the **biggest** / oldest green museum in the world.

2 The climate in the dome is **cool and dry** / **hot and humid**.

3 The team's goal is to make the exhibits more **accessible** / **lifelike**.

4 The water in the aquarium comes from **a human-made lake** / **the ocean**.

5 The aquarium has the **deepest** / **widest** tank for a coral reef in the world.

C   **Complete the information below.** Circle the correct answers.

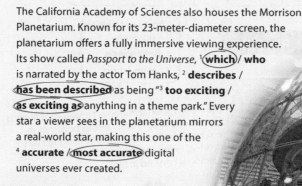

The California Academy of Sciences also houses the Morrison Planetarium. Known for its 23-meter-diameter screen, the planetarium offers a fully immersive viewing experience. Its show called *Passport to the Universe*, [1] **which** / who is narrated by the actor Tom Hanks, [2] **describes** / **has been described** as being "[3] too exciting / **as exciting as** anything in a theme park." Every star a viewer sees in the planetarium mirrors a real-world star, making this one of the [4] **accurate** / **most accurate** digital universes ever created.

After You Watch

Talk with a partner. What is the most interesting museum you have visited? What made it so interesting?
Answers will vary.

In recent years, the color green has become synonymous with words like *eco-friendly*, *environmentally friendly*, and *sustainable*. In the context of this video, the word *green* refers to both the appearance of the museum exhibit (i.e., green color) and the museum's eco-friendly design features. The California Academy of Sciences has won awards for its sustainable design and construction.

WHILE YOU WATCH

A   Tell students they will watch the video and they should check four things that can be found at the California Academy of Sciences. Have a student read the list of things aloud, as students follow along in their books.

▶ 8.2   Play Video 8.2. Play it again, if necessary.

Check answers.

A Complete the sentences. Use the adjectives in the box. One adjective is extra.

expensive	fast	hungry	old	tall

1 Why do we have so many _____ *tall* _____ buildings? They block out the sun!

2 A Banksy painting sold for more than $12 million in 2019. That's really _____ *expensive* _____.

3 The McLaren F1 is a super _____ *fast* _____ car—it can reach speeds of up to 386 kilometers per hour.

4 The Ponte Sant'Angelo bridge in Rome is very _____ *old* _____. It was built around A.D. 134.

B Correct the error in each sentence.

1 I think James is older ~~as~~ *than* Barbara.

2 Jennifer is just as ~~prettier~~ *pretty* as her sister.

3 Eduardo is ~~to~~ *too* young to go on the roller coaster.

4 Aaron is the ~~more~~ *most* talented person I know.

5 Eun-joo is finally ~~enough old~~ *old enough* to vote.

C Complete the sentences. Use words from the word web on page 99.

1 Where did you park your _____ *car* _____?

2 How many country stamps do you have in your _____ *passport* _____?

3 You can collect your _____ *luggage* _____ at the Baggage Claim area.

4 Have you ever flown _____ *first-class* _____? I hear it's very expensive.

SELF CHECK   Now I can …

☐ talk about architectural and engineering wonders

☐ use language for describing and comparing things

☐ describe an extreme railway journey in Africa

Unit 8 **101**

B Tell students that they will watch the video again and they should circle the correct answers to complete the sentences. Have students read the sentences silently before watching again.

▶ 8.2 Play Video 8.2. Play it again, if necessary.

Check answers.

CHALLENGE Have students complete **B** after their first viewing of the video for **A**. Then play the video for students to check answers.

C Tell students to circle the correct answers to complete the paragraph.

Have students do the task. Check answers.

AFTER YOU WATCH

Tell students they will get into pairs and talk about interesting museums like the museum in the video.

As students follow along in their books, read the questions aloud.

Have students do the task.

CHALLENGE Have students work in pairs to do more research about the California Academy of Sciences. Tell them to find out about another attraction there, or something interesting about how the Academy was built. For example, the Academy has a 2.5-acre garden on its roof. Give each pair time to do research. Tell them to find information that will add on to what the class already learned in the video. Have each pair take turns sharing what they found with the class.

REVIEW

Explain to students that they are going to review the material from the unit, and this will help them remember what they have studied.

A Explain that activity **A** reviews vocabulary from the unit. Have students use the adjectives in the box to complete the sentences. Point out that one adjective is extra and will not be used. Check answers as a class.

B Explain that activity **B** reviews the grammar from the unit. Have students correct the error in each sentence. Check answers.

C Point out that activity **C** reviews words from **VOCABULARY** activity **B**.

Have students use the words from the word web on page 99 to complete the sentences. Check answers.

SELF CHECK

These *I can* statements provide vital feedback on students' perceived ability to use the language from the unit. If you find students are reluctant to check they can do the skills, consider asking them to rate themselves from 1 (not very confident) to 3 (very confident).

SUPPORT For each skill, have students say sentences demonstrating their ability.

UNIT 9
HE'S A GREAT ACTOR, ISN'T HE?

9
HE'S A GREAT ACTOR, ISN'T HE?

CONTENT AREA: HISTORY AND CULTURE

Topic: movies

Vocabulary: adjectives to describe movies: interesting, gorgeous, overrated, superb, dull, plain, predictable, unrealistic, stunning, spectacular, amazing, incredible, exciting; **words related to movies:** plot, soundtrack, costume, actor, special effects, opening scene, ending, plot, characters, theater; **other words:** identify, response, curious, factor, mood, appeal

Grammar: tag questions

Extra material: some easy-to-read English movie reviews

Other useful vocabulary: jobs related to movies: director, assistant director, producer, sound crew, camera operator, casting coordinator, music composer, costume designer, animator, editor, hair stylist, makeup artist, postproduction coordinator, stunt actor

END OF UNIT PROJECT Tell students they will get into pairs and do research about a popular movie celebrity. Explain to students that they should think critically about their research to write a (pretend) interview between the celebrity and a news reporter. Tell them that they will present this interview to the class.

Have students brainstorm contexts in which these types of interviews happen, providing additional ideas if necessary (e.g., before the release of a new movie, before the Academy Awards, after the announcement that the

ABOUT THE PHOTO

This photo shows Australian actor Chris Hemsworth on the set of the movie *Thor: The Dark World*. To date, the actor has starred in more than 30 movies, some of which include *Rush* (2013) and *Men in Black: International* (2019). However, he is best known for his portrayal of Thor in the series of movies by the Marvel Cinematic Universe. In 2019, *Forbes* named Chris Hemsworth as one of the highest-paid actors in the world, with earnings of about $76.4 million that year.

102

celebrity will get a star on the Hollywood Walk of Fame).

Assign the research and interview preparation as homework.

In the next lesson, have pairs present their interviews to the class.

After all the presentations are finished, have a class discussion about facts that were surprising. Also, have students discuss attitudes, experiences, or qualities that different celebrities have in common, and ask the students to give theories about why this might be.

CONTENT NOTE: MOVIES

The 2011 movie *Thor* is the story of the thunder deity Thor Odinson from Marvel Comics. Thor makes appearances in many other Marvel films as well, such as *The Avengers* (2012), *Thor: The Dark World* (2013), *Avengers: Age of Ultron* (2015), *Thor: Ragnarok* (2017), and *Avengers: Infinity War* (2018).

Chris Hemsworth on the set of *Thor: The Dark World*

PREVIEW

A 🎧 9.1 **Listen to four conversations about different movies and TV shows.** Does each person want to watch the movie or TV show again? Write **Y** (yes) or **N** (no).

1 Megan ___Y___   3 Ling ___N___

2 Junko ___Y___   4 Terry ___Y___

B 🎧 9.1 **Listen again.** Circle the correct answers.

1 Megan thinks the plot of the first *Thor* movie was very (**interesting**) / **dull**.

2 Junko says the costumes in *Beauty and the Beast* are (**gorgeous**) / **quite plain**.

3 Ling thinks *Frozen 2* is a bit **predictable** / (**overrated**) but she likes the soundtrack.

4 Terry says the acting in *Stranger Things* is **unrealistic** / (**superb**).

C **Talk with a partner.** Describe a recent movie or TV show you have seen. Share what you liked or didn't like about it. Answers will vary.

> I saw the new *Wonder Woman* movie recently. The story was pretty exciting!

> How was the acting?

HISTORY AND CULTURE

UNIT GOALS

- talk about what makes movies successful or unsuccessful
- use language to ask for confirmation or information
- learn about why people enjoy feeling scared

103

The 2017 live-action remake of Disney's *Beauty and the Beast* starred Emma Watson as Belle and Dan Stevens as a computer-graphic version of the Beast.

Frozen 2 (2019) is the long-awaited follow-up to the 2013 Disney phenomenon *Frozen*. Although generally well-received by audiences globally, the critical reviews were not as kind.

The Netflix series *Stranger Things* follows the story of a group of friends who are led on a frightening adventure after one of

them suddenly disappears. The first season was so popular that additional seasons were immediately planned.

PREVIEW

Have students study the photo for a moment. Read the unit title and the photo caption aloud, as students follow along. Explain that in this unit they will learn to talk about movies. Tell them they will also learn to ask for confirmation or information.

A Tell students that they will listen to four short conversations about different movies and TV shows. Have them listen for whether the speaker wants to watch the movie or TV show again, and write **Y** or **N**.

🎧 9.1 Play Audio Track 9.1. Play it again, if necessary. Check answers.

B Tell students that they will listen again and they should circle the correct answers to complete the sentences.

🎧 9.1 Play Audio Track 9.1. Play it again, if necessary. Check answers.

OPTIONAL Have students raise their hands if they have seen any of the movies or the TV show. Ask those students whether they agree with the opinions of the speakers in the conversations, giving reasons for their answers.

C Tell students they are going to get into pairs and talk about a recent movie or TV show they have seen.

Model the conversation with a student. Point out that students should tell their partner what they liked or didn't like about the movie or TV show.

Have students do the task.

CHALLENGE Have students name different jobs that are needed to produce a movie. (See **Other useful vocabulary**.) Then have students talk about which ones they would be interested in learning more about.

UNIT GOALS

Direct students' attention to the **UNIT GOALS** box. Explain that these are some of the things students will learn in this unit. Point out that this unit is about history and culture. As students follow along, read each of the unit goals to the class. Explain any words students do not know. Remind students that at the end of the unit there is a self check that allows them to see if they have accomplished each goal.

LANGUAGE FOCUS

A Tell students they will listen to a conversation between Nadine and Maya.

🎧 **9.2** Play Audio Track 9.2 as students listen and follow along in their books.

As students follow along, read the question, *What don't Nadine and Maya want to miss?* Have students answer.

Have students work in pairs and practice the conversation once. Point out the bold words. Tell students to practice the conversation two more times, changing the bold words each time and swapping roles after the first time.

CHALLENGE Ask students to share their own stories about watching a movie after waiting a long time. Encourage them to talk about whether or not the movie lived up to their expectations.

REAL ENGLISH

Direct students' attention to the expression in the **REAL ENGLISH** box. Explain that *Same here* is used in informal English to agree with what the other person just said or to say you have had the same experience that is being talked about. Its use is similar to the expression *Me, too.* The phrase can be a good way for showing agreement or empathy with a speaker. For example:

A: The traffic was horrible yesterday, so I was late for work.

B: Yeah, same here. My boss wasn't very happy.

B Ask students to look at the chart. Explain that they will study how to turn a statement into a question to confirm something, using tag questions.

🎧 **9.3** Have students follow along as they listen to Audio Track 9.3.

LANGUAGE FOCUS

A 🎧 **9.2 Listen and read.** What don't Nadine and Maya want to miss? Then repeat the conversation and replace the words in **bold**. *They don't want to miss the opening scene.*

> **REAL ENGLISH** Same here.

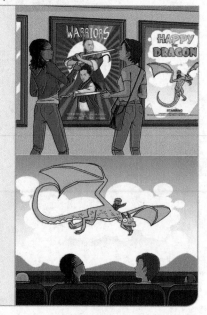

Nadine: I've been waiting **so long** to see this movie. (**forever / a long time**)

Maya: Same here. The poster looks great, doesn't it?

Nadine: Yeah, it does. You know, I really love the actors in this movie.

Maya: And I've heard the **costumes are gorgeous**. (**plot is really interesting / special effects are stunning**)

Nadine: Everyone says the opening scene is **spectacular**. (**amazing / incredible**)

Maya: So let's hurry! I don't want to miss it.

Nadine: Hey, what's this?

Maya: Oh, no! **We must be** in the wrong theater! (**I think we're / It looks like we're**)

B 🎧 **9.3 Look at the chart.** Then circle the correct answers below.

ASKING FOR CONFIRMATION OR INFORMATION (USING TAG QUESTIONS)	
Leonardo DiCaprio **is** a good actor, **isn't he**?	Yes, he is.
That TV show **was** amazing, **wasn't it**?	Yes, it was.
You **liked** the ending of the movie, **didn't you**?	Yeah, I did.
You **haven't** been to the new movie theater, **have you**?	No, I haven't.
Meryl Streep **will** star in a new TV series next year, **won't she**?	Actually, she won't.
You **can't** see that movie until you're 18, **can you**?	No, I can't.

1 We use tag questions when we expect the listener to ⟨agree⟩ / disagree with us.

2 When a statement is in the affirmative, the question tag is in the **affirmative** / ⟨**negative**⟩.

3 When a statement is in the negative, the question tag is in the ⟨**affirmative**⟩ / **negative**.

Tell students that the words after the comma in the question is called a *tag*. Point out that the main verb of the sentence is repeated in the tag and in the answer to the question.

Explain to students that there are three things they should ask themselves when forming tag questions:

1 *What is the verb (a* be *verb or another verb) and what is the tense of the verb in the main sentence?* Explain that the verb and tense should be the same in both the main sentence and the tag.

2 *Is the main sentence positive or negative?* Explain that if the verb in the main sentence is positive, the verb in the tag is negative, and if the main verb is negative, the verb in the tag is positive. Ask students to identify whether each of the verbs and tags in the sentences in the chart is positive or negative, to reinforce this point.

3 *Do I need to use a pronoun to form the tag question?* Have students identify examples of this in the chart.

C Complete the tag questions. Then ask and answer the questions with a partner.

1 Special effects make movies more exciting, _____don't they_____ ?

2 You didn't watch TV last night, _____did you_____ ?

3 You haven't seen every *Star Wars* movie, _____have you_____ ?

4 Most romantic comedies are really predictable, _____aren't they_____ ?

5 You don't like action movies very much, _____do you_____ ?

6 You're not a fan of superhero movies, _____are you_____ ?

D 🎧 9.4 Complete the conversation. Write appropriate tag forms and answers. Then listen and check.

Sam: Do you like the actress Scarlett Johansson?

Kylie: She was in the *Avengers* movies, ¹ _____wasn't she_____ ?

Sam: Yes, ² _____she was_____ . She played Black Widow.

Kylie: Yeah, I think she's really talented. By the way, I'm taking my nephew out for a movie tomorrow. Do you have any suggestions?

Sam: Hmm … He likes animated movies, ³ _____doesn't he_____ ?

Kylie: Yeah, ⁴ _____he does_____ . What do you have in mind?

Sam: How about the latest *Lego* movie? He hasn't seen that yet, ⁵ _____has he_____ ?

Kylie: I don't think so. Maybe we'll watch that. Thanks for the suggestion.

E Work in groups. Talk about the topics below. Ask follow-up questions. Answers will vary.

favorite actors/actresses	action movies	movie soundtracks	animated movies
science fiction movies	favorite books	new TV shows	pop music

You like action movies, don't you?

Of course!

Have you seen the new Keanu Reeves movie?

OPTIONAL Have students get into pairs and take turns asking and answering the questions in the chart. Then have them practice again, personalizing the answers by giving their own opinions. Tell students to replace *That TV show* (second question), *the movie* (third question), and *that movie* (last question) with the titles of actual movies or TV shows. If necessary, review the different ways students can answer (e.g., *Hmm, I'm not sure. / Actually, I didn't see that movie. / Actually, I've never heard of him.*).

Draw students' attention to the three statements under the chart. Have students circle the correct answers. Check answers.

C Have students complete the questions by adding the correct tags.

Check answers as a class.

Then have students work in pairs and take turns asking and answering the questions.

D Have students complete the conversation by writing the appropriate tag forms and answers. Tell them they will listen and check their answers.

🎧 9.4 Play Audio Track 9.4. Check answers.

E Tell students they are going to get into groups and talk about the topics in the box. Ask a student to read the topics aloud.

Model the example with a student. Point out that the first speaker asks a follow-up question. Emphasize that the students should do this, too.

Have students get into small groups and do the task. Walk around the classroom, providing assistance as necessary.

Explain that all the tag questions in the chart require *yes/no* answers. Have students rephrase the *Actually* response to include *yes/no* (e.g., *Actually, no, she won't.*).

Explain that negative sentences can be difficult to answer. Give an example by asking, *That movie wasn't very interesting, was it?* Ask students how to answer before

explaining that if they agree, they should answer *No, it wasn't.* However, if they disagree and think the movie was interesting, they would probably start by saying *Actually*. Remind them that *Actually* here is used to introduce a different point of view to show disagreement. Explain that the person might answer, *Actually, I really liked it.*

THE REAL WORLD

Ask students to look at the photo. Have a student read the title and the caption aloud. Ask students if they have seen the movie or read the book *A Wrinkle in Time*.

A Tell students they are going to watch a video about movies that don't make money. Tell them to circle **T** if the statement is true or **F** if it is false. Before they watch the video, have students read the statements silently.

▶ 9.1 Play Video 9.1. Play it again, if necessary. Check answers.

DO YOU KNOW?

Read the sentence and answer choices aloud, as students follow along in their books. Have students guess the answer before providing it (b).

CONTENT NOTE: BLOCKBUSTER

The expression *blockbuster* was originally used during World War II to describe a bomb that could devastate a whole city block at once. Then the term began to be used to describe a shocking event or unexpected news. It began to be used to refer to money-making movies in the 1950s.

B Tell students they will watch the video again, and they should match each movie with the reason it was unsuccessful. Have students read the movie titles and reasons silently before watching again.

▶ 9.1 Play Video 9.1. Play it again, if necessary. Check answers.

C Tell students to look at the chart and decide which movies are flops, based on the definition in the video.

Have students do the task. Check answers.

THE REAL WORLD

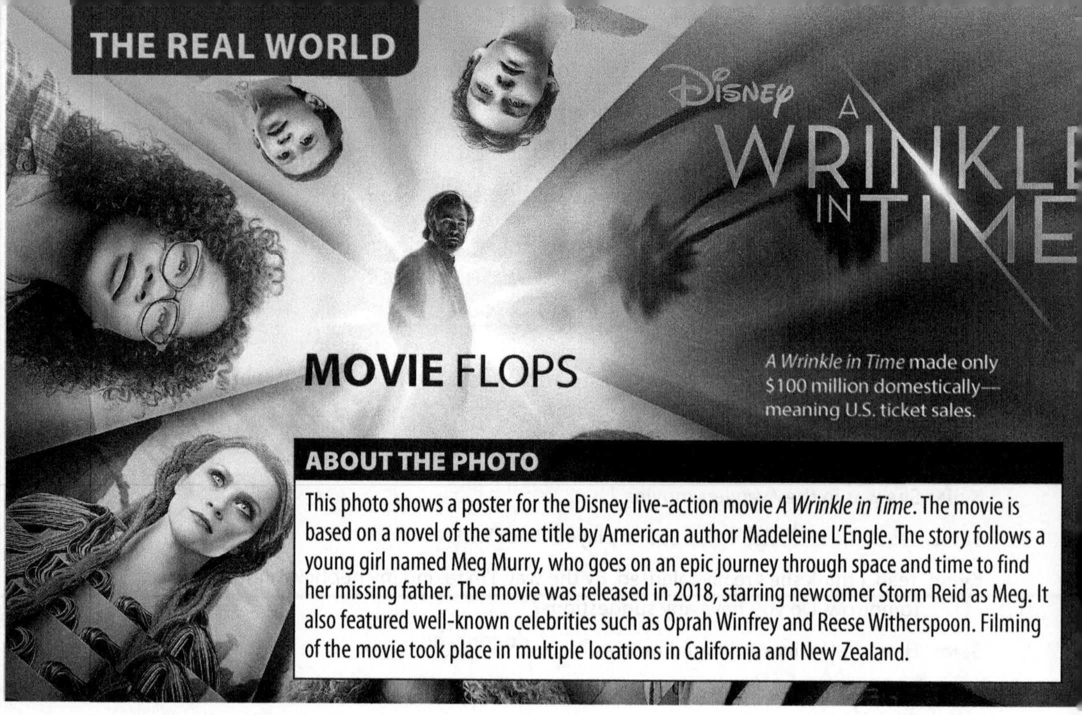

MOVIE FLOPS

A Wrinkle in Time made only $100 million domestically—meaning U.S. ticket sales.

ABOUT THE PHOTO

This photo shows a poster for the Disney live-action movie *A Wrinkle in Time*. The movie is based on a novel of the same title by American author Madeleine L'Engle. The story follows a young girl named Meg Murry, who goes on an epic journey through space and time to find her missing father. The movie was released in 2018, starring newcomer Storm Reid as Meg. It also featured well-known celebrities such as Oprah Winfrey and Reese Witherspoon. Filming of the movie took place in multiple locations in California and New Zealand.

A ▶ 9.1 **Watch the video.** Circle **T** for true or **F** for false.

1 The movie *Mortal Engines* is considered a flop. (T) F
2 The movie *Warcraft* did poorly outside of North America. T (F)
3 *Blade Runner* was a big success when it was first released. T (F)

B ▶ 9.1 **Watch again.** Match each movie with the reason it flopped.

1 *Treasure Planet* — a miscast actor/actress
2 *John Carter* — poor timing
3 *Aloha* — poor marketing
4 *A Wrinkle in Time* — bad reviews

DO YOU KNOW?

A movie that's a massive hit is a ______.
a double feature
(b) blockbuster
c midnight movie

C **Look at the chart below.** Based on the definition in the video, which of these movies are flops? Circle the movie titles.

Movie	Production cost	North America ticket sales	International ticket sales
Tomb Raider (2018)	$94 million	$58 million	$216 million
(*Robin Hood* (2018))	$100 million	$30 million	$54 million
Blade Runner 2049 (2017)	$150 million	$92 million	$168 million
(*King Arthur* (2017))	$175 million	$39 million	$107 million

OPTIONAL Have students identify which movie was the biggest flop (*King Arthur*) and which was the biggest success (*Tomb Raider*). Then ask students to raise their hands if they have seen any of the movies. Have students talk about some of the good or bad points of that movie.

D CRITICAL THINKING

As students follow along, read the task aloud. Explain that a *pitch* is an idea for a new movie. Give students time to read the pitches and think about or write down their ideas first. Then have students get into pairs and share their ideas and opinions. Emphasize to students that they should continue to brainstorm ideas as they discuss. Encourage them to give reasons to support their ideas.

PROJECT As students follow along, read the project instructions aloud. Explain that they will research about another movie flop. Give students time to search the internet and make notes. If necessary, suggest the search term *movie flops*.

D CRITICAL THINKING Speculating **Talk with a partner.** Read these "pitches" for possible movies. Which do you think is most likely to succeed? Which is most likely to flop? Why? Answers will vary.

Make *Black Panther* into an animated movie. Add some talking animals and a few musical numbers.

Make a drama about Genghis Khan. Include big battle scenes. Cast Leonardo DiCaprio as Khan.

Make a sequel to the movie *Titanic*. Cast Kate Winslet as Rose again. Show her life after the shipwreck.

PROJECT Think of a movie you like that generally did poorly. Find out how much money it lost. Why did it flop? What did you like about it?

PRONUNCIATION intonation in tag questions

A 🎧 9.5 **Listen and repeat.**

1 That actor is really overrated, isn't he? (asking for confirmation)

2 You don't like movie sequels, do you? (asking for information)

B 🎧 9.6 **Listen.** Mark each question tag with the intonation pattern ↗ or ↘. Then listen again and repeat the questions.

1 That film was awesome, wasn't it?

2 Anime comes from Japan, doesn't it?

3 You don't like 3D movies, do you?

4 Movie tickets are so expensive, aren't they?

COMMUNICATION

A **Look at the sentences below.** Write the name of a classmate in each blank that you think makes the sentence true. Answers will vary.

1 _____ doesn't like romantic comedies.

2 _____ watches a lot of shows on Netflix.

3 _____ enjoys reading comic books.

4 _____ didn't play any video games last week.

5 _____ has never seen the movie *Titanic*.

B **Talk to the people in A.** Check your predictions using tag questions. Answers will vary.

You don't like romantic comedies, do you?

No, I don't. / Actually, I do.

Unit 9 **107**

Explain that students will listen and repeat the questions. Tell them to pay attention to how the intonation goes up or down and to mimic it as best as they can. Make sure students understand that falling intonation is used to ask for agreement or confirmation, while rising intonation is used to ask for information.

🎧 9.5 Play Audio Track 9.5, pausing after each question so students can repeat.

B Tell students to listen and mark each question tag with a rising or falling arrow to indicate the intonation pattern.

🎧 9.6 Play Audio Track 9.6. Check answers.

🎧 9.6 Play Audio Track 9.6 again, pausing after each question so students can repeat.

COMMUNICATION

Tell students they are going to talk to some of their classmates, but first they are going to make guesses about which statement is true for which classmate.

A Tell students to complete each sentence with the name of one of their classmates. Explain that students are making predictions only.

Have students do the task.

B Explain that students will now check their predictions by talking to the classmates whose names they wrote down. Tell them to use tag questions to check their predictions.

Model the example with a student.

Have students do the task.

You might want to assign the research as homework. Then in the next lesson, have students share with the class what they learned.

OPTIONAL If the students in your class come from different countries, encourage them to choose a movie from their respective home countries. Tell them to include information about the movie's plot. Have students share in small groups instead of pairs.

PRONUNCIATION

Tell students they will practice their intonation in tag questions.

A Tell students they will study how to use the rise and fall of their voice to show whether they are asking the other person for their confirmation or for information. Point out that this difference is very important in avoiding miscommunication.

READING

Ask students to look at the photo. As students follow along, have a student read the title aloud.

___

OPTIONAL Personalize the content by asking students to share their impressions and how they feel when they look at the photo. Encourage them to say whether it makes them feel scared and why.

___

TEACHING NOTE: PERSONALIZATION

Encourage students to personalize the content and develop personal opinions about it. This encourages them to apply the content. It also gives them the opportunity to use the language presented in the unit.

A   Tell students they will make predictions about the article based on the title. As students follow along, read the question and answer choices aloud.

Have students do the task. Check answers.

___

OPTIONAL Have a class discussion about the other two questions (**a** and **c**). Encourage students to provide reasons for their opinions.

B   Tell students they will skim the article and add headings (**1–4**) to the correct places. As students follow along in their books, have a student read the headings aloud. Point out that one heading is extra and will not be used. Remind students that skimming involves reading quickly.

Have students do the task. Check answers.

C   Ask students to scan paragraph D and underline the three components of horror movies.

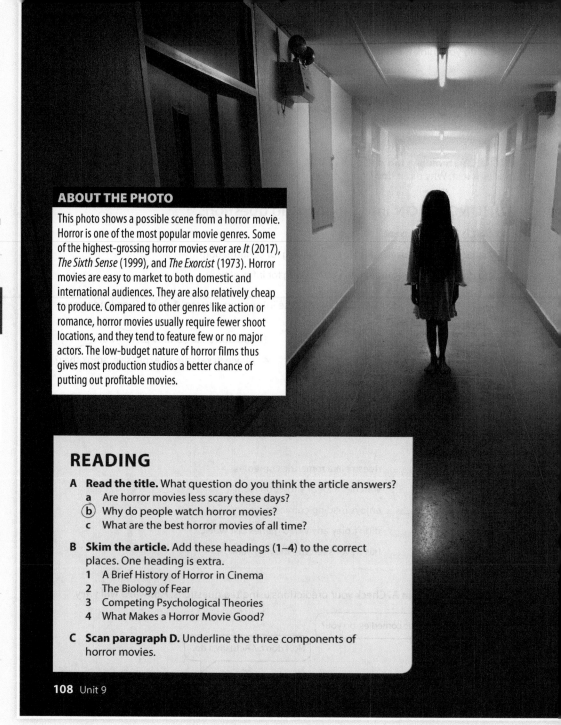

ABOUT THE PHOTO

This photo shows a possible scene from a horror movie. Horror is one of the most popular movie genres. Some of the highest-grossing horror movies ever are *It* (2017), *The Sixth Sense* (1999), and *The Exorcist* (1973). Horror movies are easy to market to both domestic and international audiences. They are also relatively cheap to produce. Compared to other genres like action or romance, horror movies usually require fewer shoot locations, and they tend to feature few or no major actors. The low-budget nature of horror films thus gives most production studios a better chance of putting out profitable movies.

READING

A   Read the title. What question do you think the article answers?
   a   Are horror movies less scary these days?
   (b)   Why do people watch horror movies?
   c   What are the best horror movies of all time?

B   Skim the article. Add these headings (1–4) to the correct places. One heading is extra.
   1   A Brief History of Horror in Cinema
   2   The Biology of Fear
   3   Competing Psychological Theories
   4   What Makes a Horror Movie Good?

C   Scan paragraph D. Underline the three components of horror movies.

___

CHALLENGE Before students do **C**, have them name some famous horror movies. Have students name the types of things that are in these movies (e.g., ghosts, zombies, witches, vampires) and the actions that make people scared (e.g., being chased by an unknown predator, torture, being eaten alive).

___

After completing the task, have students read the article in more detail so they can answer the **COMPREHENSION** questions.

OPTIONAL The text can also be used as a listening activity. Have students close their books. Tell students they will listen to the passage.

🎧 **9.7**   Play Audio Track 9.7. Ask students to get into pairs and discuss what information they heard. Then have them read the article more carefully.

OUR ATTRACTION TO
FRIGHT

A 🎧 9.7 Do you enjoy watching horror movies? Many people do, and scientists are interested in finding out why.

B Millions of years of human evolution have made us afraid of certain things. For example, we are afraid of the dark for good reason—sometimes wild animals or other dangers hide in the dark. In a way, fear has helped humans avoid danger and has helped us survive.

C __2__ Scientists have **identified** an area of the brain that is linked to fear: the amygdala. This area of the brain produces stronger **responses** when people view pictures of animals—compared to pictures of people, places, or objects. Perhaps this is why so many scary movies have animal-like monsters. However, brain research also shows that horror movies don't actually create fear responses in the amygdala. This makes researchers **curious** to know the kinds of emotions people are really feeling when they watch a horror movie.

D __4__ It's important to understand what creates horror in movies. Psychologist Glenn D. Walters has identified three **factors**. One is <u>tension</u>, created through mystery, fear, shock, and **mood**. The second is <u>relevance</u>: There are basic fears we all share, such as fear of the unknown. The third factor is <u>unrealism</u>. In one study, students were shown horrible scenes from documentaries. Most students couldn't watch them. But these same students paid money to see even worse scenes in horror movies. Why? They knew the movie was not real.

E __3__ The attraction to fear is interesting on a psychological level. Many theories have tried to explain its **appeal**. One theory suggests that young people like horror movies because adults tend to frown upon them or think that horror movies are not suitable for young viewers. For adults, the appeal may be a sort of dark curiosity, similar to what happens when we stop to look at a car accident. Another theory claims that people enjoy watching horror movies because of the feeling of confidence they experience afterward.

F Although many theories have been suggested, we still don't fully understand our fascination with horror movies. But whatever reasons people have for watching them, one thing is clear—horror movies are not going anywhere.

Unit 9 **109**

4 Does the author think horror movies are going to become less popular? (No. The phrase *not going anywhere* suggests their popularity will continue indefinitely.)

Vocabulary Practice and Expansion

Help students remember new words from the article by playing a word-association game.

Write one of the new words (e.g., *mood* in paragraph D) and make sure students understand its meaning (how you feel at a certain moment). Have students name as many types of moods that they can think of (e.g., happy, sad, scared, angry, upset).

Divide the class into groups. Write another new word on the board, confirm the meaning, and then give the teams a few minutes to think of related words or phrases. When they have finished, have teams take turns saying their words. They may need to explain why they associated a specific word. Award one point for each word or one point for each word that other teams don't have. At the end, have teams add up their points. The team with the most points is the winner.

Developing Critical Thinking

Remind students that making a movie can be very expensive, as they learned in the **REAL WORLD** section. Encourage students to think critically about what they have read in the text and to draw their own conclusions by asking them to discuss whether they think moviemaking is a good way to spend that amount of money. Then ask them if their opinion is different for horror movies.

If some students believe the money could be spent in a better way, have students get into small groups with at least one student who has this opinion. Ask them to discuss what a government that wants to help its people might do with that much money.

Additional Activities to Use with the Reading

Additional Comprehension Questions

1 According to the article, why do many horror movies have images of animal-like monsters? (People have stronger responses to them than to other things, including people.)

2 Why are researchers curious about people's emotional responses to horror movies? (They are curious because research has shown that horror movies don't create fear responses in the brain.)

3 According to the article, why do people want to see what happened at the scene of a car accident? (because of dark curiosity, which is curiosity that stems from wanting to know about things that are generally considered mysterious or taboo)

COMPREHENSION

A EXAM PRACTICE

The focus of multiple-choice questions varies.

Both **main idea** and **purpose** items require students to think about the entire passage. As a *global* question, students need to think about what the author (or speaker) wants to emphasize. One way to do this is to ask for an alternative title or the main topic. Students can usually eliminate any distractor that is only applicable to one part of the passage. Another way to test purpose is to ask for the purpose of one section of the passage.

Detail items test students' understanding of the information in the reading (or listening) passage. Although the passage and question may use the same words, synonyms are also used. These items are generally more straightforward and less complex than other types of multiple-choice questions.

Have students read the questions to themselves and circle the correct answers.

After they have finished, check answers as a class.

IDIOM

As students follow along in their books, read the sentence and answer choices aloud. Have them guess the answer before providing it (c). Give an example:

I was scared stiff when my cat suddenly jumped out from behind the sofa.

B Tell students to read the statements and circle **T**, **F**, or **NG**.

Have students do the task. Check answers.

COMPREHENSION

A Answer the questions about *Our Attraction to Fright*.

1 PURPOSE The main purpose of paragraph B is to _____.

   a give an introduction to human evolution

   b list the reasons why some people are scared of the dark

   (c) explain why we fear some things

2 INFERENCE Horror movies often make use of music to add to the _____.

   (a) tension   b relevance   c unrealism

3 DETAIL It's easier for people to watch scary scenes in movies than in documentaries because they know that the scenes in movies _____.

   (a) aren't real   b aren't important   c aren't as exciting

4 VOCABULARY In paragraph E, *frown upon* means _____.

   a to be unafraid of

   (b) to show disapproval of

   c to refuse to see

5 COHESION The following sentence would best be placed at the end of which paragraph?

   They feel better about themselves because they made it through the horror safely.

   a paragraph C   b paragraph D   (c) paragraph E

B Read the statements. Circle **T** for true, **F** for false, or **NG** for not given.

1 There are evolutionary reasons for why we fear certain things.   (T)   F   NG

2 The amygdala responds more strongly to pictures of places than of objects.   T   F   (NG)

3 Scary movies activate fear responses in the amygdala.   T   (F)   NG

4 One way to build tension in a movie is through the use of mystery.   (T)   F   NG

5 People in their 20s watch more horror movies than anyone else.   T   F   (NG)

C CRITICAL THINKING Justifying an Opinion **Talk with a partner.** Do you think watching horror movies is harmful in any way? Give reasons for your opinion. Answers will vary.

IDIOM

Someone who is very scared is "scared _____."

a stone

b scream

(c) stiff

OPTIONAL As the class checks answers, ask students to point out the paragraph in the passage where they found the information for the true statements. (**1** paragraph B; **4** paragraph D) Ask them to also correct the false statement. (**3** Scary movies do not activate fear responses in the amygdala.)

C CRITICAL THINKING

As students follow along, read the question aloud. Have students get into pairs and discuss their ideas.

OPTIONAL Have a class sharing session during which each student contributes an opinion about watching horror movies. Encourage them to give reasons to support their ideas and opinions.

VOCABULARY

A Find the words below in the article. Then complete the sentences using the words in the box.

appeal	curious	factors	identify	mood	response

1 Your ___response___ to an action or event is your reaction to it.

2 The ___appeal___ of something is what makes it attractive or interesting to others.

3 The ___mood___ of a story is the general feeling that you get from it.

4 When you ___identify___ something, you discover its existence and are able to name it.

5 ___Factors___ are the parts or elements that contribute to a particular result.

6 If you are ___curious___ about something, you are interested in it and want to know more about it.

B Read the information below. Then write true sentences using the words in **bold** (1–4).

Answers will vary.

> One way to help remember new vocabulary is to write true sentences using each word. This gives you a personal connection to the word, helping you to remember it more easily.
>
> **horror:** *Horror movies scare most people, but not me.*

1 **afraid:** _____

2 **tension:** _____

3 **horrible:** _____

4 **fascination:** _____

WRITING

A Read the movie review.

B Choose a movie you watched recently. Make notes about it.

C Write a movie review using your notes. Describe the movie and share what you liked or didn't like about it.
Answers will vary.

◄ ► ⌂ MovieReviewForum.com

MOVIE REVIEW

A fun family movie ★★★★☆

I watched *Aladdin* recently. The movie is a live-action remake of Disney's 1992 animated film of the same name. I really liked the music and the characters, especially the Genie, who was played by Will Smith. I would recommend this movie to everyone because …

VOCABULARY

A Ask a student to read the words in the box aloud. Have students find the words in the **READING** passage.

Have students use the words in the box to complete the sentences. Check answers.

B As students follow along, read the information in the box aloud. Tell students to write sentences using the words in bold. Point out that the sentences should be true.

Have students do the task. Check answers.

CONTENT NOTE: HORROR MOVIES

Horror movies have existed as long as the movie industry has. Researchers who study human behavior created the term *horror paradox* to refer to the apparent contradiction between the suffering and fear in horror movies and people's willingness to watch these grotesque movies. While brain scans show we don't have fear responses in our brains when we watch horror movies, there are other physical effects. The heart can beat as much as 15 beats more per minute, causing blood pressure to go up. The viewers' palms may become sweaty, their muscles may tighten, and their skin temperature may go down.

WRITING

Tell students they are going to write a short review of a movie they have seen recently. Explain that a movie review talks about the good and bad points of the movie, and people often read movie reviews before deciding whether to watch a movie.

A As students follow along, read the example review aloud. Point out that the review starts with a four-word summary of the author's opinion, along with how many stars the author is giving the movie. Have students identify the other aspects of the review (e.g., movie title, plot summary, information or impressions about the movie's characters and the story, the author's recommendation).

SUPPORT If you brought in some easy-to-read movie reviews, distribute them to the students and have them read through the reviews to get a better idea of what goes into a movie review.

B Give students time to think of a movie they want to write a review about and make notes. Have students talk about other things they could include, such as the names of actors or the director, as well as opinions about how the acting was, or if the soundtrack was good.

C Have students write their reviews using their notes from **B**. You might want to assign the writing as homework, and set a minimum number of sentences students must write (e.g., 10).

VIDEO

Tell students they are going to watch the trailer for a film called *Free Solo*. As students follow along in their books, read the sentence about the video aloud. If needed, elicit or explain the meaning of *documentary* (a movie that provides a factual retelling or report of a subject).

OPTIONAL Ask students to guess what they think the word *free* refers to in *Free Solo*. If necessary, explain that *free* means the climber is free of ropes or other safety equipment.

CONTENT NOTE: FREE SOLOING

Free soloing is considered a risky sport, even for seasoned rock climbers. Climbing without safety equipment can mean that one small slip will lead to death. Free soloing is actually quite controversial in the rock-climbing world, as many expert climbers think it is a reckless interpretation of the sport.

BEFORE YOU WATCH

Tell students that they will watch a trailer, or a short video that previews scenes from a longer movie. As students follow along, read the discussion questions aloud. Have students get into pairs and write down their ideas. Tell them that they will use their notes again in **AFTER YOU WATCH**.

OPTIONAL Have students share with the class their ideas about what makes a good movie trailer.

WHILE YOU WATCH

A Tell students to watch the trailer and circle their answer for what they would expect to see in the documentary.

▶ 9.2 Play Video 9.2. Play it again, if necessary. Check answers.

FREE *SOLO*

Before You Watch

Work with a partner. You are going to watch the trailer for the documentary *Free Solo*. What makes a good movie trailer? What should a trailer include? Note your ideas.

Answers will vary.

While You Watch

A ▶ 9.2 **Watch the video.** Based on the trailer, what would you expect to see in the documentary?

  a Alex Honnold's attempt to climb El Capitan in record time

  (b) Alex Honnold's quest to climb El Capitan without ropes or equipment

  c how a team of climbers rescued Alex Honnold after he fell from El Capitan

B ▶ 9.2 **Watch again.** Circle the correct answers.

1 Alex says that having a girlfriend makes his life (better in every way) / harder in some ways.

2 Alex's girlfriend (is) / isn't interviewed in the documentary.

3 The director Jimmy Chin has mixed feelings about shooting the film because he almost died once while climbing El Capitan / (he's afraid that Alex will fall and die.)

C **Look at these expressions from the video.** Choose the correct meanings of the words in **bold**.

1 "People who really know exactly what he's doing are **freaked out**."

  a extremely happy   (b) very anxious

2 "I'm starting to **get kind of psyched**."

  a feel a little scared   (b) become very excited

3 "Hey, Jimmy, **do you copy**? Just started climbing."

  (a) do you hear me   b are you doing the same thing as me

After You Watch

Talk with a partner. Look back at your notes from **Before You Watch**. Assess the trailer for *Free Solo*. Does it meet your criteria for a good movie trailer? Did it make you want to watch *Free Solo*?

Answers will vary.

Alex Honnold (in red) training for his free solo climb up El Capitan, or El Cap, in Yosemite National Park

112 Unit 9

OPTIONAL Have students talk about whether they would like to see the documentary and why.

B Tell students that they will watch the video again and they should circle the correct answers to complete the sentences. Have students read the sentences silently before watching the video.

▶ 9.2 Play Video 9.2. Play it again, if necessary. Check answers.

OPTIONAL Have students share any background information they know about El Capitan or Yosemite National Park. (See **CONTENT NOTE**.)

CONTENT NOTE: EL CAPITAN

The granite formation El Capitan, called El Cap by climbers like Alex, is in Yosemite National Park in northern California. The towering wall of rock stands 2,307 meters above sea level. Most visitors who want to

ABOUT THE PHOTO

This photo shows American free solo climber Alex Honnold training for a climb up El Capitan in Yosemite National Park. Alex climbs without ropes or other safety equipment. In 2017, he became the first person to free solo El Capitan, completing the climb in a remarkable 3 hours and 56 minutes. This amazing achievement was filmed by director Jimmy Chin, who documented the entire ascent. In 2019, *Free Solo* was awarded an Oscar for Best Documentary (Feature).

A Complete the sentences. Circle the correct answers.

1 The acting was **overrated** /(**superb**) It was some of the best I've ever seen.

2 The costumes were (**spectacular**) / **uninteresting**. Everyone looked amazing.

3 I found the movie's plot quite **exciting** /(**dull**) I fell asleep in the theater!

4 The characters are so **predictable** /(**unrealistic**) No one behaves or talks that way.

B Complete the questions. Write appropriate tag forms.

1 Your sister has acted in a movie, _____hasn't she____ ?

2 They're not planning to see the movie tonight, ____are they____ ?

3 He went to the wrong movie theater, ____didn't he___ ?

4 You can't see that movie without a parent, ___can you___ ?

5 You haven't bought tickets for the movie yet, ___have you___ ?

C Complete the sentences. Use the words in the box.

afraid	fascination	horrible	tension

1 The sight was so ___horrible____ that I had to turn away.

2 Why do some people have such a(n) ___fascination___ with snakes? I find them terrifying.

3 I wasn't ___afraid____ while watching the movie, but the music did create some ___tension____ .

SELF CHECK   Now I can …

☐ talk about what makes movies successful or unsuccessful

☐ ask for confirmation or information

☐ discuss why people enjoy feeling scared

Unit 9 **113**

CHALLENGE As a critical thinking exercise, ask students to make their own discussion questions about the video (e.g., *What kind of person do you think is good at free soloing? How do you think Honnold's friends felt while watching him climb?*). Give students time to write their questions, then have them get into small groups and take turns asking and answering them.

REVIEW

Explain to students that they are going to review the material from the unit and this will help them remember what they have studied.

A Explain that activity **A** reviews vocabulary from the unit. Have students circle the correct answers to complete the sentences. Check answers as a class.

B Explain that activity **B** reviews the grammar from the unit. Tell students to complete the questions with appropriate tag forms.

Have students do the task. Check answers.

C Point out that activity **C** reviews words from **VOCABULARY** activity **B**. Have students use the words in the box to complete the sentences. Check answers.

SELF CHECK

These *I can* statements provide vital feedback on students' perceived ability to use the language from the unit. If you find students are reluctant to check they can do the skills, consider asking them to rate themselves from 1 (not very confident) to 3 (very confident).

OPTIONAL Have students complete the **SELF CHECK** before doing the **REVIEW** activities. After reviewing the unit, have students once again check their confidence for each statement.

experience the view at the top of El Capitan take a half-kilometer intermediate-level hiking path there. Alex's climb was the first-ever successful free solo climb of El Capitan. The rock's name, El Capitan, is Spanish for "the captain."

C Tell students to read the quotations from the video and circle the correct meanings of the words in bold.

Have students do the task. Then have them get into pairs and compare answers with a partner.

OPTIONAL Have pairs write new sentences with the expressions. Have them read one of their sentences to the class. Ask others to say whether they think the use is correct. If it isn't correct, ask the other students if they can help to revise the sentence.

AFTER YOU WATCH

Have students get into pairs and assess the trailer, using their notes from **BEFORE YOU WATCH**. Remind them to give reasons to support their opinions.

I WISH I COULD BE AN OLYMPIC ATHLETE!

CONTENT AREA: PEOPLE AND PLACES

Topic: wishes and hopes

Vocabulary: wishes: cure diseases, be an athlete, travel back in time, be a famous architect, fly, see through walls, read people's minds, be invisible, meet someone famous, play a musical instrument; **other words:** represent, invention, inspire, event, pressure, reality

Grammar: using *wish, would* + verb

Extra material: a world map

Other useful vocabulary: words with meanings similar to *cure*: abolish, eliminate, wipe out, drug, remedy, medicine

END OF UNIT PROJECT Tell students they will give a presentation about a researched topic or about an idea of their own. If students have access to software that can create presentation slides, encourage them to create slides for their presentations.

Remind students that in the **READING** section, they learned about four young people who are making the world a better place; in the **REAL WORLD** section, they heard people talk about superpowers; and in the **VIDEO** section, they learned about a new futuristic technology that humans have developed. Tell students they should choose one of the following topics for their presentation:

1 a teenager who is making a difference in the world

2 a new technology being developed that is like a superpower

10

I WISH I COULD BE AN OLYMPIC ATHLETE!

A ski jumper in mid-air

114

3 an imaginary new kind of technology designed by you that can help make a difference in the world

Assign the research and presentation preparation as homework. Remind students to list the sources they used on the last slide, or last page, of their presentation.

In the next lesson, have students share their research with their classmates. For each new technology, have a class discussion about how probable the predictions about the technology are.

CONTENT NOTE: SKI JUMPING AS AN OLYMPIC SPORT

The first Winter Olympics was held in 1924 in Chamonix, France. While ski jumping has been an official event from the start, over the years the sport's presence at the Olympic Games has grown to include three different events: normal hill, large hill, and team large hill.

Technology has played a big role in the development of ski jumping. Improvements

ABOUT THE PHOTO

This photo shows a ski jumper in action. Ski jumping is a sport whereby an athlete aims to jump as far down a hill as possible after skiing down a ramp. In addition to the distance jumped, competitor's style and other factors such as wind also affect the final score. Sondre Norheim, a Norwegian, is widely regarded as the pioneer of modern ski jumping. In 1866, he won the world's first ski jumping competition, which was held in Høydalsmo, Norway. Since then, the sport has evolved to include different jumping techniques and styles, allowing athletes to jump farther. (See **CONTENT NOTE** for more information.)

PREVIEW

A 🎧 **10.1 Listen.** Four students are discussing their wishes. Number the wishes (1–4).

__4__ cure diseases

__2__ be an athlete

__1__ travel back in time

__3__ be a famous architect

B 🎧 **10.1 Listen again.** What would the students do if their wishes came true? Write two words for each blank.

1 John would meet Albert Einstein and __interview him__.

2 Gabriela would set a(n) __Olympic record__.

3 Luke would design __interesting buildings__.

4 Sara would find a cure __for cancer__.

C **Talk with a partner.** Look at the wishes in **A**. Which wish would you choose? Why? _Answers will vary._

> I wish I could travel back in time. That way, I could find the answers to ancient mysteries!

> When would you go back to?

PEOPLE AND PLACES

UNIT GOALS

- talk about your wishes and hopes
- learn language for talking about wishes and imaginary situations
- learn about teenagers who are making a difference in the world

115

---

in skis, slopes, and safety systems have helped athletes to break records and reduce injuries. Thanks to developments in engineering, ski jumpers can even train during the summer season now.

PREVIEW

Have students study the photo for a moment. Read the unit title and the photo caption aloud, as students follow along. Explain that in this unit they will learn to talk about wishes and imaginary situations.

A Tell students that they will listen to four short conversations. Ask them to listen and number each student's wish, from 1 to 4.

🎧 **10.1** Play Audio Track 10.1. Play it again, if necessary. Check answers.

CHALLENGE Have students also try to catch the name of each speaker talking about a wish. Tell them to write the person's name next to each wish (*John, Gabriela, Luke, Sara*). Check answers.

B Tell students that they will listen again for more details about each speaker's wish. Tell them to write two words for each blank to say what each speaker would do if their wish came true.

🎧 **10.1** Play Audio Track 10.1. Play it again, if necessary.

Check answers.

C Tell students they are going to get into pairs and talk about which wish they would choose from **A** and why.

Model the conversation with a student. Point out that students should ask each other follow-up questions to talk more about their wish.

Have students do the task.

SUPPORT Note that students will learn how to talk about wishes on the next page, and some might not be familiar with using *would* to ask a question about wishes yet. For lower-level classes, encourage them to use question words such as *What, When, Where, Why,* and *How* to ask follow-up questions in the discussion.

CHALLENGE Have students talk about their own imaginary wishes instead of using the ones from the audio.

UNIT GOALS

Direct students' attention to the **UNIT GOALS** box. Explain that these are some of the things students will learn in this unit. Point out that this unit is about people and places. As students follow along, read each of the unit goals to the class. Explain any words students do not know. Remind students that at the end of the unit there is a self check that allows them to see if they have accomplished each goal.

LANGUAGE FOCUS

A Tell students they will listen to a conversation between Stig and Ming.

🎧 **10.2** Play Audio Track 10.2 as students listen and follow along in their books.

As students follow along, read the question, *What superpower would Stig like to have?* Have students answer.

Have students work in pairs and practice the conversation once. Point out the bold words. Tell students to practice the conversation two more times, changing the bold words each time and swapping roles after the first time.

CHALLENGE Ask students to share their own ideas of imaginary superpowers that they would like to have. Encourage them to talk about what they would do with that superpower.

REAL ENGLISH

Direct students' attention to the expression in the **REAL ENGLISH** box. Explain that *You mean …?* is used to confirm what the other person just said. It is short for *Do you mean …?* For example:

A: I wish I could fly to work to avoid traffic.

B: You mean you wish you had a flying car?

B Ask students to look at the chart. Explain that they will study how to talk about wishes and imaginary situations.

▶ **10.3** Have students follow along as they listen to Audio Track 10.3.

Read the sentences in the first row of the chart aloud. Explain to students that the wishes and situations being talked about in the chart either aren't true right now or are not real.

LANGUAGE FOCUS

A 🎧 **10.2** **Listen and read.** What superpower would Stig like to have? Then repeat the conversation and replace the words in **bold**. *He'd want to control people's minds.*

> **REAL ENGLISH** You mean …?

Stig:	Do you ever wish you had a superpower?
Ming:	You mean like being able to **fly**? (**see through walls** / **travel back in time**)
Stig:	Yeah. What do you wish you could do?
Ming:	I wish I could breathe underwater.
Stig:	That would be **cool**! (**awesome** / **amazing**)
Ming:	What superpower would you **want to have**? (**like to have** / **wish for**)
Stig:	I'd want to control people's minds.
Ming:	Why's that?
Stig:	If I could do that, I could make **all my teachers give me A's**! (**other people do all my chores** / **my friends buy me food every day**)

B 🎧 **10.3** **Look at the chart.** Then circle the correct answers below.

TALKING ABOUT WISHES AND IMAGINARY SITUATIONS (USING *WISH, WOULD* + VERB)

I **wish** I	**were** famous. / **didn't have** so much homework. / **could play** an instrument.
If you **were** rich, **would** you **use** the money to travel?	Yes, I **would**. I**'d use** it to go to Antarctica. No, I **wouldn't**. I**'d donate** the money to charity.
If you **could have** any superpower, what **would** it **be**?	I**'d like** to be able to fly.
Where **would** you **go if** you **could go** anywhere in the world?	**If** I **could go** anywhere in the world, I**'d go** to Australia and New Zealand.

1 The examples in the chart refer to imaginary situations in the **past** / (**present or future**)

2 We talk about wishes using subject + *wish* + subject + the (**past**) / **present** tense.

3 When talking about unlikely or imaginary situations, we use the (**past**) / **present** tense in the *if*-clause and **will** / (**would**) + base verb in the main clause.

116 Unit 10

Direct students' attention to the questions in the second and third rows on the left side of the chart. Ask students how these questions are different from each other. (The first question is about a situation, while the second question is about an ability.) Have students identify which verb tense is used in the first clause of each question, providing the answer if necessary (past tense for situations, *could* + present tense verb for ability).

Have a student read the first question and the responses in the chart aloud, as students follow along. Point out that *yes/no* responses use *would*.

Have two students read the remaining questions and responses aloud. Explain that the *if*-clause can be omitted in the responses because the situation is already understood, so it is fine to say *I'd like to be able to fly* instead of *If I could have any superpower, I'd like to be able to fly.*

C **Complete the sentences.** Use the correct form of the phrases in the box.

be older	be more hours in a day	~~can go back in time~~
can sing well	be fewer words in English	

1 I wish I ___could go back in time___ . It would be interesting to meet Abraham Lincoln.

2 I'm too young to drive. I wish I ___were older___ .

3 I never have enough time to see my friends. I wish there ___were more hours in a day___ .

4 I wish I ___could sing well___ . It would be fun to enter a talent competition.

5 I wish there ___were fewer words in English___ . There are too many to remember!

D 🎧 10.4 **Complete the conversations.** Write the correct form of the words in parentheses. Use contractions where possible. Then listen and check your answers.

1 **Kay:** What would you do if you [1] ___were___ (**be**) rich?

   Hugh: I [2] ___'d buy___ (**buy**) a nice house for my parents.

2 **Ahmed:** If you [3] ___could have___ (**can have**) any superpower, what superpower [4] ___would___ you ___want___ (**want**)?

   Sandy: I think I'd want to be able to predict the future.

3 **Erin:** If you [5] ___could live___ (**can live**) forever, would you be happy?

   Bruno: No way. I [6] ___wouldn't want___ (**not want**) that.

4 **Trevor:** If you [7] ___didn't have to___ (**not have to**) go to school, how different would your life be?

   Haruko: It [8] ___wouldn't be___ (**not be**) different at all. I'd still want to go to school.

E **Work in groups.** Imagine you have been granted three wishes. What would you wish for? Share your wishes with your group members. *Answers will vary.*

I wish I could talk to animals.

Why?

I'd like to know what they think of us.

Unit 10   **117**

Point out that the main clause in the questions uses *would* and the present tense form of the verb. Explain that the grammar in the *if*-clause follows the same patterns as the sentences in the first row of the chart.

Tell students that when the *if*-clause is at the beginning of the statement or question, it must be followed by a comma, but when it is after the main clause, no comma is used.

SUPPORT Have students summarize the grammatical form to be used in statements with *if*-clauses, providing assistance as necessary.

Structure of statements using *if*-clauses without *could*:

if-clause (*if* + subject + past tense form of the verb or *were*) + main clause (subject + *would* + present tense form of the verb)

Structure of statements using *if*-clauses with *could*:

if-clause (*if* + subject + *could* + present tense form of the verb) + main clause (subject + *would* + present tense form of the verb)

OPTIONAL Have students get into pairs and take turns asking and answering the questions in the chart. Have them give their own answers.

Draw students' attention to the three statements under the chart. Have students circle the correct answers. Check answers.

C Have students complete the sentences using the correct form of the phrases in the box. Check answers.

D Have students complete the conversations by writing the correct form of the words in parentheses. Remind them to use contractions where possible, so that the conversations will sound natural.

Tell students they will listen and check their answers.

🎧 10.4 Play Audio Track 10.4. Check answers.

OPTIONAL Have students get into pairs and practice the conversations twice, swapping roles after the first time.

E Tell students they are going to get into groups and talk about what they would wish for if they were granted three wishes.

Model the example with a student. Point out that the speaker is asked a follow-up question. Emphasize that group members should do this, too.

Have students do the task.

SUPPORT Have the class brainstorm a list of possible wishes to talk about. Write them on the board to support students during the discussion.

Unit 10   **117**

THE REAL WORLD

Ask students to look at the photo. Have a student read the title and the caption aloud.

OPTIONAL Have each student share with the class one superpower they wish they had.

A Tell students they are going to watch a video in which National Geographic Explorers—made up of scientists, artists, engineers, and researchers—are interviewed about their dream superpower. Tell them to circle the superpower that they think will be the most common wish.

Before they watch the video, have students read the choices silently and circle their answer.

▶ **10.1** Play Video 10.1. Check answers.

DO YOU KNOW?

Read the sentence and answer choices aloud, as students follow along in their books. Have students guess the answer before providing it (c).

CONTENT NOTE: LADYBUG

The insect known as the ladybug in North America is a small beetle that commonly has a red back with black spots on it. However, there are actually around 5,000 types of ladybugs with various color combinations. In England, the insect is known as a *ladybird*, rather than a *ladybug*.

B Tell students they will watch the video again and they should match each National Geographic Explorer with the superpower they wish they had. Have students silently read the names and superpowers before watching the video.

▶ **10.1** Play Video 10.1. Play it again, if necessary. Check answers.

C Tell students to circle the correct answers to complete the sentences.

THE REAL WORLD

WHAT *SUPERPOWER* DO YOU WISH *YOU HAD?*

ABOUT THE PHOTO

This photo shows some attendees of the 2014 Awesome Con in Washington, D.C. Awesome Con is an annual pop culture convention in Washington, D.C. It celebrates all aspects of geek culture including comics, movies, television, and video games. Awesome Con began in 2013, and is held at the Walter E. Washington Convention Center every year. Many people come dressed as their favorite comic book or movie character. Participants can take part in costume contests, buy fan-made goods, and meet well-known comic artists or television/movie actors.

Attendees of Awesome Con 2014, Washington, D.C.

A ▶ **10.1** **Predict.** You are going to watch 10 National Geographic Explorers talk about superpowers they wish they had. What do you think is the most common wish? Circle **a**, **b**, or **c**. Then watch the video and check your prediction.

a to be able to read people's minds

b to be able to fly

ⓒ to be invisible

DO YOU KNOW?

Some people say you should make a wish if a _____ lands on your hand.
a moth
b blackbird
ⓒ ladybug

B ▶ **10.1** **Watch again.** Match each Explorer with the superpower they wish they had.

1 Andrés Ruzo — the ability to magically make people understand
2 Neil deGrasse Tyson — invisibility
3 Ricky Qi — the power to read other people's minds
4 Albert Lin — the power to turn anything into any kind of food

118 Unit 10

Have students do the task.

Note that students will likely decide their answers based on which option sounds more incredible or superhuman-like. If time permits, have students research the information online to verify their answers.

Check answers. Then ask, *Which ability do you think is the most incredible?*

Have students show their vote by raising their hands. Ask some students to share their reasons why.

D **CRITICAL THINKING**

As students follow along in their books, read the task aloud. Give students time to rank the superpowers, from 1 (most appealing) to 3 (least appealing). Then have them get into pairs to discuss their rankings. Remind them to give reasons for their rankings.

SUPPORT Go over each superpower to ensure that students are clear about what it means to have each superpower. Make sure

C **Complete these sentences describing real superhuman abilities.** Circle the correct answers. Which ability do you think is the most incredible?

1 In 2006, American Dean Karnazes ran **5** /(**50**) marathons in 50 days, in all 50 U.S. states.

2 Anne Jones, a retired teacher from England, can read up to **470** /(**4,700**) words in one minute. The average adult can read 220–300 words per minute.

3 Known as the "human computer," Shakuntala Devi of India could solve 7,686,369,774,870 × 2,465,099,745,779 in 28 (**seconds**) / **minutes**—in her head.

D **CRITICAL THINKING Ranking** **Of the superpowers below, which appeals to you the most?** Rank them from **1** (most appealing) to **3** (least appealing). Then share your ranking and reasons with a partner. Answers will vary.

_____ being able to fly   _____ being able to teleport   _____ being invisible

> **PROJECT Talk to three family members.** Ask them what superpower they wish they had. Share their answers with a partner.

PRONUNCIATION contractions: *'ll* and *'d*

🎧 10.5 **Listen.** Circle the words you hear. Then listen again and repeat the sentences.

1 **I'll** /(**I'd**) go to the White House.

2 (**He'll**) / **He'd** visit Brazil.

3 **She'll** /(**She'd**) be a famous athlete.

4 (**I'll**) / **I'd** buy a new car.

COMMUNICATION

Play a game. Work with a partner. Read the questions below. Guess what your partner's answers will be. Then check your guesses and ask follow-up questions. Answers will vary.

Questions	My guesses	My partner's answers
Which would you choose to spend one day as—a cat or a bird?		
If you could be very rich or very good-looking, which would you choose?		
If you had to give up pizza or burgers, which would you never eat again?		
If you had to lose your hearing or your sense of taste, which would it be?		

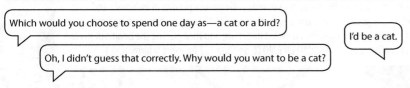

Which would you choose to spend one day as—a cat or a bird?

I'd be a cat.

Oh, I didn't guess that correctly. Why would you want to be a cat?

Tell students they will hear four sentences and they should circle the words they hear.

🎧 **10.5** Play Audio Track 10.5. Play it again, if necessary. Check answers.

SUPPORT Ask students when each sentence should be used. (**1** and **3** are examples of talking about a wish or imaginary situation; **2** and **4** are examples of talking about a decision or plan to take action in the future.)

🎧 **10.5** Play Audio Track 10.5 again, pausing after each sentence so students can repeat.

TEACHING NOTE: REPEATING

Having the whole class chorally repeat is one way to get in pronunciation practice. However, always using the same style for repeating can get boring for students and become less effective as a result. Try different formations when students repeat in class. For example, rather than always having the students repeat in chorus (as a class), divide the class by rows and have them repeat.

COMMUNICATION

Tell students they are going to play a game where they will guess their partner's answers to four questions. Tell them the winner is the partner who guesses the most answers correctly.

As students follow along, have a few students read the questions aloud. Tell students to write what they think their partner will say.

Model the conversation with a student. Emphasize that students should ask follow-up questions.

Have students get into pairs to check their guesses and ask follow-up questions. When everyone has finished, find out which partner in each pair guessed the most answers correctly.

---

students understand that to *teleport* means to move your body to any location instantly.

PROJECT As students follow along, read the project instructions aloud. Explain that they will interview their family members to find out their preferred superpower. Encourage students to ask their family members their reasons for wanting that particular superpower.

Assign the project as homework. In the next lesson, have students get into pairs and share what their family members said.

CHALLENGE Have advanced-level classes (or students) interview their family members in English, instead of just presenting the results of the interview in English. Encourage them to take a video of the entire interview to show to the class.

PRONUNCIATION

Tell students they will practice their pronunciation of the contractions *'ll* and *'d*.

READING

Ask students to look at the photos. As students follow along, have a student read the captions aloud. Then have another student read the title aloud.

A Tell students they will preview the topic of the article by looking closely at the title. As students follow along, read the question and answer choices aloud.

Have students do the task. Check answers.

OPTIONAL Ask students to give some examples of making a difference. Then tell them the article is about teenagers making a difference. Encourage students to make predictions about how these teenagers are making a difference.

B Have students scan the article and underline the places where the teenagers are from. If necessary, remind students that scanning involves looking quickly for specific information, and that place names will start with a capital letter.

Have students do the task. Check answers.

OPTIONAL Have students scan the article again and make a note of all the places mentioned (*Sierra Leone, the United States, Bali, Indonesia, Rio de Janeiro*). Then have them find these locations on a world map.

C Have a student read the questions aloud. Have students get into pairs and discuss their ideas.

After completing the task, have students read the article in more detail so they can answer the **COMPREHENSION** questions.

READING

A **Read the title.** What does it mean to "make a difference"?
  a become famous by accident
  b do the opposite of what others say or do
  c have a positive impact on a person or situation

B **Scan the article.** Where are the teenagers from? Underline the places.

C **Talk with a partner.** Do you know of other young people who have made a difference in the world? What did they do?
Answers will vary.

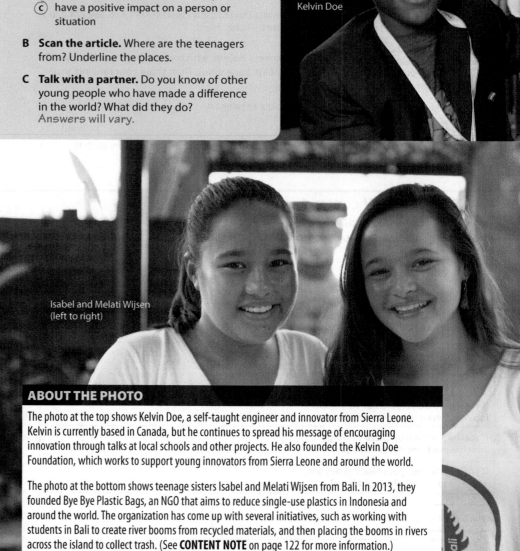

Kelvin Doe

Isabel and Melati Wijsen
(left to right)

ABOUT THE PHOTO

The photo at the top shows Kelvin Doe, a self-taught engineer and innovator from Sierra Leone. Kelvin is currently based in Canada, but he continues to spread his message of encouraging innovation through talks at local schools and other projects. He also founded the Kelvin Doe Foundation, which works to support young innovators from Sierra Leone and around the world.

The photo at the bottom shows teenage sisters Isabel and Melati Wijsen from Bali. In 2013, they founded Bye Bye Plastic Bags, an NGO that aims to reduce single-use plastics in Indonesia and around the world. The organization has come up with several initiatives, such as working with students in Bali to create river booms from recycled materials, and then placing the booms in rivers across the island to collect trash. (See **CONTENT NOTE** on page 122 for more information.)

120   Unit 10

OPTIONAL The text can also be used as a listening activity. Have students close their books. Tell students they will listen to the passage.

🎧 **10.6** Play Audio Track 10.6. Ask students to get into pairs and discuss what information they heard. Then have them read the article more carefully.

Additional Activities to Use with the Reading

Additional Comprehension Questions

1 How many times has the film about Kelvin been viewed? (millions of times)

2 What kind of event did Melati and Isabel organize at first? (a beach cleanup)

MAKING A DIFFERENCE

🎧 10.6 **The Inventor**

Kelvin Doe was born during Sierra Leone's civil war. He was six when the war ended. Today, he **represents** how this West African country is moving forward. A short film about him has already been viewed millions of times
5 on YouTube.

Kelvin is a self-taught engineer. At age 11, he began digging through trash to find electronic parts to create things. Since then, he has built a battery, a generator to provide electricity, and a radio station from recycled materials.

At age 15, Kelvin won a competition that took him to the United States. There,
10 he spoke to students about his **inventions**. He also appeared on television, and was a speaker at TEDxTeen. He has helped **inspire** and educate people through these **events**.

The Environmentalists

Melati Wijsen, 18, and her sister Isabel, 16, are fighting plastic pollution in
15 their home of Bali, in Indonesia. In 2013, they started a campaign called Bye Bye Plastic Bags, after being inspired by a school lesson on significant people. They went home that day and asked themselves, "What can we do now, as children living in Bali, to make a difference?" The answer was right in front of them, on the plastic-covered beach.

20 The sisters organized beach cleanups, collected signatures calling for a ban on single-use plastic bags, and used social media to **pressure** the local government. They even gave a TED Talk. Their efforts paid off. In 2019, the governor of Bali announced a ban on single-use plastics. The sisters are thrilled, but want to do more to reduce plastic pollution around the world.

25 **The Journalist**

Like many teenagers in Rio de Janeiro, Rene Silva is interested in computer games, soccer, and music. But he also has another interest—he wants people to understand what the poor neighborhoods, or *favelas*, are really like. Many people see Rio's favelas as dangerous places. Rene has used social media to
30 show a more positive side.

When Rene was 11, he set up a neighborhood newspaper for his favela. He worked hard writing reports for the paper. At 17, he became famous for tweeting about a police raid there. On his blog, he corrected mistakes made by TV reporters. Soon, his followers increased from a few hundred to tens
35 of thousands.

At age 19, Rene wrote his first book about the favelas. If he could have one wish, it would be to educate others about the people living there. "Today," Rene says, "there is more recognition of the people who are trying to do good and change the **reality** of the place where they live."

Unit 10 **121**

Understanding Cohesion

Tell students that when we write an essay, we need to make sure the ideas are connected well so the reader can understand them clearly. Explain that, as readers, we should notice how ideas are connected through the author's language choice. Explain that coherence is developed in an essay through cohesive devices such as words and phrases that help connect ideas together.

Read through the article again together to point out and find examples of cohesion. Point out that on line 6, the information *At age 11* helps us understand the order of events. Have students provide other examples of words or phrases within the sentences that help us connect the ideas together. For example, we understand the order of events by references to time: line 2, *when*; line 3, *Today*; line 15, *In 2013*; line 22, *In 2019*; line 31, *When Rene was 11*; line 32, *At 17*; line 36, *At age 19*. The term *but* shows contrast (lines 24, 27).

Explain that pronoun references are another tool for cohesion. Have students find three examples in the article (e.g., line 3: *this West African country* = Sierra Leone; line 12: *these events* = speaking to students and at TEDxTeen, and his appearances on television; line 15: *they* = the Wijsen sisters).

Explain to students that cohesion is also at the paragraph level. Point out that the author groups similar ideas together. For example, the author didn't mix information about the different teenagers in the same paragraph. Remind students that a paragraph should be about one topic. Have them identify the topics of the first three paragraphs (e.g., summary of Kelvin's importance, Kelvin's engineering ability, Kelvin's inspiration for many people).

3 What is the stereotype of Rio de Janeiro's *favelas* that Rene wants to challenge? (the idea that they are dangerous places, and hence, by inference, people shouldn't go there)

Developing Critical Thinking

Encourage students to think critically by having them make their own discussion questions. Then have them get into pairs and take turns asking and answering the questions. If necessary, you might want to give students additional discussion questions such as:

1 If you could meet any of these teenagers, who would you meet and why?

2 Which teenager do you think is the most inspiring? Why?

3 How do you think the civil war in Sierra Leone might have affected Kelvin?

4 Why do you think Kelvin might have been interested in developing generators and batteries?

COMPREHENSION

A Have students read the questions to themselves and circle the correct answers.

After they have finished, check answers as a class.

B EXAM PRACTICE

A Venn diagram is a graphic organizer that has two or more circles. The diagram is included in standardized tests such as the PTE Academic Speaking Test, which requires students to study the diagram for a short time before describing it.

A Venn diagram organizes information into groups, each representing how one set of things is related to others (e.g., as a subset, with some similarities but other differences). The diagram provides a visual representation that allows for easy comparison and contrast. In a two-circle diagram, for example, students should notice things that are in (1) only one set, (2) both sets, (3) neither set. In a three-circle diagram, like the one in **B**, students should notice what is in

---

COMPREHENSION

A Answer the questions about *Making a Difference*.

1 DETAIL According to the article, what is true about Kelvin Doe?

a He fought in Sierra Leone's civil war.

b He studied engineering in the United States.

ⓒ He taught himself how to make a generator.

2 CAUSE-EFFECT What gave Melati and Isabel Wijsen the idea to start Bye Bye Plastic Bags?

a learning about plastic pollution at school

b realizing how much plastic they use

ⓒ seeing plastic trash on a beach

3 VOCABULARY In line 22, *paid off* means _____.

a received a big donation ⓑ resulted in success c became well known

4 DETAIL Rene Silva is trying to _____ in Rio's favelas.

a improve children's access to education

ⓑ educate people about life

c create more job opportunities

5 SEQUENCE Which activity happened last?

ⓐ Rene wrote a book about the favelas.

b Rene set up a newspaper in his neighborhood.

c Rene became famous for tweeting about a police raid.

B Look at the descriptions (a–g) below. Write them in the Venn diagram.

a wrote a book
b won a competition
c used social media
d started a newspaper
e was/were inspired by a school lesson
f is/are involved in recycling or reducing pollution
g is/are using their influence to educate people

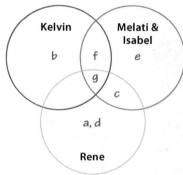

C CRITICAL THINKING Applying **Talk with a partner.** In what way(s) could you make a difference in your community? Answers will vary.

---

(1) only one set, (2) two sets, (3) all three sets, (4) no sets.

Tell students that they should write the letters representing the descriptions (**a–g**) in the correct places in the Venn diagram. Point out that the places where the circles overlap are for information that two or all of the teenagers in the article share. As students follow along in their books, have a student read the descriptions (**a–g**) aloud.

Have students do the task. Check answers.

OPTIONAL Have students go back to the article and add more information about the teenagers to the Venn diagram.

C CRITICAL THINKING

As students follow along, read the question aloud. Have students get into pairs and discuss their ideas.

VOCABULARY

A Find the bold words below in the article. Then circle the correct answers.

1 If you **represent** a country, you (are a symbol of it) / leave it for another place.

2 Examples of **inventions** include (TVs and computers) / happiness and excitement.

3 If you **inspire** people to do something, they *no longer want* / (have a strong desire) to do it.

4 An example of an **event** is a high school (dance) / teacher.

5 If you **pressure** someone, you *take a photo of them* / (try to persuade them to do something.)

6 The **reality** of a situation is how (it actually is) / you wish it was.

IDIOM

If something is "beyond your wildest dreams," it's _____ you imagined.
a worse than
b exactly as
(c) better than

B Read the information below. Then complete the sentences (1–4) with expressions from the box. Two expressions are extra.

There are many expressions containing the word *wish*:

make a wish	*wish list*	*against (someone's) wishes*
grant a wish	*dying wish*	*wish (someone) good luck*

1 My grandmother's ___dying wish___ was to see the ocean one last time.

2 Be sure to ___make a wish___ before you blow out the candles on your birthday cake.

3 My cousin called to ___wish___ me ___good luck___ in my new job.

4 She was angry because her brother posted a photo of her on Facebook ___against___ her ___wishes___.

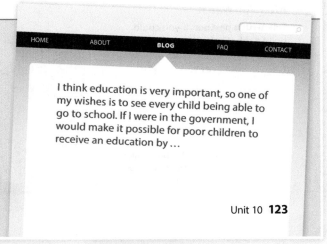

WRITING

A Read the blog post.

B Think about three changes you would like to see in the world. Note your ideas.

C Write a blog post using your notes. What three changes would you wish for? What would you do to make these changes happen? Answers will vary.

I think education is very important, so one of my wishes is to see every child being able to go to school. If I were in the government, I would make it possible for poor children to receive an education by …

Unit 10 **123**

OPTIONAL Have a class sharing session during which each student contributes an idea about how to help the community. Encourage them to add on to each other's ideas. Guide them to make at least one plan that sounds doable.

VOCABULARY

A Have students find the bold words in the **READING** passage.

Have students circle the correct answers to complete the sentences. Check answers.

B As students follow along, read the information in the box aloud. Tell students to use expressions from the box to complete the sentences. Point out that two expressions are extra and will not be used.

Have students do the task. Check answers.

SUPPORT Go over the meaning of each expression in the box, if necessary. Provide students with examples of contexts for when each expression can be used.

WRITING

Tell students they are going to write a blog post about three changes they would like to see in the world.

A As students follow along, read the example blog post aloud. Point out that it only has part of the first paragraph, which is focused on the first wish. Explain to students that they should write about each change wished for in a separate paragraph.

Have students identify elements of the blog post (e.g., what the wish is, why it is important, how the author could help make the change, and why the world would be better with the change). Tell students that each paragraph of their post should include this information about one of their wishes.

B Have students think about three changes they would like to see in the world and make notes about their ideas.

C Have students write their blog posts using their notes from **B**. Assign the writing as homework and collect the blog posts in the next lesson.

IDIOM

As students follow along in their books, read the sentence and answer choices aloud. Have them guess the answer before providing it (c). Give an example:

A: How was your trip to New York?

B: It was beyond my wildest dreams. I saw two shows on Broadway, visited the Empire State Building and the Statue of Liberty, and ate some fantastic food. It was amazing!

VIDEO

Tell students they are going to watch a video called "RoboBees." As students follow along in their books, read the sentence about the video aloud.

BEFORE YOU WATCH

Have students look at the photo. Ask a student to read the photo caption aloud.

Tell students that they will guess what Robert Wood's robots are like. As students follow along in their books, have a student read the features aloud. Have students check the ones that they believe are true about Robert Wood's robots.

WHILE YOU WATCH

A   Tell students they will watch the video and check their answers to the question in **BEFORE YOU WATCH**.

    ▶ **10.2** Play Video 10.2. Play it again, if necessary.

    Check answers.

B   Tell students that they will watch the video again and they should circle the correct answers to complete the sentences. Have students read the sentences silently before watching the video.

    ▶ **10.2** Play Video 10.2. Play it again, if necessary.

    Check answers.

CHALLENGE Encourage students to think more critically about the kind of attitude a person needs in order to build new technology like RoboBees.

Read them the following quote by Robert Wood from the video, then lead a class discussion about his attitude toward design and invention:

Many of our designs don't work. We build and test the robots over and over again. But every time we fail, we're able to learn something new and improve our designs.

ROBOBEES

Before You Watch

Look at the photo below. What do you think Robert Wood's robots are like? Check (✓) the features.

- [✓] small
- [✓] cheaper to make
- [ ] can lift heavy things
- [✓] soft
- [✓] can fly
- [ ] built from recycled materials

While You Watch

A   ▶ **10.2** **Watch the video.** Check your answers to the **Before You Watch** question.

B   ▶ **10.2** **Watch again.** Circle the correct answers.

1. Robert hopes his robots will be useful in ~~exploring space and deep oceans~~ / **monitoring people's health**.

2. Robert's team gets ideas from (nature) / machines.

3. Robert believes that in the next **5** / (**20**) years, his robots will be able to help people do dangerous tasks.

4. Robert's team wants to build robots that (work in groups like) / **are as independent as** bees.

C   **Discuss with a partner.** How effective do you think Robert's robot insects will be at these tasks? Would success require a single RoboBee or a group of RoboBees? Answers will vary.

detecting gas leaks	surveying disaster zones	pollinating crops
delivering supplies	spying on people	tracking marine life

After You Watch

Talk with a partner. If you could build a robot, what kind of robot would you want to build?
Answers will vary.

A robot created by Robert Wood and his team

124   Unit 10

C   Tell students that they will get into pairs and discuss how effective they think Robert's robot insects will be at certain tasks, and whether success would require a single RoboBee or a group of RoboBees.

Have a student read the tasks in the box aloud. Then have students get into pairs and share their ideas. Remind them to give reasons to support their opinions.

SUPPORT Review the language that students can use to politely disagree with each other during their discussions. Explain that although it is possible to say *I disagree* or *I don't think so*, it is more polite to use "softer" language, such as:

I see what you mean, but . . .
You may be right, but . . .
I understand what you are saying, but I think . . .
I understand your point, but I believe . . .
I don't really agree because . . .

A   Complete the sentences. Use the phrases in the box (a–d).

> a cure diseases
> b meet someone famous
> c play a musical instrument
> d travel back in time

1 I wish I could __d__. It would be cool to see real dinosaurs.
2 I wish I could __a__. Then people would live much longer.
3 I wish I could __c__. It would be fun to perform with a band.
4 I wish I could __b__. If I had a choice, I'd meet Barack Obama.

B   Complete the sentences. Write the correct form of the words in parentheses. Use contractions where possible.

1 If I ___could cure___ (**can cure**) only one disease, I ___'d cure___ (**cure**) diabetes.

2 If you ___were___ (**be**) rich, what ___would___ you ___buy___ (**buy**) first?

3 Bryan ___wishes___ (**wish**) he ___didn't have___ (**not have**) so much homework every week.

4 Sebastian ___wouldn't attend___ (**not attend**) school if he ___didn't have to___ (**not have to**).

C   Complete the sentences. Use the words in the box. Two words are extra.

> against   good   grant   list   luck   make

1 Visiting Japan is at the top of my wish ___list___.
2 Hae-Soon went to the party ___against___ her mother's wishes.
3 I'd like to wish everyone ___good___ ___luck___ for the exam tomorrow.

SELF CHECK   Now I can …

☐ talk about my wishes and hopes
☐ use language for talking about wishes and imaginary situations
☐ talk about teenagers who are making a difference in the world

Unit 10   **125**

REVIEW

Explain to students that they are going to review the material from the unit, and this will help them remember what they have studied.

A   Explain that activity **A** reviews vocabulary from the unit. Have students use the phrases in the box (**a–d**) to complete the sentences. Check answers as a class.

B   Explain that activity **B** reviews the grammar from the unit. Tell students to complete the sentences using the correct form of the words in parentheses. Remind them to use contractions where possible.

Have students do the task. Check answers.

C   Point out that activity **C** reviews words from **VOCABULARY** activity **B**.

Tell students to use the words in the box to complete the sentences. Point out that two words are extra and will not be used.

Have students do the task. Check answers.

SELF CHECK

These *I can* statements provide vital feedback on students' perceived ability to use the language from the unit. If you find students are reluctant to check they can do the skills, consider asking them to rate themselves from 1 (not very confident) to 3 (very confident).

SUPPORT For each skill, have students say sentences demonstrating their ability.

OPTIONAL Have students complete the **SELF CHECK** before doing the **REVIEW** activities. After reviewing the unit, have students once again check their confidence for each statement.

CONTENT NOTE: ROBOBEES

The possibilities for the RoboBees are endless, but one immediate use is the pollination of crops. Bees pollinate almost 35 percent of all food crops produced, but bees have been dying at alarming rates.

AFTER YOU WATCH

Tell students they will get into pairs and talk about what kind of robot they would like to build. Remind them to use the language they have learned for talking about imaginary situations.

CHALLENGE Have students work in pairs to create a manual for their robot. Explain that the manual should include a description of the robot, a drawing of the robot, an explanation of its use and purpose, and how to operate the robot. In the next lesson, have each pair present their robot and manual to the class.

UNIT 11
WHAT WOULD YOU DO?

Topic: ethical dilemmas

Vocabulary: actions: pickpocketing, stealing, cheating, refuse to turn down the music, refuse to clear the trash, lose something, damage something, find a handbag, find a wallet; **advice:** tell the teacher, call the police, tell the store manager, take it to the police station; **other words:** experiment, split, rob, blame, crime, connect

Grammar: review—present perfect progressive and passive form; giving advice and talking about imaginary situations; describing probability

Extra material: examples of thought experiments

Other useful vocabulary: tear a page (from a book), drop something, littering, spread rumors, vandalize something

END OF UNIT PROJECT Tell students they will make a poster about a thought experiment. Remind students that they read about thought experiments in the **READING** section. Explain that the poster topic should be one of the following:
- a well-known thought experiment
- a thought experiment that they designed

Explain that students will use a famous thought experiment or make up one of their own. Tell them to interview at least five people to gather data for their thought experiment. Remind them that the more people they interview, the more accurate their survey results will be. Tell them to interview a range

WHAT WOULD *YOU* DO?

126

of people if possible, not just their classmates or peers their own age.

Give students time to write their thought experiment or research a famous one online. If you brought in examples of thought experiments, students can choose from those experiments as well.

Assign the survey and poster as homework. Explain that the poster should explain the thought experiment and include information about the answers they received from the people they interviewed.

In the next lesson, put up the posters around the classroom, and give students time to look at them. Then have students take turns explaining the thought experiments they conducted and the results.

CONTENT NOTE: PICKPOCKETING

A disproportionate amount of pickpocketing occurs in busy places like popular tourist sites and major train stations. According to the British Transport Police, pickpocketing has been on the rise on the London

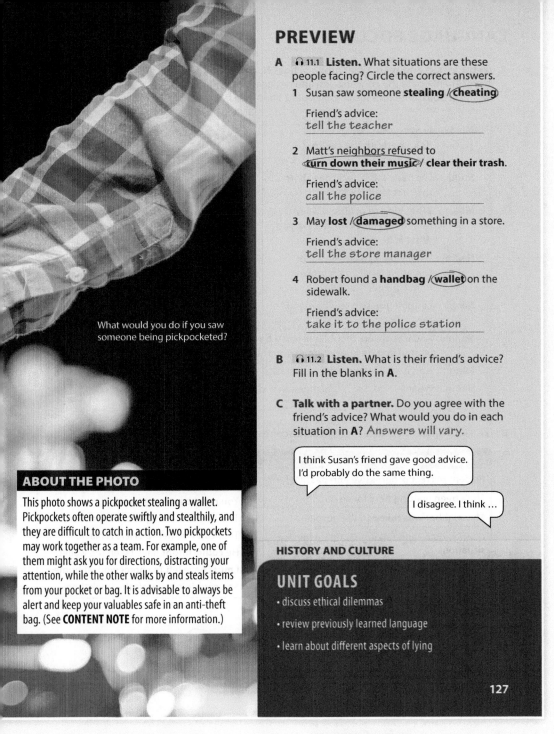

What would you do if you saw someone being pickpocketed?

PREVIEW

A 🎧 11.1 **Listen.** What situations are these people facing? Circle the correct answers.

1 Susan saw someone **stealing** / **cheating**

   Friend's advice:
   tell the teacher

2 Matt's neighbors refused to **turn down their music** / **clear their trash**.

   Friend's advice:
   call the police

3 May **lost** / **damaged** something in a store.

   Friend's advice:
   tell the store manager

4 Robert found a **handbag** / **wallet** on the sidewalk.

   Friend's advice:
   take it to the police station

B 🎧 11.2 **Listen.** What is their friend's advice? Fill in the blanks in **A**.

C **Talk with a partner.** Do you agree with the friend's advice? What would you do in each situation in **A**? Answers will vary.

> I think Susan's friend gave good advice. I'd probably do the same thing.

> I disagree. I think …

HISTORY AND CULTURE

UNIT GOALS

- discuss ethical dilemmas

- review previously learned language

- learn about different aspects of lying

127

B Tell students that they will listen to the full conversations and they should fill in the blanks in **A** by writing the advice that each friend offers.

🎧 11.2 Play Audio Track 11.2. Play it again, if necessary.

Check answers for **A** and **B**.

C Tell students they are going to get into pairs and take turns talking about each piece of advice and whether they agree with it. Ask them to think about what they would do in a similar situation. Encourage them to give reasons for their ideas.

Model the example with a student.

Have students do the task.

SUPPORT Remind students that the grammar they learned in **UNIT 10** is useful for talking about imaginary situations. Write the following sentence starter on the board to support students' discussions: *If I were in that situation, I'd …*

CHALLENGE To encourage active listening, tell students that when they have finished discussing, you will randomly call on several students, who must tell the class what their partner would do in one of the situations mentioned in **A**.

UNIT GOALS

Direct students' attention to the **UNIT GOALS** box. Explain that these are some of the things students will learn in this unit. Point out that this unit is about history and culture. As students follow along, read each of the unit goals to the class. Explain any words students do not know. Remind students that at the end of the unit there is a self check that allows them to see if they have accomplished each goal.

Underground. In 2016–2017, there were 3,730 cases of theft reported; this number increased to 6,825 in 2018–2019. The police suggest taking the following precautions to avoid being pickpocketed:

- Hold on tightly to your bags, purses, and wallets.
- Zip your bags shut.
- Keep your bags in front of you. (Don't wear backpacks on your back.)
- Don't show your money, jewelry, or wallet unnecessarily.

PREVIEW

Have students look at the photo. Read the unit title and the photo caption aloud, as students follow along. Explain that in this unit they will learn to talk about personal and ethical dilemmas.

A Tell students that they will listen to the first half of four conversations. Tell students to circle the situation that each person is facing.

🎧 11.1 Play Audio Track 11.1. Don't check answers yet.

LANGUAGE FOCUS

A Tell students they will listen to a conversation between Ming and Nadine.

🎧 **11.3** Play Audio Track 11.3 as students listen and follow along in their books.

As students follow along, read the question, *What problem does Nadine have?*

As the class discusses, make sure students also recognize that the item that Nadine lost belongs to Ming.

Have students work in pairs and practice the conversation once. Point out the bold words. Tell students to practice the conversation two more times, changing the bold words each time and swapping roles after the first time.

OPTIONAL Ask students to share any similar personal experiences about losing something that didn't belong to them. Have them tell their partners about it, or for more advanced-level classes, have students share the experience with the class.

REAL ENGLISH

Direct students' attention to the expression in the **REAL ENGLISH** box. Explain that we use *What a relief!* to express a feeling of reassurance when something is over or isn't as bad as we had expected. For example:

A: What did the doctor say?
B: She told me it's just a cold.
A: What a relief! I was worried it might be something more serious.

B Ask students to look at the chart. Explain that they will review some of the grammar they have learned so far.

🎧 **11.4** Have students follow along as they listen to Audio Track 11.4. Go over the chart as a class. Have students read each of the sentences and review the grammatical form and use of each.

LANGUAGE FOCUS

A 🎧 **11.3** **Listen and read.** What problem does Nadine have? Then repeat the conversation and replace the words in **bold**. *She has lost something that she borrowed from Ming.*

> **REAL ENGLISH** What a relief!

Ming:	Is everything OK, Nadine? (**Is something the matter / Are you OK**)
Nadine:	I've been thinking all day about this problem I have.
Ming:	**What kind of problem**? Maybe I can help. (**What's bothering you / What is it**)
Nadine:	What would you do if you lost something that you borrowed from a friend?
Ming:	I'd apologize and tell the friend the truth.
Nadine:	And if you were that friend, **you'd be angry, wouldn't you**? (**would you be angry / don't you think you'd be angry**)
Ming:	Not at all! Everyone makes mistakes.
Nadine:	What a relief! So … remember that **video game** I borrowed? (**book / scarf**)

B 🎧 **11.4** **Look at the chart.** Then circle the correct answers below.

LANGUAGE REVIEW	
Present perfect progressive and passive form	**Describing probability**
She**'s been waiting** here for an hour.	You **must** be very relieved.
My neighbor **was taken** to the hospital.	This bag **could/might** belong to Ben.
Giving advice and talking about imaginary situations	That **can't** be her car. Hers is black.
	He **could/might** have taken the wallet.
You **should apologize** for saying that.	I **must** have left my homework at home.
If I **saw** a crime, I**'d call** the police.	She **couldn't** have left the book there.

1 We use (should)/ **will** + base verb to give advice.

2 In passive sentences, the person who does the action **is** /(isn't) always important.

3 We use *must* when we are (very) / **not very** sure about something.

Remind students of the unit that each grammar point comes from if they need to go back and review one more fully:

- Present perfect progressive—**UNIT 2**
- Passive form—**UNITS 4** and **5**
- Giving advice—**UNIT 3**
- Talking about imaginary situations—**UNIT 10**
- Describing probability—**UNIT 7**

SUPPORT Have students use the grammar patterns to write sentences of their own. Collect the students' sentences and correct them before the next lesson.

In the next lesson, return the papers. Have students think of a second, incorrect grammar structure for each sentence, so that they can play a quiz game with their partners.

When students have finished thinking of their alternative sentences and have written them down, organize students into pairs. Have them take turns reading their sentences, providing both the correct and the incorrect grammar choices for each. Explain that their partner should guess which option is grammatically correct, before giving the answer.

C 🎧 **11.5** **Complete the conversations.** Circle the correct answers. Then listen and check.

1 **Amy:** If you had an extra $1,000, what ¹(**would**)/ **must** you do with it?

Hector: That's a lot of money. ²(**I'd**)/ **I'll** buy a new computer. ³ **I was using** /(**I've been using**) this one for five years.

2 **Seo-jun:** I heard that the answers to today's test ⁴ **were being stolen** /(**were stolen**). They ⁵ **took** /(**were taken**) off Mr. Lee's desk when he left to make a call.

Kelly: No way! Does he know who ⁶(**did**)/ **was done** it?

3 **Peter:** Do you know whose backpack this is?

Isobel: It ⁷ **would** /(**might**) be Jennifer's. She has a blue bag.

Peter: No, it ⁸(**can't be**)/ **might not have been** hers. Look—the initials "T. R." are on it.

D **Complete the sentences.** Use your own ideas. Answers will vary.

1 Feng was up all night studying. She must _____ now.

2 I don't see Richard anywhere. He must have _____ .

3 If you need career advice, I think you should _____ .

4 Allie has been _____ for over a year.

E **Work in groups.** Talk about what you would do in each situation below. Answers will vary.

- You are given the ability to communicate with one animal species.
- You accidentally break the handle off a mug in a store.
- You see your favorite celebrity on the street.
- You are mistakenly given an A+ by your teacher.
- You can go back in time and change one historical event.
- You are allowed to change one law in your country.

What would you do if you were given the ability to communicate with one animal species?

I'd communicate with humpback whales. I'd want to know …

Unit 11 **129**

OPTIONAL Have students get into pairs and practice the conversations twice, swapping roles after the first time.

D Have students complete the sentences using their own ideas. Check answers by randomly calling on students to give their answers. Point out that their answers will vary but that the grammar being used in each sentence should be the same.

SUPPORT Collect answers and write some of the sentences on the board to examine the grammar with the class. Use each example anonymously. If there is a mistake, encourage students to offer ideas about how to fix it.

E Tell students they will get into groups of three or four and discuss some situations. Have a few students read the situations aloud, as students follow along in their books. Note that the situations range from possible dilemmas to imaginary situations.

Explain that, in their groups, they will take turns asking and answering what they would do in each situation.

Have groups do the task. Circulate around the classroom as groups discuss, to offer support as needed.

OPTIONAL Encourage students to brainstorm other reactions than those they would normally have to the situations in **E**.

CHALLENGE Ask each group to prepare a role play for one of the situations. You might want to assign situations, so that all the situations are covered. Have each group role-play their situation in front of the class, showing what they would do if they encountered such a situation.

CHALLENGE To help students check their understanding of the grammar (and practice the vocabulary in the Student's Book), have students get into pairs. Explain that the first person must say part of a sentence using grammar from the chart, and their partner must complete the sentence. Explain that they will take turns completing each other's sentences. To encourage students to use various grammar points and new vocabulary, have students use each grammar structure only once.

Draw students' attention to the three statements under the chart. Have students circle the correct answers. Check answers.

C Have students circle the correct answers to complete the conversations.

Tell students they will listen and check their answers.

🎧 **11.5** Play Audio Track 11.5. Check answers.

THE REAL WORLD

Ask students to look at the photo. As students follow along, have a student read the title and the caption aloud.

A Tell students they are going to watch a video that shares research about how often and why humans lie. Explain that students will predict what the research says by answering the questions before watching **Part 1** of the video.

Have students do the task.

▶ 11.1 Play Video 11.1. Check answers.

B Tell students they will watch **Part 2** of the video, and they should complete the summary using words from the video.

▶ 11.2 Play Video 11.2. Play it again, if necessary. Check answers.

C Explain that students will read some examples of lies, and they should determine the reason for each lie (**a–c**), based on what they learned from the video.

Have students do the task. Check answers.

D CRITICAL THINKING

As students follow along, read the task aloud. Have students get into pairs and talk about their ideas. Remind them to support their opinions with reasons.

PROJECT As students follow along, read the project instructions aloud. Explain that they are being asked to talk about the last lie they told, which was likely a white lie and not significant. Tell them to use the information they learned in the video to analyze and explain their lie.

SUPPORT If you think sharing personal stories about lying might be uncomfortable for your students, change the assignment to a written one.

CHALLENGE Ask students to also talk about a significant lie they once told. Have them compare and contrast the two lies they told, explaining the reasoning behind each and evaluating whether it was an acceptable lie or not.

DO YOU KNOW?

Read the sentence and answer choices aloud, as students follow along in their books. Have students guess the answer before providing it (a).

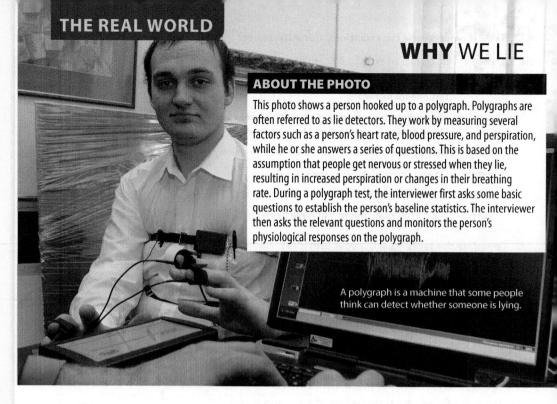

WHY WE LIE

ABOUT THE PHOTO

This photo shows a person hooked up to a polygraph. Polygraphs are often referred to as lie detectors. They work by measuring several factors such as a person's heart rate, blood pressure, and perspiration, while he or she answers a series of questions. This is based on the assumption that people get nervous or stressed when they lie, resulting in increased perspiration or changes in their breathing rate. During a polygraph test, the interviewer first asks some basic questions to establish the person's baseline statistics. The interviewer then asks the relevant questions and monitors the person's physiological responses on the polygraph.

A polygraph is a machine that some people think can detect whether someone is lying.

A ▶ 11.1 **Guess the answers to these questions.** Then watch **Part 1** of the video and check your guesses.

1 How many times a day do adults lie on average?
   ⓐ 1–2   b 5–6   c 10–12

2 Which age group lies the most?
   a people aged 6–8   ⓑ people aged 13–17   c people aged 25–35

3 Which age group lies the least?
   ⓐ people aged 6–8   b people aged 13–17   c people aged 25–35

B ▶ 11.2 **Watch Part 2 of the video.** Complete the summary below using words from the video.

Most lies are told so that people can ¹ _____protect_____ or promote themselves. Fewer lies are told for the sake of other people. For example, we lie to cover up our ² _____mistakes_____, to avoid other people, to gain economic and personal ³ _____advantage_____, or even to make people laugh.

130 Unit 11

PRONUNCIATION

Tell students they will practice their pronunciation of a final *t* and *d* sound with an initial *y* sound. Remind students that the sound of individual letters sometimes changes depending on what other letters are next to it. Explain that the sound of *d* or *t* at the end of a word, when followed by *y* at the beginning of the next word, changes to *j* or *ch*, respectively.

A Tell students to listen to the sentences and repeat.

C Read these examples of lies. Write the reason for each lie: **a** = to protect yourself, **b** = to promote yourself, or **c** = to help or hurt someone else.

1 You don't like Seth, so you told him you have to work on Friday so that you won't have to see him. __a__

2 You were mad at your coworker, so you told everyone that she was stealing money. __c__

3 You told someone that you can speak five languages, which isn't true. __b__

4 Your little brother broke a vase in a store, but you said that you did it. __c__

5 You spilled juice on the kitchen floor but told your parents that the cat knocked it off the table. __a__

D CRITICAL THINKING Reflecting **Talk with a partner.** In the video, Erika Bergman says people lie "because it's easy." Do you agree? Is it ever OK to lie? If so, under what circumstances? Answers will vary.

> PROJECT **Think about the last lie you told.** When was it? Why did you lie? If you faced the same situation, would you lie again?

PRONUNCIATION final *t* or *d* with initial *y*

A 🎧 11.6 **Listen and repeat.**

1 I want you to be honest.   2 What would you do?

B 🎧 11.7 **Listen.** Write the words you hear. Then listen again and repeat the sentences.

1 How ___did you___ get here?

2 I don't ___want you___ to be angry.

3 ___Would you___ like to play a game?

4 Why won't the teacher ___let you___ leave early?

> **DO YOU KNOW?**
> When making moral decisions, people tend to use areas of the brain related to ___.
> (a) emotion
> b logic

COMMUNICATION Answers will vary.

Debate an issue. Your school wants to ban cell phones in class. Work in groups of four. Two students are Team A, and two students are Team B. **Team A:** Turn to page 150. **Team B:** Turn to page 152.

> We don't support the ban because we think cell phone use promotes critical thinking. For example, …

Unit 11 **131**

---

have them get into pairs and take turns reading their sentences.

COMMUNICATION

Tell students they are going to get into groups of four and debate whether the school should ban cell phones in class.

Explain that a debate is an in-depth discussion about a topic, and it allows us to think about all sides of an issue. Explain that during a debate, ideas need to be clear. Also, tell students that they should discuss the topic and shouldn't attack the individual speaker (e.g., by saying *You're stupid* or *That's a dumb idea*).

Model the example. Point out the speaker gives a reason and will next support that reason with an example.

Have students get into groups. Decide which group will be Team A and which will be Team B. Tell Team A to turn to page 150, and Team B to turn to page 152. Have the teams read the information on their respective pages silently. Give each team time to come up with points to talk about that support their side of the argument. Encourage students to take notes on their ideas and practice how to present them before the debate begins.

After each debate, have the rest of the class vote on which team they think won the debate. If possible, offer constructive criticism about how a team can improve on their debating skills or their arguments.

TEACHING NOTE: DEBATING

How we try to persuade people varies by cultures. If your students are unfamiliar with giving direct arguments and reasons, you may need to explain that in English-speaking countries, it is generally a good thing to be able to clearly and concisely give your opinion. If your students are from cultures where consensus is valued more than individual opinion, this may be particularly challenging for them.

🎧 11.6 Play Audio Track 11.6, pausing after each sentence so students can repeat. Play it again, and have students repeat one more time, if necessary.

SUPPORT To practice reducing the final *t* or *d* with an initial *y*, have students say the last word in the question or statement. Then have them say the last two words. Have students continue to add one word and progressively work from the end of the sentence until they can say the entire line with the words correctly reduced.

B Tell students to listen and write the words they hear to complete the sentences.

🎧 11.7 Play Audio Track 11.7. Play it again, if necessary. Check answers.

🎧 11.7 Play Audio Track 11.7 again, pausing after each sentence so students can repeat.

CHALLENGE To give students further pronunciation practice, have them write their own sentences using the final *t* or *d* with initial *y*. After students have finished writing,

READING

OPTIONAL Ask students to look at the photo. Have students ask questions about how the photo might possibly connect to the content of the article. Tell them to think of one question each about the photo or the article. For example, *Is this an article about trains?* Call on several volunteers to give their question. Write each question on the board. Use this as a warm-up to get students thinking about the content ahead of time. After students have read the article, come back to the questions on the board and try to answer them. For example, *No, the article isn't about trains.* Star any question on the board that ends up being relevant.

A As students follow along in their books, have a student read the title aloud. Ask students what they think thought experiments are. Have a class discussion to share ideas about what a thought experiment is. Accept and encourage all ideas during the discussion. Have students check their ideas as they read the article for **C**.

B Have students scan the first paragraph to find out who designs thought experiments.

Check answers. If necessary, explain the meaning of *philosopher* (a person who studies thought, morality, and human nature).

SUPPORT Point out that students have been reading and talking (i.e., philosophizing) about moral dilemmas throughout the unit already. Explain that a thought experiment has no right or wrong answer.

READING

A Look at the title. What do you think thought experiments are?
Answers will vary.
B Scan the first paragraph. Who designs thought experiments?
philosophers
C Read the article. As you read, think about what you would do in each situation. Share your ideas with a partner. Answers will vary.

ABOUT THE PHOTO

This photo represents a famous ethics thought experiment called "The Trolley Problem" (or "The Runaway Train"), developed in 1967 by English philosopher Philippa Foot. It is used to demonstrate two conflicting schools of thought—is an action ethical because it ensures maximum well-being of the individuals involved, or is an action itself morally right or wrong, regardless of the consequences? There is no clear answer, but that is the point of thought experiments—they usually present ethical dilemmas or "What if" scenarios in which there are no straightforward answers. Thought experiments have been used in philosophy and other fields, such as physics and economics, to break down complicated issues and analyze them from various angles.

-132 Unit 11

C As students follow along in their books, read the task aloud. Have students read the article first, then get into pairs to discuss their ideas.

After completing the task, if necessary, have students read the article again so they can answer the **COMPREHENSION** questions.

OPTIONAL The text can also be used as a listening activity. Have students close their books. Tell students they will listen to the passage.

🎧 **11.8** Play Audio Track 11.8. Ask students to get into pairs and discuss what information they heard. Then have them read the article more carefully.

THOUGHT EXPERIMENTS

🎧 11.8 Like scientists, philosophers use **experiments** to test their ideas. But unlike scientists, they don't need labs or expensive equipment. Instead, they use moral dilemmas to better understand the human mind. Moral dilemmas are situations where a difficult decision has to be made.
5 There are no right or wrong answers to the questions raised by the following thought experiments.

The Runaway Train

You are walking along some train tracks. You look ahead and see five people—they've been tied up and left on the tracks. They're unable to
10 move and are shouting for help. An out-of-control train is speeding toward them. It's going to hit and kill them if you do nothing.

You see that the train tracks **split**. Next to you is a lever. All you need to do is pull the lever to make the train go onto the other track. However, a person is crossing that other track. If you pull the lever, the train will
15 kill the lone person, but you'll save the five people who are tied up.

The Prisoner's Dilemma

You and a friend **robbed** a bank, and both of you have been arrested. You are brought to the police station and placed in two different rooms.

A police officer comes in and questions you. You can either remain silent
20 or **blame** your friend for the **crime**. If you blame your friend and your friend remains silent, you can go free and your friend will go to prison for five years. If you remain silent but your friend blames you, your friend will go free and you'll go to prison for five years. If you both blame each other, you'll both go to prison for three years. If you both remain silent, you'll
25 both go to prison for only one year.

The Famous Pianist

You wake up and find yourself in a hospital bed, covered with tubes. These tubes **connect** you to a famous pianist. The pianist is very sick, and only your blood type can save him. He'll die if you remove the tubes now.
30 On the other hand, if you choose to remain connected for the next three months, he'll definitely get better. Although you have to stay in bed for three months, there'll be no danger to your health.

What would you do in each of these situations? Philosophers are very interested in studying the different responses people give. They want to
35 find out how people think or react in various situations.

Unit 11 **133**

Additional Activities to Use with the Reading

Additional Comprehension Questions

1 What do philosophers use to conduct experiments? (make-believe situations involving moral dilemmas)

2 In line 10, what does *out-of-control* mean? (cannot be controlled)

3 In line 19, what does *remain silent* mean? (not say anything)

Vocabulary Expansion—The Prefix *un-*

Have students find *unlike* (line 2) and *unable* (line 9). Remind students that *un-* means *not*, and when *un-* is added to some words, an opposite meaning is made. Ask students to find words (or forms of the words) in the text that would have the opposite meaning if *un-* were added (e.g., line 4: *made–unmade*; line 9: *tied–untied*; line 33: *do–undo*).

Listening and Pronunciation (Focused)

Remind students that we blend words that end in *t* or *d* when they are followed by a word that starts with *y*.

Have students look at the article on page 133 and mark all the places where they would expect to hear this blending (line 15: *but you'll*; line 20: *and your*; line 21: *and your*; line 22: *but your*; line 23: *and you'll*; line 27: *find yourself*; line 28: *connect you*; line 33: *would you*).

If students think the words *silent* and *you* in line 21 should be blended, ask them to look at the punctuation more closely, reminding them that when there is a comma, we normally pause briefly.

Tell students to listen and check their predictions.

🎧 11.8 Play Audio Track 11.8. Ask students if they heard blending in each place they marked.

🎧 11.8 Play Audio Track 11.8 again, pausing after each instance of blending so students can repeat.

Vocabulary Review

Tell students that they will review the new vocabulary in the **READING** by playing a game. The game can be played in small groups, or it can be played as a class. Encourage students to include vocabulary from the last few units to increase the challenge.

Explain that one student begins to draw a picture (on the board or on a piece of paper) representing one of the new words. While the student is drawing—before it becomes clear what the picture is—the other students ask questions until they figure out the object. The first person to guess the object then becomes the artist for the next word.

COMPREHENSION

A EXAM PRACTICE

Standardized tests regularly ask the test taker to make inferences from the reading and listening passages. In order to achieve the highest scores on the Listening and Reading sections of the TOEIC test, for example, students must be able to infer the main idea, the purpose, and basic details, even when the information is indirect. The TOEFL test includes items such as *Which of the following can be inferred ...?*

Students should remember the following:

- The answer must be inferred from the passage, not just true, and should not contradict the main idea.
- Students should be able to point to explicit information in the passage that supports their inference.

Have students read the questions to themselves and circle the correct answers.

After they have finished, check answers as a class.

IDIOM

As students follow along in their books, read the sentence and answer choices aloud. Have students guess the answer before providing it (a).

Explain that we use this idiom when we are in a situation where there is no good solution or the decision is very hard. Tell students to imagine something being crushed between a rock and a hard place (e.g., a brick wall) so that they can remember the idiom more easily. Give an example:

A: My two best friends have both planned their weddings on the same day! I don't know which one to attend.

B: That's an impossible choice. You're between a rock and a hard place.

COMPREHENSION

A Answer the questions about *Thought Experiments*.

1 [MAIN IDEA] What is true about thought experiments?

  a They were first created by scientists.

  b They have a single correct answer.

  (c) They are used to test the human mind.

2 [DETAIL] In "The Runaway Train," if you want to let things happen naturally, you'd _____ .

  a get help   b pull the lever   (c) do nothing

3 [VOCABULARY] Which of the following has a different meaning from the word *lone* in line 15?

  a single   (b) lonely   c solitary

4 [DETAIL] In "The Prisoner's Dilemma," is it possible for you to avoid prison time?

  (a) Yes, if you blame your friend.

  b Yes, if you remain silent.

  c No, it isn't possible.

5 [INFERENCE] Which of the following is NOT true in the case of "The Famous Pianist"?

  a You have a very rare blood type.

  (b) To help the pianist, you'll have to break the law.

  c It involves a life-or-death decision.

B Match each thought experiment with the question it raises.

1 "The Runaway Train"   Should you make personal sacrifices to help someone live?

2 "The Prisoner's Dilemma"   Is there a difference between killing someone and allowing them to be killed?

3 "The Famous Pianist"   Do you trust someone enough?

C [CRITICAL THINKING Evaluating] **Talk with a partner.** Would your responses to the thought experiments depend on other factors not mentioned in the article? What kinds of factors would change your decisions? Answers will vary.

IDIOM

If someone is "between a rock and a hard place," the person is in a situation with _____ choices.

(a) unpleasant
b confusing
c too many

B Have students match each thought experiment with the question it raises. Read the questions aloud, as students follow along.

Have students do the task. Check answers.

C [CRITICAL THINKING]

As students follow along, read the questions aloud. Have students get into pairs and discuss their ideas. Encourage students to give examples and reasons to support their ideas.

SUPPORT If students are having difficulty thinking about factors that might change their decisions, have the class brainstorm ideas, providing a few at the beginning if necessary (e.g., in "The Runaway Train," the lone person is one of your family members; in "The Prisoner's Dilemma," the other robber saved your life last year so you owe him).

VOCABULARY

A **Find the words below in the article.** Then complete the sentences using the correct form of the words in the box.

blame	connect	crime	experiment	rob	split

1 A hallway __connects__ the bedroom to the living room.

2 The two men __robbed__ a department store and stole thousands of dollars.

3 The __experiment__ is designed to test why some people lie more than others.

4 Shoplifting is a serious __crime__ .

5 I don't __blame__ anyone for the accident but myself.

6 Turn right where the road __splits__ , then continue walking.

B **Read the information below.** Complete the sentences (1–4) with the words in the box. Then decide if each sentence is in the present or past tense, and circle your answer.

> Some verbs, such as *split* and *cut*, have the same form in the simple present tense and in the simple past tense. You can usually determine which tense is being used from the context.

cut	hurt	quit	split

1 She __quit__ her job after only two weeks.   present **(past)**

2 My knees __hurt__ , so I think I should see a doctor.   **(present)** past

3 The teacher __split__ the class into three groups.   present **(past)**

4 This knife doesn't __cut__ very well.   **(present)** past

WRITING Answers will vary.

A **Read the paragraph.**

B **Do you think this project is a good idea?** Why or why not? Make a list of pros and cons, and choose a side.

C **Write a persuasive essay.** Introduce the topic and present your point of view. Give reasons for your argument.

A developer has proposed turning a large area of forested land on the edge of town into a new mall. Some local residents are for the project, but some aren't. I support this project because I think it will bring many benefits to the town. Firstly, ...

Unit 11 **135**

VOCABULARY

A Ask a student to read the words in the box aloud. Have students find the words in the **READING** passage.

Have students use the correct form of the words in the box to complete the sentences.

Check answers.

B As students follow along, read the information in the box aloud. Then have a student read the words in the gray box aloud.

Have students use the words in the box to complete the sentences. Point out that they should also decide if each sentence is in the present or past tense, and circle their answer.

Check answers.

WRITING

Tell students they are going to write a persuasive essay in response to the situation described in the model. Explain that they should think about both sides of the argument, and then choose a side.

A Read the paragraph aloud, as students follow along. Point out that this is just the beginning of the essay, but that it explains the situation that students will respond to in their own essays.

B Tell students to make a list of pros and cons, as well as brainstorm ideas about each pro or con, so they can decide which side they support and explain why they are for or against the project. Give students time to make their lists and take notes. Encourage them to use a graphic organizer such as a T-chart.

C Have students write their essays, using their notes from **B**. Remind them that the argument they make should be supported with reasons. You might want to assign the writing as homework, and set a minimum number of paragraphs students must write (e.g., three).

CHALLENGE Have students do peer editing. Have them get into pairs and exchange papers, correcting each other's first draft and writing questions in the margins when they don't understand something.

After they have finished their peer editing, have them return the papers to their partner. Encourage students to think critically about their partner's suggested changes, and review the text and changes before writing a second draft. Emphasize that not all errors may have been caught, and that some things may have been marked incorrect even though they were correct. Have students write second drafts. Collect both drafts and grade them, including the corrections. In the next lesson, return the drafts and have pairs look over how their corrections were evaluated by you.

VIDEO

Tell students they are going to watch a video called "Test of Character." As students follow along in their books, have a student read the sentence about the video aloud.

BEFORE YOU WATCH

Have students look at the main photo on the page. As students follow along, read the task aloud. Make sure students understand that the experiment involves one person seeing a stranger being robbed, and the researchers are looking to see if the person tries to help or not. Read the question, *How many people do you think tried to help the woman?* Point out that students should guess how many people out of 10 people tried to help.

Have students get into pairs and share their ideas.

WHILE YOU WATCH

A Tell students they will watch **Part 1** of the video, and they should match the people in the photos with their reactions. Have a student read the list of reactions aloud, as students follow along in their books.

Tell students to also watch for the answer to the **BEFORE YOU WATCH** question.

▶ **11.3** Play Video 11.3. Play it again, if necessary. Check answers.

B Explain that students will watch **Part 2** of the video, which is about another experiment. Tell students to write words from the video to complete the summary. Have students read the paragraph silently before watching the video.

▶ **11.4** Play Video 11.4. Play it again, if necessary. Check answers.

OPTIONAL Ask students what they would have done in the situations outlined in **A** and **B**. Encourage students to give reasons to support their answers.

TEST OF CHARACTER

Before You Watch

Talk with a partner. In an experiment, a lone person sees a thief trying to steal a woman's handbag. The experiment was conducted 10 times. How many people do you think tried to help the woman?

Answers will vary.

While You Watch

A ▶ **11.3 Watch Part 1 of the video.** Match the people below with their reactions.

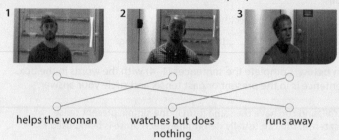

helps the woman   watches but does nothing   runs away

B ▶ **11.4 Watch Part 2 of the video.** Complete the summary of the experiment.

The experiment took place in a restaurant with hidden [1] _____cameras_____ . An actor walked past customers and fell to the ground. The lone diner took [2] _____4_____ seconds to help the man. The group of diners took [3] _____10_____ seconds. This is an example of the "bystander effect." When people are in a group, they wait for [4] _____someone else_____ to take control.

C **Read the information below.** What kind of impact do you think social media has on the bystander effect? Do you know of any other situations like this? Discuss in groups. *Answers will vary.*

> In 2013, a fire broke out on a residential street in Pincourt, Canada. Observers took videos of the house burning to the ground and uploaded them to social media—but nobody called the fire department.

After You Watch

Talk with a partner. Describe an actual situation where you needed to help someone. What did you do? Have you ever been affected by the bystander effect? *Answers will vary.*

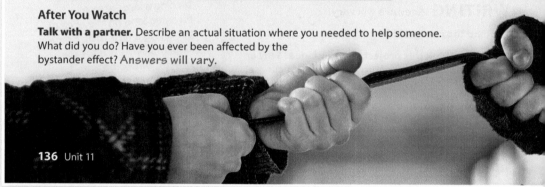

136 Unit 11

CONTENT NOTE: BYSTANDER EFFECT

Social psychologists Bibb Latané and John Darley are credited with popularizing the term "bystander effect," after a group of people watched a woman being murdered in New York in 1964. Latané and Darley concluded that no one intervened to help the woman because each onlooker believed that since no one else was doing anything, their help was unnecessary.

C Tell students they will get into groups of three or four and discuss the bystander effect. Read the information in the box aloud. Then read the discussion questions.

Have students get into groups and discuss their ideas. After they have finished their discussions, ask them to share with the class one or two points they talked about.

ABOUT THE PHOTO

This photo shows a snatch thief committing a robbery. The photo is related to the video, which presents a social experiment to illustrate the "bystander effect"—a psychological term that suggests the greater the number of bystanders in a situation such as a robbery or an accident, the less likely someone will intervene to help.

However, a 2019 study by Dr. Richard Philpot and his team at Lancaster University in the United Kingdom found that the bystander effect may not always hold true. The team studied surveillance footage of violent situations in several countries, and discovered that 90 percent of the time, one or more bystanders stepped in to help.

A Complete the sentences. Use the words in the box.

> cheat   damaged   manager   police   refused   teacher

1 I saw a classmate ___cheat___ on the exam today. Should I tell the ___teacher___ ?

2 I was in a café last night, and two customers got into a fight. They ___damaged___ some of the furniture but ___refused___ to apologize to the owner.

3 Someone broke into my apartment while I was out. I called the ___manager___ of my apartment block as soon as I got home. She then called the ___police___ .

B Complete the sentences. Circle the correct answers.

1 I'm so happy that the baby panda **rescued** / **(was rescued)**

2 I'd help if I saw someone **(fall)** / **fell** to the floor.

3 You got 100 percent on the exam? You **(must be)** / **might have been** thrilled!

4 You're the one who broke the glass. You **would** / **(should)** apologize.

5 Mariko **to lie** / **(has been lying)** about her age for a long time.

C Complete the sentences. Use the words in parentheses. In each set, one word is extra.

1 Did it ___hurt___ when you ___cut___ your finger? (**cut, hurt, quit**)

2 Tony ___quit___ the race after he fell and ___hurt___ himself. (**hurt, quit, split**)

SELF CHECK   Now I can ...

☐ discuss ethical dilemmas

☐ use previously learned language

☐ talk about why people lie

Unit 11   **137**

OPTIONAL If some groups finish quickly, have them think of other situations and discuss them. When all the groups have finished **C**, you might want to have them think of a situation where social media could have a positive impact on helping others quickly. If cell phones are allowed in your classroom, have students go online to research whether such a situation has happened in real life.

CONTENT NOTE: MORALITY

One's beliefs about what is acceptable and how one evaluates his or her own thoughts, feelings, and actions are part of a person's morality. Scientists say that in the months before turning age two, children begin to understand what is right and wrong. Before this age, children don't care if they violate adults' standards or definitions of what is acceptable. Around the age of two, children begin to test their hypotheses of right and wrong by seeing which rules they can break without getting into trouble.

AFTER YOU WATCH

Tell students they will get into pairs and talk about their own personal experiences.

As students follow along in their books, read the task aloud.

Have students do the task.

CHALLENGE Have students write the experience as a first-person narrative story. Ask them to write two versions: one version telling what actually happened, and one version telling what might have happened if they had acted differently. Have partners swap stories and guess which one is the real one.

REVIEW

Explain to students that they are going to review the material from the unit, and this will help them remember what they have studied.

A Explain that activity **A** reviews vocabulary from the unit. Have students use the words in the box to complete the sentences. Check answers as a class.

B Explain that activity **B** reviews grammar from past units. Have students circle the correct answers to complete the sentences. Check answers.

C Point out that activity **C** reviews words from **VOCABULARY** activity **B**.

Have students use the words in parentheses to complete the sentences. Point out that in each set, one word is extra and will not be used. Check answers.

SELF CHECK

These *I can* statements provide vital feedback on students' perceived ability to use the language from the unit. If you find students are reluctant to check they can do the skills, consider asking them to rate themselves from 1 (not very confident) to 3 (very confident).

UNIT 12

WHOLE GRAINS ARE GOOD FOR YOU

CONTENT AREA: SCIENCE AND TECHNOLOGY

Topic: health and nutrition

Vocabulary: foods: vegetables, fruits, processed food, whole grains, red meat, poultry, juice, nuts, banana, coffee, tea, soda, Greek yogurt; **diseases:** high blood pressure, heart disease; **things in food:** protein, vitamins, minerals, salt, sugar, fat; **activities:** exercising, meditating, reading, taking a nap, getting plenty of sleep; **other words:** signal, calculate, source, boost, produce, solve

Grammar: review—gerunds; describing and comparing things; tag questions; non-defining relative clauses

Extra material: simple public service announcements

Other useful vocabulary: whole grains: barley, corn, oats, quinoa, rice, rye, wheat; **foods with lots of fat:** fast food, fried foods

WHOLE GRAINS ARE GOOD FOR YOU

ABOUT THE PHOTO

This photo shows a loaf of rye bread. Rye bread is made from mixing rye flour and grains with other types of flour like white flour or wholemeal flour. Depending on the ratio of the flour used, rye bread can be light or dark. In general, rye bread is denser than regular white bread and has a stronger, earthier taste. It is commonly eaten in northern Europe and is said to have many health benefits. As it is high in fiber, it is more filling when consumed. Rye bread also has a low glycemic index, meaning that the carbohydrates in the bread are broken down slowly, which helps with blood sugar control.

138

END OF UNIT PROJECT Tell students they are going to get into small groups and create a public service announcement (PSA) about being healthy. Explain that a PSA is like a commercial, but instead of selling something, the government or a group wants to teach people more about something. Ask students whether they have seen any PSAs and what those PSAs were about.

If you brought in some PSAs, show them to the students.

Talk about what makes a PSA effective, providing additional ideas as necessary. For example:

- a clear message
- effective use of visuals (e.g., movies, pictures, images)
- short (e.g., 20 to 40 seconds)

Explain to students that they can make the PSA by recording it on their phone/camera. (Allow students to use editing software to increase their ability to use technology.) Also give students the option of acting it out in class.

Have students get into groups and brainstorm ideas for their PSAs (e.g., introduce the idea of superfoods, talk about what a "balanced diet" means, discuss how to build exercise into your daily lifestyle so it doesn't take a lot of time).

Have students prepare their PSAs before the next lesson.

In the next lesson, have students take turns presenting their PSAs to the class.

At the end of the PSAs, you might want to have a secret ballot so students can decide which PSA was the most convincing. If you do

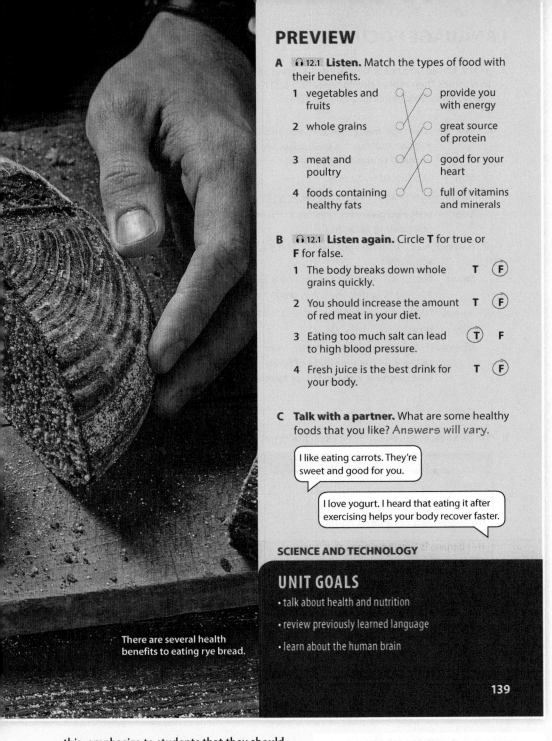

There are several health benefits to eating rye bread.

PREVIEW

A 🎧 12.1 **Listen.** Match the types of food with their benefits.

1 vegetables and fruits — provide you with energy
2 whole grains — great source of protein
3 meat and poultry — good for your heart
4 foods containing healthy fats — full of vitamins and minerals

B 🎧 12.1 **Listen again.** Circle **T** for true or **F** for false.

1 The body breaks down whole grains quickly.   T   **(F)**

2 You should increase the amount of red meat in your diet.   T   **(F)**

3 Eating too much salt can lead to high blood pressure.   **(T)**   F

4 Fresh juice is the best drink for your body.   T   **(F)**

C **Talk with a partner.** What are some healthy foods that you like? *Answers will vary.*

> I like eating carrots. They're sweet and good for you.

> I love yogurt. I heard that eating it after exercising helps your body recover faster.

SCIENCE AND TECHNOLOGY

UNIT GOALS

- talk about health and nutrition
- review previously learned language
- learn about the human brain

139

OPTIONAL Before students open their books, ask them whether they eat junk food, and, if so, how often. Ask them if they think they are healthy eaters, and why they think so.

A Tell students that they will listen to a talk about healthy eating. Tell them to listen and match the types of foods with their benefits. If necessary, explain that *benefit* refers to a positive impact.

🎧 12.1 Play Audio Track 12.1. Play it again, if necessary. Check answers.

B Tell students that they will listen again and they should circle **T** if the statement is true or **F** if it is false. Have a few students read the statements aloud, as others follow along.

🎧 12.1 Play Audio Track 12.1. Play it again, if necessary. Check answers.

OPTIONAL Have students correct the false statements to make them true. (**1** The body breaks down whole grains slowly; **2** You should decrease the amount of red meat in your diet; **4** Water is the best drink for your body.)

C Tell students they are going to get into pairs and talk about healthy foods that they like.

Model the conversation with a student.

Have students do the task.

UNIT GOALS

Direct students' attention to the **UNIT GOALS** box. Explain that these are some of the things students will learn in this unit. Point out that this unit is about science and technology. As students follow along, read each of the unit goals to the class. Explain any words students do not know. Remind students that at the end of the unit there is a self check that allows them to see if they have accomplished each goal.

---

this, emphasize to students that they should not just vote for their friends but for the best PSA. Alternatively, have students get into groups and talk about which PSAs were most effective and why.

CONTENT NOTE: HEALTHY EATING

The Centers for Disease Control and Prevention (CDC) suggest that people who want to start eating healthily focus on all of the foods they are allowed to eat rather than focusing on the foods they are not allowed to eat. The CDC also encourages eating a variety of foods, not just the same types of food all of the time.

PREVIEW

Have students study the photo for a moment. Read the unit title and the photo caption aloud, as students follow along. Explain that in this unit they will learn to talk about health and nutrition.

LANGUAGE FOCUS

A Tell students they will listen to a conversation between Nadine, Stig, and Ming.

🎧 **12.2** Play Audio Track 12.2 as students listen and follow along in their books.

As students follow along, read the question, *Why doesn't Maya give advice to Nadine?* Have students answer.

Have students work in threes and practice the conversation once. Point out the bold words. Tell students to practice the conversation two more times, changing the bold words each time and swapping roles after the first time.

CHALLENGE Ask students to share their own advice for Nadine. Encourage them to talk about what helps them to relax when they are stressed and overly busy.

REAL ENGLISH

Direct students' attention to the expression in the **REAL ENGLISH** box. Explain that *Any ideas?* is used in informal English to ask others to share their thoughts or suggestions. Its use is similar to the expression *What do you think I should do?* For example:

A: It's almost Mother's Day. Have you gotten your mom a gift yet?

B: No. Any ideas? I gave her flowers last year and a book the year before. I'm not sure what to get her this year.

B Ask students to look at the chart. Point out that the chart, like the one in **UNIT 11**, will help them to review previous grammar points from the Student's Book. Note that students will review gerunds, tag questions, describing and comparing things, and non-defining relative clauses.

LANGUAGE FOCUS

A 🎧 **12.2 Listen and read.** Why doesn't Maya give advice to Nadine? Then repeat the conversation and replace the words in **bold**. *because she's asleep*

> **REAL ENGLISH** Any ideas?

Nadine: I have **too many things to do**. I'm so stressed out! (**such a busy schedule / so many things I need to do**)

Stig: You should try to relax.

Nadine: That's easier said than done. Any ideas?

Stig: Well, **exercising** is a great way to relax. (**meditating / reading**)

Nadine: Yeah, I know. It's just hard to find the time sometimes.

Ming: And you should think about reducing the amount of **coffee** you drink. (**soda / tea**)

Nadine: I do drink a lot of **coffee**, don't I? (**soda / tea**)

Stig: What's your advice, Maya?

Nadine: If Maya were awake, she'd tell me **to take a nap!** (**to get plenty of sleep / that sleeping is the best way to relax**)

B 🎧 **12.3 Look at the chart.** Then circle the correct answers below.

LANGUAGE REVIEW	
Gerunds	**Tag questions**
Exercising is a great way to relax.	Nuts **are** good for you, **aren't they**?
Describing and comparing things	**Non-defining relative clauses**
This banana is (**not**) **as ripe as** that one. I'm not going out today. I'm **too tired**. This coffee is (**not**) **sweet enough**.	My aunt, **who studied medicine**, always gives good health advice. Greek yogurt, **which has a lot of protein**, is good for you.

1 We use **adjective +** *enough* / (**as + adjective + as**) to say that two things are equal.

2 Tag questions can be used to (**check**) / **add** information.

3 If we remove a non-defining relative clause from a sentence, the sentence (**still makes**) / **makes no** sense.

140 Unit 12

Point out that even though this is a review, all the example sentences are about the unit's topic of health and nutrition.

🎧 **12.3** Have students follow along as they listen to Audio Track 12.3.

SUPPORT Give students simple sentences (e.g., *I like to exercise.*). Have students work in pairs and make four new sentences, one for each grammar pattern. Point out that they will need to add more information. Check answers.

For example:

> *Exercising is great!*
> *Exercising is healthier than watching lots of TV.*
> *Exercising, which can be done alone or with friends, is good for you.*
> *Exercising is good for you, isn't it?*

Give students more sentences and have them do the activity again.

C 🎧 12.4 **Complete the paragraph.** Circle the correct answers. Then listen and check.

Having a good night's sleep feels great, [1] **does** /**doesn't** it? [2] **Get** /**Getting** the right amount of sleep is important for teens, [3] **who** / **which** need energy to study or play sports. But during the teenage years, there is a reset of the body's internal "clock." This reset tells a person to fall asleep later and wake up later. Many teens don't get [4] **sleep enough** /**enough sleep** because they go to sleep late but wake up early for school. School life is busy, and getting through a full day without enough rest isn't as [5] **easy** / **easier** as you might think. So, if you're feeling [6] **too tired** / **tired enough** to give your best during the day, you're probably not getting the eight to nine hours of sleep experts say you need.

D **Match the phrases to form statements.** Then talk with a partner. Do you agree or disagree with each statement?

1 A healthy mind — than a meat-based diet.

2 A vegetarian diet is healthier — before and after a workout.

3 Exercising 30 minutes a day — who is the best person to give advice.

4 It's important to stretch — is long enough to keep yourself fit.

5 If you're unwell, talk to a doctor, — is just as important as a healthy body.

E **Work with a partner.** Decide if each statement is a health fact or a health myth, and circle your answer. Then check the answers on page 151. Do any surprise you?

1 Being out in cold weather causes colds.   Fact **Myth**

2 Laughing helps increase blood flow in the body.   **Fact** Myth

3 Chocolate causes acne, which is a common skin condition among teens.   Fact **Myth**

4 Everyone should drink at least eight glasses of water a day.   Fact **Myth**

5 Eating spicy food causes stomach ulcers.   Fact **Myth**

6 Drinking water before a meal can help with weight loss.   **Fact** Myth

Being out in cold weather causes colds, doesn't it?

I'm not so sure. I …

Unit 12 **141**

Draw students' attention to the three statements under the chart. Have students circle the correct answers. Check answers.

C Have students circle the correct answers to complete the paragraph. Tell them they will listen and check their answers.

🎧 12.4 Play Audio Track 12.4. Play it again, if necessary.

Check answers.

SUPPORT When checking answers, note which grammar pattern(s) students had the most difficulty with. Go back and review the unit(s) as necessary.

- Gerunds—**UNIT 1**
- Non-defining relative clauses—**UNIT 6**
- Describing and comparing things—**UNIT 8**
- Tag questions—**UNIT 9**

D Have students match the phrases to form statements. Then have them work in pairs to check answers and talk about whether they agree or disagree with each statement. Encourage students to provide reasons to support their opinions.

CONTENT NOTE: BENEFITS OF A VEGETARIAN DIET

A vegetarian diet involves eating only plant-based meals, so there is no meat or seafood. Vegetarianism is beneficial to both humans and the environment for a number of reasons. For example, people who follow a vegetarian diet are overall healthier than those who eat meat; specifically, they suffer less from food-related diseases and heart problems. Livestock farms take up a large amount of land globally, use an abundance of water, and are one of the main emitters of greenhouse gases. Without these farms, land could be returned to nature, less water would be wasted, and carbon emissions would be reduced.

E Tell students they are going to get into pairs, read some statements about health, and decide if each statement is a fact or a myth. Have students get into pairs. Tell them to read each statement aloud together and discuss if they think it is a fact or myth. Emphasize that they should discuss each point together before circling their answers.

Model the conversation with a student.

After students have finished the task, have them turn to page 151 to check their answers. Randomly call on students to share with the class which answer surprised them and why.

OPTIONAL Before doing the activity, as homework, have students research the facts for each statement. In the next lesson, have them bring in their research and have the discussions, providing reasons for their opinions.

THE REAL WORLD

Ask students to look at the photo. Have a student read the title and the caption aloud. Ask students if they have ever eaten a macaron. Then ask if any of them have ever eaten a cricket macaron!

A Tell students they are going to watch a video about using insects for food. Tell them to circle **T** if the statement is true or **F** if it is false, as they watch the video. Before they watch the video, have students read the statements silently.

▶ **12.1** Play Video 12.1. Play it again, if necessary. Check answers.

DO YOU KNOW?

Read the sentence and answer choices aloud, as students follow along in their books. Have students guess the answer before providing it (b).

B Tell students they will watch the video again and they should check all the advantages of eating insects mentioned in the video. Have students read the advantages silently before watching again.

▶ **12.1** Play Video 12.1. Play it again, if necessary. Check answers.

C Read the instructions aloud, as students follow along. Tell students to read the clauses in the box and complete the menu items with the correct clauses (**a–d**).

Have students do the task. Check answers. Then ask students which item they would choose if they had to order one of the menu items. Encourage them to give reasons for their answers.

OPTIONAL Have students work in pairs to add one more item containing insects to the menu, be it an actual food item that they know of or an imaginary one. Tell them to write a description of the item, using a *which* clause to add more information.

EDIBLE INSECTS

Macarons made with insect powder

ABOUT THE PHOTO

This photo shows macarons made from insects. This dessert is produced by Micronutris, a French company that makes food products from insects for human consumption. The company advocates the consumption of insects as a healthier, alternative source of protein. Micronutris operates a farm in the South of France, where it raises mealworms and crickets. These insects are fed organic vegetables like carrots and zucchinis. Micronutris currently offers a range of insect-based foods, such as crackers, chocolates, energy bars, and pasta.

A ▶ **12.1** **Watch the video.** Circle **T** for true or **F** for false.

1 More than one-quarter of the world's population currently eats insects. **(T)** F

2 The most popular edible insect is the beetle. **(T)** F

3 Most farmed insects are now used to feed people. T **(F)**

4 Insects are currently being used in cosmetics. **(T)** F

DO YOU KNOW?

Most edible ants are said to taste like ____.

a salt
(b) lemon
c pepper

B ▶ **12.1** **Watch again.** Check (✓) all the advantages of eating insects mentioned in the video.

☐ They help improve people's memory.

☑ They are full of protein.

☑ They require less food than birds and mammals.

☐ They help people lose weight.

☑ They require less land to produce than traditional farm animals.

142 Unit 12

D CRITICAL THINKING

As students follow along, read the questions aloud. Ask if any students have ever eaten insects. Have them share their experiences with the class.

Then have students get into pairs and share their opinions. Emphasize to students that they should give reasons to support their opinions.

PROJECT As students follow along, read the project instructions aloud. Explain that students will research three food products that contain insects. Tell them to research products different from those mentioned in **C**. Give students time to search the internet and make notes. If necessary, suggest the search term *food made from insects*.

You might want to assign the research as homework. Then in the next lesson, have students get into pairs and share what they learned. Encourage them to bring in pictures to show their partner, if possible.

C **Below are actual menu items containing insects (1–4).** Complete these menu items with the clauses in the box (a–d). If you had to order one of these items, which would you choose?

| a which have been sweetened with honey | c which is made with skim milk |
| b which contrast nicely with the garden greens | d which are usually filled with meat |

1 **Beetle dip:** This healthy dip, _c_ , gets its flavor from roasted beetles.

2 **Cricket cheesecake:** Sticky crickets, _a_ , top a creamy cheesecake with a cricket flour crust.

3 **Grasshopper tacos:** Tacos, _d_ , get a fresh twist when filled with fried grasshoppers.

4 **Salad with crispy worms:** Try a fresh summer salad with lightly roasted worms, _b_ .

D CRITICAL THINKING Reflecting **Talk with a partner.** How do you feel about eating insects? Would you ever eat them regularly? Answers will vary.

PROJECT **Go online.** Find three food products for sale that contain insects. What are they, and what insects are used? Are the products advertised as containing insects?

PRONUNCIATION pausing between thought groups

A 🎧 12.5 **Listen and repeat.**

1 Large-scale insect farming / for human food / will begin soon.

2 In Uganda, / a kilogram of grasshoppers / is more expensive / than a kilogram of beef.

B 🎧 12.6 **Mark the pauses in these sentences with a slash (/).** Then listen and check your answers.

1 A healthy mind/is just as important/as a healthy body.

2 A vegetarian diet/is healthier/than a meat-based diet.

3 If you're unwell,/talk to a doctor,/who is the best person/to give advice.

COMMUNICATION Answers will vary.

A **Work in groups.** Imagine you have been asked to help market a new food product that contains insects. Choose one of the food products below, and note your ideas for it.

Type of food product: _a breakfast cereal / an energy bar / an ice cream bar_

- What to name it
- What insect(s) to use
- Its key selling points
- Who to market it to

B **As a group, present your product to the class.** Then vote on which food product is most likely to become the top-selling item.

Unit 12 **143**

OPTIONAL Have pairs find a recipe for a dish made with insects. Have them rewrite the recipe in their own words. Then have each pair perform a short imaginary cooking show for the class in which they show how to cook their dish.

PRONUNCIATION

Tell students they will practice pausing between groups of ideas.

A Explain that when we speak naturally, we use pauses to convey meaning. Explain that pausing in different places can subtly change the meaning of what is being said. Tell students to listen to the sentences and repeat.

🎧 12.5 Play Audio Track 12.5, pausing after each sentence so students can repeat. Play it again and have students repeat one more time, if necessary.

B Tell students to mark where they think the pauses in each sentence should be. Then have them listen and check their answers.

🎧 12.6 Play Audio Track 12.6. Check answers.

SUPPORT Have students make rules for places where we usually pause, such as:

- at the end of a sentence or question
- at every punctuation mark (e.g., comma)
- at the end of a clause or independent idea

COMMUNICATION

Tell students they are going to work in groups to help market a new food product that contains insects.

A Have students get into groups and decide on the type of food product their group will help market (a breakfast cereal, an energy bar, or an ice cream bar). Tell them to next brainstorm and choose the product's name, the insect that will be used, what the product's key selling points (i.e., benefits) are, and who their target market is.

Have students do the task.

OPTIONAL Have groups draw a picture of the product to include in their presentations in **B**.

B Explain that groups will now present their products to the class. Tell students that every group member should participate in the presentation.

Have groups do their presentations. Then have the class vote on the product that they think will most likely become the top-selling item.

READING

Ask students to look at the photo. As students follow along, have a student read the caption aloud.

A Have a student read the title aloud. Tell students they will make predictions about the article based on the title. As students follow along, read the question aloud.

Have a class discussion to talk about possible answers. Ask students to share any background knowledge they know about the brain.

CONTENT NOTE: THE BRAIN

The brain is a huge system of over 100 billion nerves. It combines information from our senses and processes them before enabling us to act. The brain has many parts, including the frontal lobe, which controls and directs the operation of the various brain systems and cognition, and the temporal lobes, which are found along the sides of our brain above our ears and are used for processing both language and non-language sounds (e.g., music). The temporal lobes are also involved in memory.

The brain stem, which is connected to the spinal cord, regulates functions such as blood pressure, heartbeat, and respiration, as well as the nerves and muscles for sight, hearing, movement, speech, and eating. All information going to or from the brain passes through the brain stem.

The cerebellum controls muscle coordination and muscle tone. The occipital lobe is where sight is controlled. The parietal lobe is the part of the brain that controls visual and spatial perception.

B Tell students that they will make some more predictions about the article. Ask them to read the sentences silently and check the ones that they think are true.

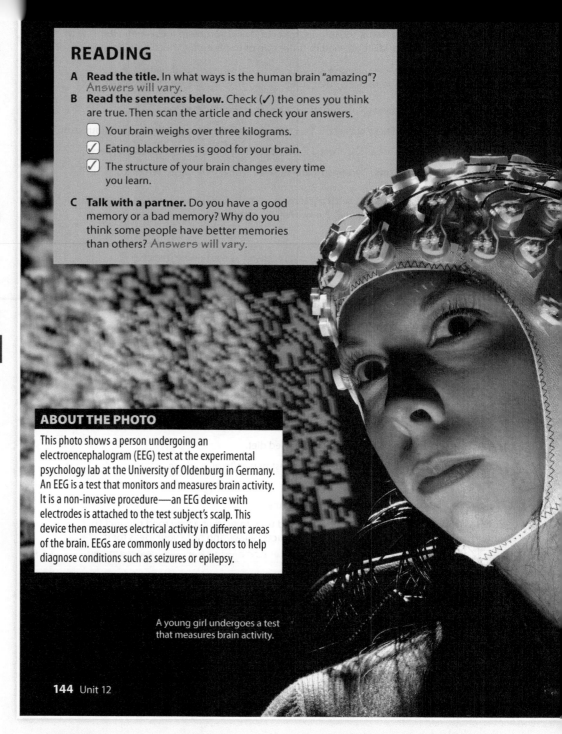

READING

A **Read the title.** In what ways is the human brain "amazing"? Answers will vary.

B **Read the sentences below.** Check (✓) the ones you think are true. Then scan the article and check your answers.

- ☐ Your brain weighs over three kilograms.
- ☑ Eating blackberries is good for your brain.
- ☑ The structure of your brain changes every time you learn.

C **Talk with a partner.** Do you have a good memory or a bad memory? Why do you think some people have better memories than others? Answers will vary.

ABOUT THE PHOTO

This photo shows a person undergoing an electroencephalogram (EEG) test at the experimental psychology lab at the University of Oldenburg in Germany. An EEG is a test that monitors and measures brain activity. It is a non-invasive procedure—an EEG device with electrodes is attached to the test subject's scalp. This device then measures electrical activity in different areas of the brain. EEGs are commonly used by doctors to help diagnose conditions such as seizures or epilepsy.

A young girl undergoes a test that measures brain activity.

144 Unit 12

Then tell them to scan the article to check their answers.

Have students do the task.

C Read the questions aloud, as students follow along. Make sure students understand that *memory* in this case refers to a person's ability to remember something, not a specific memory about a past event.

Have students get into pairs and discuss their ideas.

After completing the task, have students read the article in more detail so they can answer the **COMPREHENSION** questions.

YOUR *AMAZING* BRAIN

A 🎧 **12.7** You carry a 1.3-kilogram mass of fatty material in your head that controls everything your body does. It lets you think, learn, create, and feel emotions. What's this amazing machine? It's your brain—a structure that scientist James Watson called "the most complex thing we have yet discovered in our universe."

Your brain is more powerful than a supercomputer.

B Imagine you see a cat about to step onto a hot stove. Your brain reads the **signals** from your eyes and quickly **calculates** when, where, and at what speed you need to run to save her. Then it tells your muscles to move. No computer can match your brain's ability to download, process, and react to the flood of information from your eyes, ears, and other sensory organs.

Neurons can send information extremely quickly.

C Your brain contains about 100 billion nerve cells called neurons. If a bee lands on your foot, sensory neurons in your skin send this information to your brain at a speed of more than 240 kilometers per hour. Your brain then uses motor neurons to send a message back to your foot: Shake the bee off quickly!

The right foods make you healthier.

D Your brain can benefit from a healthy diet, just like the rest of your body. Whole grains release glucose—the brain's main **source** of energy—into the blood slowly, helping you stay focused throughout the day. Oily fish, which contain omega-3 fatty acids, can potentially fight off brain-related illnesses such as Alzheimer's disease. Dark berries help improve brain function. Eating leafy greens **boosts** memory and learning.

Exercise helps make you smarter.

E Exercising is great for your body and can even improve your mood. But scientists have also learned that your body **produces** a chemical after you exercise that makes it easier for your brain to learn. So, the next time you can't figure out a homework problem, go out and play soccer, and then try the problem again. You might find that you're able to **solve** it!

When you learn, you change the structure of your brain.

F Riding a bike seems impossible at first, but you eventually master it. How? As you practice, your brain sends "bike riding" messages along certain neural pathways again and again, forming new connections. In fact, the structure of your brain changes every time you learn, as well as whenever you have a new thought or memory.

Unit 12 **145**

OPTIONAL The text can also be used as a listening activity. Have students close their books. Tell students they will listen to the passage.

🎧 **12.7** Play Audio Track 12.7. Ask students to get into pairs and discuss what information they heard. Then have them read the article more carefully.

Additional Activities to Use with the Reading

Developing Critical Thinking

Having students compare data is a good way to develop critical thinking. Have students reread the first sentence of the article. Then tell them more about how our brains compare to the brains of other animals. For example,

the average sperm whale's brain weighs about 8 kilograms. On the other hand, the bottlenose dolphin's brain weighs 1.5 to 1.7 kilograms, just slightly more than an adult human brain. A cat has a brain that averages 25 to 30 grams in weight, and an alligator's brain weighs only around 9 grams.

Have students research the average weight of other animals' brains and report back to the other students in the next lesson.

Developing Fluency

Tell students that they will get into pairs and talk about the topic of the **READING** for one minute. Show students a stopwatch, your watch, or the classroom clock, and tell them they will be timed. Tell them they should not stop the discussion before the allocated time has ended, and that they cannot use their native language. If necessary, give students a minute to jot down some important vocabulary.

Explain that if they are not certain what to say, they can use fillers in English. Tell students that these are used when we need time to think. Write some fillers on the board (e.g., *uh, mmm, well, hmm*). Practice saying them as a class.

Have students get into pairs. Tell them that when you say *Go*, they should start talking about the topic. After one minute, say *Stop*. If some pairs have done well, praise them. If some pairs didn't try very hard, encourage the class, as a whole, to try to do better.

Explain that next, they are going to get into new pairs and discuss the topic again, but this time they will talk for 90 seconds (or two minutes). Have them get into new pairs and do the task.

When they have finished, have students talk about whether the first or second time was easier, giving reasons for their answers.

COMPREHENSION

A EXAM PRACTICE

A **cohesion** question asks students to add a new sentence somewhere in the passage. These are also sometimes called **sentence insertion** questions. Students must recognize where in a paragraph or passage the sentence will best fit. Students must consider the order and flow of ideas in the paragraph to decide where the new sentence fits logically and smoothly. Students should:

- recognize content connections between sentences.
- use trial and error by trying the new sentence after each sentence suggested in the answer choices to see where it fits best.
- think about the flow in the presentation of ideas in a paragraph.

Have students read the questions to themselves and circle the correct answers.

After they have finished, check answers as a class.

IDIOM

As students follow along in their books, read the sentence and answer choices aloud. Have them guess the answer before providing it (c). Explain that we use *pick someone's brain* to seek advice when we know that person has more information or experience than we do in relation to the topic. Give an example:

I know you're a good writer. Can I pick your brain about my essay?

B Tell students to use the words in the box to complete the summary. Point out that one word is extra and will not be used.

Have students do the task. Check answers.

COMPREHENSION

A Answer the questions about *Your Amazing Brain*.

1 **GIST** What could be another title for the article?
   - (a) Understanding the Brain and How It Works
   - **b** New Trends in Brain Research
   - **c** How to Train Your Brain to Think Faster

2 **VOCABULARY** In paragraph B, *the flood of information* means _____ of information.
   - **a** a lack
   - **b** a variety
   - (c) a huge amount

3 **DETAIL** According to the article, which of the following is NOT true?
   - **a** The brain's processing power allows you to react quickly in an emergency situation.
   - **b** The human brain contains about 100 billion neurons.
   - (c) The brain gets most of its energy from omega-3 fatty acids.

4 **INFERENCE** If you were stuck on a homework problem, the author might suggest _____.
   - (a) going to the gym
   - **b** playing a musical instrument
   - **c** doing a crossword puzzle

5 **COHESION** The following sentence would best be placed at the end of which paragraph?
   A recent report suggests that a daily serving of spinach could make your brain 11 years younger.
   - **a** paragraph A
   - (b) paragraph D
   - **c** paragraph F

B Complete the summary below. Use the words in the box. One word is extra.

connections	food	glucose	illnesses	neurons	think

Your brain is incredibly powerful. It allows you to [1] __*think*__, to feel, and to learn. When you sense an emergency, your brain reads the signals and uses your motor [2] __*neurons*__ to tell your muscles to move. But the brain needs the right [3] __*food*__ to function well. Whole grains, oily fish, berries, and leafy greens all help improve brain function and possibly fight off certain [4] __*illnesses*__. Exercising also helps make it easier for you to learn. Every time you learn something new, the structure of your brain changes as it forms new [5] __*connections*__.

C **CRITICAL THINKING Comparing and Contrasting** **Talk with a partner.** Do you think male and female brains are better at different tasks? If so, what kinds of tasks? *Answers will vary.*

IDIOM

If someone wants to "pick your brain," they'll probably _____.
- **a** give you a brain scan
- **b** look at your test scores
- (c) ask you questions

C **CRITICAL THINKING**

As students follow along, read the questions aloud. Have students get into pairs and discuss their ideas.

OPTIONAL Have a class sharing session during which each student contributes an opinion about the question, providing reasons for their opinion.

VOCABULARY

A Ask a student to read the words in the box aloud. Have students find the words in the **READING** passage.

Have students use the words in the box to complete the sentences. Check answers.

B As students follow along, read the information in the box aloud. Tell students to circle the correct answers to complete the sentences.

Have students do the task. Check answers.

VOCABULARY

A **Find the words below in the article.** Then complete the information using the words in the box.

boost	calculate	produce	signals	solve	source

The human brain is a ¹ ___source___ of wonder. Check out these facts about the brain:

- The brain interprets pain ² ___signals___, but it doesn't actually feel pain.
- The brain can combine individual memories to ³ ___solve___ problems.
- Playing classical music to babies can potentially ⁴ ___boost___ their brain power.
- Even while asleep, your brain can ⁵ ___produce___ enough energy to power a 25-watt light bulb.
- It's possible to ⁶ ___calculate___ numbers in your head faster by learning a few mental tricks.

B **Read the information below.** Then circle the correct answers.

> The word root *sens-* means "feel." Many words can be formed using this root, such as:
>
> | sense | sensor | sensible | sensation |
> | senses | sensory | sensitive | sensational |

1 Which of your five **senses** / sensors do you think is the strongest?
2 It would have been more **sense** / **sensible** to save the money than to spend it all on shoes.
3 After his eye surgery, he was very **sensitive** / sensational to light for a few days.
4 The accident caused a loss of **sensory** / **sensation** in her right foot.

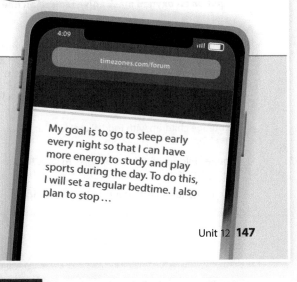

WRITING Answers will vary.

A **Read the paragraph.**

B **Choose a health-related goal.** How do you plan to achieve this goal? Note some ideas.

C **Write an action plan.** Create a step-by-step plan for achieving your goal. Use your notes from **B** to help you.

> 4:09
> timezones.com/forum
>
> My goal is to go to sleep early every night so that I can have more energy to study and play sports during the day. To do this, I will set a regular bedtime. I also plan to stop …

Unit 12 **147**

---

of vocabulary with strategies students can learn to memorize words. Students can also learn vocabulary indirectly through the teacher's use, thus emphasizing the importance of using English in the classroom whenever pragmatic.

WRITING

Tell students they are going to write an action plan for achieving a health-related goal. Explain that an action plan is a step-by-step plan to follow to achieve a goal. Tell students that the plan often (but not always) includes a timeline.

A As students follow along, read the example aloud. Point out that the plan starts with the author's goal and reason for the goal. Also point out that the plan states how the person will accomplish the goal. Tell students that their plan should include all of this information.

B Ask students to think about a health-related goal that they want to achieve and how they plan to achieve it. Encourage them to use a real goal, because we can all benefit from living healthier lives. Give students time to make notes about their ideas.

C Have students write their action plans using their notes from **B**. You might want to assign the writing as homework, and set a minimum number of steps students must write (e.g., seven). Point out that each step can be more than one sentence.

OPTIONAL Before students write their plans, give them the criteria on which you will judge their plans, such as:
- Is the plan relevant to the goal?
- Are all of the steps listed and in logical order?
- Are the ideas clear and concise?
- Is the plan realistic?

VIDEO

Tell students they are going to watch a video called "Food Allergies." As students follow along in their books, read the sentence about the video aloud.

OPTIONAL Ask students if they or someone they know can't eat certain kinds of food. Encourage students to share any personal stories connected to food allergies. Use questions to guide the discussion, if necessary.

CONTENT NOTE: FOOD ALLERGIES

The most common food allergens for children are milk, eggs, peanuts (which are legumes, not nuts), soy, wheat, tree nuts (such as cashews and walnuts), fish, and shellfish. Reactions from food allergies can produce a range of symptoms with varying levels of severity, from an upset stomach or diarrhea, to sudden inflammation, to more serious respiratory problems.

BEFORE YOU WATCH

Tell students to read the sentences silently and circle the correct answers to complete the definitions.

Have students do the task. Check answers. Then have students chorally repeat the bold words and phrases to practice pronunciation.

OPTIONAL Have students write new sentences with the bold words and phrases. Have each student read a sentence to the class. Ask others to say whether or not they think the usage is correct.

WHILE YOU WATCH

A   Explain that students will watch a video about a boy named Xaviar who has food allergies. Tell students to watch **Part 1** of the video and check the items that are true about Xaviar.

FOOD **ALLERGIES**

Before You Watch

The bold words and phrases below are used in the video. Complete the definitions. Circle the correct answers.

1   If someone is **allergic to** a food, they *can* / *(cannot)* eat it safely.

2   People with good personal **hygiene** keep themselves very *(clean)* / *well-fed*.

3   If you are **exposed to** a disease, you *(could)* / *definitely won't* get it.

4   Your **immune system** helps you *digest food* / *(fight off disease)*.

While You Watch

A   ▶ 12.2   Watch Part 1 of the video. Check (✓) the things that are true about Xaviar.

☑ He's allergic to tree nuts.   ☐ He's educated at home instead of at school.

☑ He's not allergic to eggs anymore.   ☑ He can have an allergic reaction through skin contact.

B   ▶ 12.3   Watch Part 2 of the video. Circle the correct answers.

1   The hygiene theory suggests that living in an environment that is *(too clean)* / *not clean enough* can cause children to develop allergies.

2   Dr. Robert Wood is especially concerned about the *(possibility of an accidental allergic reaction)* / *high cost of new treatments*.

3   Near the end of the video, Xaviar demonstrates how to *put on an oxygen mask* / *(give himself an injection)*.

After You Watch

Discuss with a partner. Below are a few ways to protect children with food allergies. What might be some advantages or disadvantages of each approach?   Answers will vary.

•   Ban the top allergy-causing foods (e.g., milk, wheat, nuts) from school cafeterias.

•   Encourage children with food allergies to sit separately from other kids.

•   Require children with food allergies to wear ID bracelets stating their allergies.

•   Require menus in restaurants to list all the ingredients in dishes.

148   Unit 12

ABOUT THE PHOTO

This photo shows some common food allergens: shellfish, fish, nuts, eggs, and soybeans. A food allergy is a condition in which certain foods trigger an abnormal immune response. For people with food allergies, consuming just a small amount of the food can cause an allergic reaction. Allergic reactions can range from minor ones, like a mild rash, to life-threatening symptoms, such as breathing difficulties.

People with potentially fatal food allergies usually have to carry an EpiPen with them at all times. An EpiPen is a medical device containing a shot of adrenaline. Injecting adrenaline into the body can help save someone's life in the event of a serious allergic reaction.

▶ 12.2 Play Video 12.2. Play it again, if necessary.

Check answers as a class.

B   Tell students that they will watch **Part 2** of the video, and they should circle the correct answers to complete the sentences. Have students read the sentences silently before playing the video.

▶ 12.3 Play Video 12.3. Play it again, if necessary. Check answers.

OPTIONAL Have students get into pairs to share their opinions about the hygiene theory. Tell them to say whether they agree that people now may be too hygienic. Remind students to give reasons for their opinions.

CHALLENGE As a critical thinking exercise, ask students to make their own discussion questions about the video (e.g., *Do you know anyone who might be too hygienic? What kinds of things do you think Xaviar's parents have to do for him to make sure he's safe?*). Give students time to write their questions, then have them get into small

A Look at the word groups. Cross out the odd item in each group.

1 **vegetables:**   carrots   spinach   ~~shellfish~~

2 **fruits:**   ~~onions~~   papayas   mangoes

3 **grains:**   wheat   ~~milk~~   oatmeal

4 **red meats:**   ~~chicken~~   lamb   beef

5 **processed foods:** frozen pizzas   ~~apples~~   potato chips

B Complete the sentences. Circle the correct answers.

1 These crickets are (too) / **enough** salty for me.

2 Your sister buys organic food, **does** / (doesn't) she?

3 My mother doesn't enjoy **to cook** / (cooking) very much.

4 These strawberries are not as (fresh) / **fresher** as those.

5 My friend, (who) / **which** is an aerobics instructor, is in great shape.

Common food
allergens

C Complete the sentences. Use the words in the box. One word
is extra.

| sensation | sensational | sense | senses | sensible |

1 It's not easy to lose weight. Try to be ___*sensible*___ about your
food choices.

2 When I entered the room, I didn't ___*sense*___ anything was
wrong.

3 She felt a burning ___*sensation*___ in her throat.

4 Of my five ___*senses*___, I think I appreciate taste the most!

SELF CHECK   Now I can …

☐ talk about health and nutrition

☐ use previously learned language

☐ discuss what makes the human brain special

Unit 12 **149**

REVIEW

Explain to students that they are going to
review the material from the unit and this will
help them remember what they have studied.

A Explain that activity **A** reviews
vocabulary from the unit. Have students
cross out the item that does not belong
in each group. Check answers as a class.

B Explain that activity **B** reviews grammar
from past units. Tell students to circle the
correct answers to complete the
sentences.

Have students do the task. Check
answers.

C Point out that activity **C** reviews words
from **VOCABULARY** activity **B**. Have
students read the words in the box
silently. Tell them to use the words in the
box to complete the sentences. Point out
that one word is extra and will not
be used.

Have students do the task. Check
answers.

SELF CHECK

These *I can* statements provide vital feedback
on students' perceived ability to use the
language from the unit. If you find students
are reluctant to check they can do the skills,
consider asking them to rate themselves from
1 (not very confident) to 3 (very confident).

SUPPORT For each skill, have students say
sentences demonstrating their ability.

OPTIONAL Have students complete
the **SELF CHECK** before doing the **REVIEW**
activities. After reviewing the unit, have
students once again check their confidence
for each statement.

groups and take turns asking and answering
their questions.

AFTER YOU WATCH

Tell students they will get into pairs and talk
about the video.

As students follow along in their books, read
the sentence and question aloud. Then have a
student read the four approaches aloud.

Have students get into pairs. Tell them to
reread each statement together and talk about

the pros and cons of each approach. Encourage
them to use a T-chart to list the pros and cons.

After students have finished the task, randomly
call on a few students to share some pros and
cons for each approach.

SUPPORT Go through the first approach
together with the class. Make a T-chart on the
board to show how to list the pros and cons in
a graphic organizer.

UNIT 3 LANGUAGE FOCUS

Work with a partner. Copy the words you wrote on page 33 in the blanks below. Then take turns reading each problem and evaluating the advice.

Problem 1:

I want to dress better. My [1] _____ always gives me advice. He always says, "If I were you, I'd wear more colorful [2] _____ and [3] _____. You'll look nicer." He also says that [4] _____ is a good color for me. Should I take his advice? Do you have better advice for me?

Problem 2:

I want to have a healthier lifestyle. My [5] _____ says I should eat more [6] _____ and less [7] _____. She also says I could do more sports, like [8] _____. Is this good advice? What do you suggest I do to have a healthier lifestyle?

UNIT 7 LANGUAGE FOCUS

Student A: Read your mystery story to Student B. Discuss what you think happened.

Who made the stone balls, and why?

In the 1930s, farm workers in Costa Rica discovered a collection of over 300 stone balls. The stone balls date from the 7th to the 16th centuries, and are almost perfectly round. Some are the size of a tennis ball, while others are much larger—up to two meters wide. They were made by humans, but no one knows why. What was their purpose?

UNIT 11 COMMUNICATION

Team A: Read the information below.

You **support** the ban. Think of ways the ban will benefit teachers and students. Come up with a list of arguments. Think about how cell phones can negatively affect students in the classroom. Also, think of points to counter Team B's possible arguments.

Follow these steps:

1 Team A: Present your arguments.
2 Team B: Counter Team A's arguments, and present your arguments.
3 Team A: Counter Team B's arguments, and summarize your arguments.
4 Team B: Summarize your arguments.
5 Discuss which team you think won the debate.

UNIT 4 LANGUAGE FOCUS

Student A: Skim the news article. Ask your partner questions to complete the article. Use the words in parentheses to help you form questions.

A Cry for Help

A baby manatee calls out for her mother. She doesn't hear any reply. A man finds the baby and calls a rescue service for help. He knows the baby won't survive on its own.

A rescue team rushes to the river. They lower a ¹ _____small net_____ (**what**) into the water. They manage to catch the baby manatee. They then carry her to their vehicle. Here, she is placed in a pool and then driven to a local zoo. When they arrive, the vet gives the baby manatee a checkup. The examination shows that the creature, now named Kee, is underweight. To increase her weight, Kee is given milk ³ _____every three hours_____ (**how often**).

The following month, an adult manatee arrives at the zoo. This animal, named Della, has injuries caused by an accident with a boat. A few days later, Della gives birth to a baby named Pal. This gives Virginia Edmonds, a caretaker at the zoo, an idea. She hopes Della will care for Kee like her baby. So the three manatees are placed ⁵ _____in the same pool_____ (**where**). Shortly after, Della begins to feed Kee. To everyone's joy, Della accepts Kee as her own. They're all one family now.

After four months, Della has recovered. It's time for her and her family to return to the wild. They are released into the river. "Kee is back where she belongs," says Edmonds.

UNIT 12 LANGUAGE FOCUS

Answers:

1. Myth—Viruses cause colds and the flu, not the weather. However, some viruses are more likely to spread at cooler temperatures. Cold weather may also weaken your ability to fight off illness.
2. Fact
3. Myth—There is no evidence that cocoa beans, from which chocolate is made, cause acne. However, a high-sugar or high-fat diet can increase your chances of developing the skin condition.
4. Myth—Everyone's water needs vary depending on their age, weight, level of physical activity, and the climate they live in. Also, fruits such as watermelons and strawberries, for example, contain a lot of water. These food sources contribute to your daily water intake.
5. Myth—Most stomach ulcers are caused by a particular bacterial infection or by long-term use of certain drugs. Spicy food does not cause ulcers. However, it can make existing ulcers worse.
6. Fact

UNIT 4 LANGUAGE FOCUS

Student B: Skim the news article. Ask your partner questions to complete the article. Use the words in parentheses to help you form questions.

A Cry for Help

A baby manatee calls out for her mother. She doesn't hear any reply. A man finds the baby and calls a rescue service for help. He knows the baby won't survive on its own.

A rescue team rushes to the river. They lower a small net into the water. They manage to catch the baby manatee. They then carry her to their vehicle. Here, she is placed in a pool and then driven to 2 _____*a local zoo*_____ (**where**). When they arrive, the vet gives the baby manatee a checkup. The examination shows that the creature, now named Kee, is underweight. To increase her weight, Kee is given milk every three hours.

The following month, 4 _____*an adult manatee*_____ (**what**) arrives at the zoo. This animal, named Della, has injuries caused by an accident with a boat. A few days later, Della gives birth to a baby named Pal. This gives Virginia Edmonds, a caretaker at the zoo, an idea. She hopes Della will care for Kee like her baby. So the three manatees are placed in the same pool. Shortly after, Della begins to feed Kee. To everyone's joy, Della accepts Kee as her own. They're all one family now.

After four months, Della has recovered. It's time for her and her family to return to the wild. They are released 6 _____*into the river*_____ (**where**). "Kee is back where she belongs," says Edmonds.

UNIT 11 COMMUNICATION

Team B: Read the information below.

You **don't support** the ban. Think of ways the ban wouldn't be good for teachers and students. Come up with a list of arguments. Think about how cell phones can contribute to learning. Also, think of points to counter Team A's possible arguments.

Follow these steps:

1 Team A: Present your arguments.
2 Team B: Counter Team A's arguments, and present your arguments.
3 Team A: Counter Team B's arguments, and summarize your arguments.
4 Team B: Summarize your arguments.
5 Discuss which team you think won the debate.

UNIT 5 LANGUAGE FOCUS

Student A: Ask your partner questions about balloons to complete the information below. Answer your partner's questions about dice.

How are balloons made?	How are dice made?
First, [1] _____rubber_____ is melted. Color is then added and mixed until the color is even. Balloons are made using a metal mold in the shape of a balloon. The mold is heated to a temperature of [2] _____about 90°C_____. It is then placed inside the rubber mixture. After a few seconds, the mold is removed with a thin layer of rubber still on it. A [3] _____brush_____ is used to roll up the bottom of the rubber layer. This is the part of the balloon you blow into. Finally, air is used to pull the balloons from their molds. **Fun fact:** Early balloons were made of [4] _____animal intestines_____.	First, plastic is melted. Color is then added, and the mixture is poured into a metal mold. The sides have dots, which will represent the numbers 1 to 6. Next, plastic cubes are removed from the mold and painted all over. The cubes are then rolled around in a machine. This removes all of the paint except for the paint inside the dots just below the surface. Finally, the dice are tested to make sure each side is equal. Otherwise, it will be hard to roll the number you need! **Fun fact:** Early dice were made of animal bones.

UNIT 7 LANGUAGE FOCUS

Student B: Read your mystery story to Student A. Discuss what you think happened.

Why are dogs jumping to their deaths?

In Dumbarton, Scotland, there's an old, high bridge from which many dogs have jumped. Since the 1950s, around 600 dogs have jumped off this bridge. About 50 have died. They all jump from the same place, without warning, usually on a clear day. Most are dog breeds that have long noses. Why do the dogs jump?

UNIT 5 LANGUAGE FOCUS

Student B: Ask your partner questions about dice to complete the information below.
Answer your partner's questions about balloons.

How are balloons made?	How are dice made?
First, rubber is melted. Color is then added and mixed until the color is even.	First, 5 _____ plastic _____ is melted. Color is then added, and the mixture is poured into a 6 _____ metal mold _____. The sides have dots, which will represent the numbers 1 to 6.
Balloons are made using a metal mold in the shape of a balloon. The mold is heated to a temperature of about 90°C. It is then placed inside the rubber mixture. After a few seconds, the mold is removed with a thin layer of rubber still on it. A brush is used to roll up the bottom of the rubber layer. This is the part of the balloon you blow into.	Next, plastic cubes are removed from the mold and painted all over. The cubes are then rolled around in a 7 _____ machine _____. This removes all of the paint except for the paint inside the dots just below the surface.
Finally, air is used to pull the balloons from their molds.	Finally, the dice are tested to make sure each side is equal. Otherwise, it will be hard to roll the number you need!
Fun fact: Early balloons were made of animal intestines.	**Fun fact:** Early dice were made of 8 _____ animal bones _____.

UNIT 6 COMMUNICATION

Group A: Choose an animal below. Combine two facts using a relative clause. Don't say the name of the animal. After Group B has made a guess, move on to another animal. Take turns giving clues and guessing. The group with the higher number of correct guesses at the end wins.

Albatross (bird)

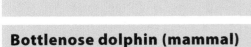

Lifespan in the wild:
About 50 years

Habitat:
Southern Ocean and North Pacific Ocean

Interesting fact 1: It drinks saltwater.

Interesting fact 2: It sometimes floats on the sea's surface.

Emperor penguin (bird)

Lifespan in the wild:
15 to 20 years

Habitat:
Antarctica

Interesting fact 1: It can dive 565 meters and stay underwater for more than 20 minutes.

Interesting fact 2: It only has one chick a year.

Bottlenose dolphin (mammal)

Lifespan in the wild:
45 to 50 years

Habitat:
Warm and tropical waters around the world

Interesting fact 1: It can swim 30 kilometers an hour and jump almost 5 meters out of the water.

Interesting fact 2: It only lets one-half of its brain sleep at a time.

Northern fur seal (mammal)

Lifespan in the wild:
Up to 26 years

Habitat:
Cold waters of the North Pacific Ocean

Interesting fact 1: It has large eyes that let it see well underwater and at night.

Interesting fact 2: It has huge flippers that help it stay cool.

Dugong (mammal)

Lifespan in the wild:
About 70 years

Habitat:
Warm coastal waters of the Red Sea, Indian Ocean, and Pacific Ocean

Interesting fact 1: It is related to elephants.

Interesting fact 2: It was sometimes mistaken for a mermaid by sailors.

Hermit crab (shellfish)

Lifespan in the wild:
Up to 30 years

Habitat:
Saltwater from shallow coastal areas to deep seas worldwide

Interesting fact 1: It is active at night.

Interesting fact 2: It often climbs over another of its kind instead of going around.

Group B's animals:

leatherback turtle	sea otter	manta ray
saltwater crocodile	stonefish	whale shark

UNIT 6 COMMUNICATION

Group B: Choose an animal below. Combine two facts using a relative clause. Don't say the name of the animal. After Group A has made a guess, move on to another animal. Take turns giving clues and guessing. The group with the higher number of correct guesses at the end wins.

Leatherback turtle (reptile)
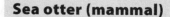

Lifespan in the wild:
About 45 years

Habitat:
Tropical and warm waters of the Atlantic, Pacific, and Indian Oceans, but seen in colder oceans, too

Interesting fact 1: It buries its eggs in the sand.

Interesting fact 2: It is endangered.

Sea otter (mammal)

Lifespan in the wild:
Up to 23 years

Habitat:
Coasts of the Pacific Ocean in North America and Asia

Interesting fact 1: It has to eat three hours a day to stay warm.

Interesting fact 2: It uses rocks to break open shellfish.

Manta ray (fish)
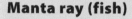

Lifespan in the wild:
Up to 20 years

Habitat:
Warm waters, often near coral reefs

Interesting fact 1: It looks like a blanket.

Interesting fact 2: It eats about 13 percent of its body weight in food each week.

Stonefish (fish)
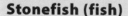

Lifespan in the wild:
Not known

Habitat:
On coral reefs and near rocks, in warm and tropical waters of the Indian and Pacific Oceans

Interesting fact 1: It is one of the most poisonous fish in the world.

Interesting fact 2: It can live outside of the ocean for 20 hours.

Saltwater crocodile (reptile)

Lifespan in the wild:
Up to 70 years

Habitat:
Freshwater and saltwater areas of eastern India, Southeast Asia, and northern Australia

Interesting fact 1: It kills one to two people every year in Australia.

Interesting fact 2: It sometimes swims far out to sea.

Whale shark (fish)

Lifespan in the wild:
60 to 100 years

Habitat:
Warm and tropical waters all over the world

Interesting fact 1: It looks dangerous but is actually very gentle.

Interesting fact 2: It can only reproduce when it is about 30 years old.

Group A's animals:

albatross   emperor penguin   bottlenose dolphin
dugong   northern fur seal   hermit crab

WORKBOOK ANSWER KEY

UNIT 1

Preview

A

1 c

2 a

3 b

4 d

B

1 drawing and mixing music

2 gardening and Instagramming

3 dancing and reading comic books

4 cooking and making videos

C Answers will vary.

Language Focus

A

1 I don't like dancing, but I enjoy singing.

2 Reading fantasy books is fun, but I like reading graphic novels more.

3 Jan likes cooking, but she doesn't enjoy baking at all.

4 I don't like watching movies on my iPad. I like seeing them in a theater.

5 I don't like doing puzzles. In fact, I can't stand it.

B

1 **A:** Does Mike like playing golf?
B: No, he can't stand it.

2 **A:** What do Hal and Linda enjoy doing?
B: They enjoy doing jigsaw puzzles.

3 **A:** Do you like cooking?
B: No, I don't really like/enjoy cooking.

4 **A:** What does Charles like doing?
B: He likes playing video games.

C

a 1

b 6

c 4

d 2

e 5

f 3

g 7

The Real World

A c

B

1 T

2 F

3 F

4 F

5 T

Reading

A Canning; soap making; beekeeping; baking; embroidery; writing

B

1 b

2 b

3 c

4 c

5 a

C

1 d

2 f

3 b

4 e

5 a

6 c

Vocabulary

A

1 appear

2 affect

3 eventually

4 average

5 post

6 leader

B

1 effect

2 council

3 advice

4 counsel

5 affect

6 advise

Writing

A watching soccer; favorite players; World Cup; tennis lessons; hope to be on the school team next year; watching movies; theater; at home; on TV; stream

B Answers will vary.

C Answers will vary.

UNIT 2

Preview

A

1 volleyball
2 taekwondo
3 archery
4 golf
5 cycling
6 swimming
7 cricket
8 baseball
9 skiing
10 tennis

B volleyball, golf, cricket, baseball, tennis

Language Focus

A

1 Kevin has been studying for over an hour.
2 What have you been doing lately?
3 How long have you and your friends been waiting here?
4 Jessica has been working at the sports center since July.

B

1 **A:** How long has Andy been going to the gym?
  B: He's / He has been going to the gym for two years.

2 **A:** Has Ana been taking tennis lessons for a long time?
  B: Yes, she's / she has been taking tennis lessons since middle school.

3 **A:** How long has it been raining?
  B: It's / It has been raining for about an hour.

4 **A:** Have you been watching TV (for) long?
  B: Yes, I've / I have been watching TV since 8:30.

C

1 c
2 a
3 d
4 b

The Real World

A table tennis; soccer

B

1 b
2 a
3 c
4 c

Reading

A a

B

1 b
2 c
3 a
4 c
5 c

C

1 c
2 a
3 e
4 b
5 d

Vocabulary

A

1 success
2 distance
3 announce
4 previous
5 determination
6 defeat

B

1 holds
2 medical
3 record time
4 world
5 break

Writing

A My name is Alison, and I'm a student at Lincoln High School.
I've been doing it for three years, and I have a yellow belt.
I also like playing basketball, but I'm not very good at it.
Do you play sports or do any martial arts?
Well, it's late now, so I'm going to bed.

B Answers will vary.

C Answers will vary.

UNIT 3

Preview

A

1 get it repaired
2 go to the library
3 join a study group
4 talk to a counselor

B

1 d

2 a

3 c

4 b

C Answers will vary.

Language Focus

A

1 should

2 getting

3 tell

4 could

5 should

B

1 Why don't you tell him the truth?

2 You could apologize / try apologizing.

3 You should talk to someone / try talking to someone.

4 Have you thought about getting a tutor?

5 If I were you, I wouldn't say anything.

C

a 1

b 4

c 8

d 3

e 6

f 7

g 5

h 2

The Real World

A

1 a

2 c

3 b

B

1 b

2 a

3 e

4 c

5 d

Reading

A b

B

1 b

2 a

3 c

4 b

5 a

C b; c; d; e

Vocabulary

A

1 e

2 c

3 a

4 f

5 b

6 d

B

1 of

2 for

3 out

Writing

A

1 fact

2 example

3 quote

4 anecdote

B Answers will vary.

C Answers will vary.

UNIT 4

Preview

A

1 b

2 d

3 e

4 a

5 c

B

1 wrapped

2 driven

3 washed

4 treated

5 released

6 attached

C Answers will vary.

Language Focus

A

1 was found

2 was given

3 was treated

4 was wrapped

5 decided

6 went

7 ran

8 was greeted

B

1 The dog is being taken to the shelter.

2 Two bears were seen near the lake.

3 The koala was released.

4 The injured owl was treated.

5 The injured animals are being tagged.

C

a 3

b 7

c 2

d 5

e 4

f 1

g 6

The Real World

A b

B

1 d

2 c

3 b

4 a

Reading

A Democratic Republic of the Congo; Rwanda

B

1 a

2 b

3 c

4 c

5 b

C

1 pet

2 buy

3 survive

4 holding

5 healthy

Vocabulary

A

1 dangerous

2 suddenly

3 cheered

4 hang

5 investigate

6 frightened

B

1 rescued; Transitive

2 arrived; Intransitive

3 help; Transitive

4 came; Intransitive

Writing

A

1 touch

2 hearing

3 hearing

4 taste

5 sight

6 hearing

B Answers will vary.

C Answers will vary.

UNIT 5

Preview

A

1 flat

2 grooves

3 lead

4 stuck

5 machine

6 sold

B

1 seen

2 placed

3 checked

4 cut

5 added

6 made

7 sold

8 put

9 designed

10 chosen

C Answers will vary.

Language Focus

A

1 love

2 are made

3 are mixed

4 is heated

5 reaches

6 are added

7 is poured

8 places

9 are removed

10 wrapped

B

1 The flavors and colors are tested by chemists.

2 The lollipops are wrapped by factory workers.

3 Each lollipop is checked by a supervisor.

4 The sweet treats are loved by kids of all ages.

C

1 got

2 's made

3 feels

4 was made

5 produce

6 bought

The Real World

A

a 3

b 2

c 1

B

1 copy

2 chemical

3 sometimes done through guessing

Reading

A plastic; metal; concrete; glass; bio-materials; food

B

1 b

2 a

3 c

4 b

5 a

C

a 5

b 4

c 2

d 6

e 1

f 3

g 7

Vocabulary

A

1 global

2 supply

3 complex

4 individual

5 combine

6 variety

B

1 network

2 brand

3 awareness

4 warming

Writing

A is shaped; is made; is added; is pressed; is closed; is cooked

B Answers will vary.

C Answers will vary.

UNIT 6

Preview

A

1 narwhal

2 seahorse

3 king crab

4 dugong

B Answers will vary.

Language Focus

A

1 which

2 who

3 who

4 which

B

1 Antarctica, which is always covered in ice and snow, is the coldest continent on Earth.

2 The emperor penguin, which is the largest penguin in the world, lives only in Antarctica.

3 Captain James Cook, who was the first explorer to sail around Antarctica, died in 1779.

C

a 4

b 6

c 1

d 2

e 5

f 3

The Real World

A b

B

1 T

2 F

3 T

4 F

Reading

A c

B

1 a

2 b

3 c

4 c

5 b

C

1 subway

2 dangerous

3 cleaned

4 rock

5 number

6 successful

Vocabulary

A

1 attract

2 popular

3 damage

4 warn

5 remains

6 shallow

B

1 He saw more than 10 sharks in the water.

2 I've gone diving nearly a dozen times.

3 We caught 20 or so fish on our trip.

4 There are about 60 fish in the tank.

Writing

A

talk—<u>speak</u>
big—<u>huge</u>
struck—<u>hit</u>
spilled—<u>leaked</u>
occurred—<u>happened</u>
protect—<u>preserve</u>

B Answers will vary.

C Answers will vary.

UNIT 7

Preview

A

1 bones; fight

2 legend

3 buried; gold

B

1 tribe

2 ruins

3 machine

4 invader

C Answers will vary.

Language Focus

A

1 might have died

2 can't be

3 could have dried up

4 might not be; might have stolen

B

1 d

2 c

3 b

4 a

C

1 must

2 could

3 could

4 might

5 might

The Real World

A

1 2001

2 1212

B

1 c

2 b

3 b

Reading

A a; b; d

B

1 b

2 c

3 a

4 c

5 b

C

1 Th

2 Th

3 Fa

4 Th

5 Fa

Vocabulary

A

1 abandon

2 lack of

3 imagine

4 collapse

5 population

6 peak

B

1 tsunami

2 flood

3 hurricane

4 avalanche

Writing

A Answers will vary.

B Answers will vary.

C Answers will vary.

UNIT 8

Preview

A

1 elevator

2 castle

3 escalator

4 bridge

5 skyscraper

6 Across: tunnel

6 Down: tower

7 train

B

1 Answers will vary.

2 Answers will vary.

Language Focus

A

1 most

2 too

3 taller; newer

4 as good as

B

1 the most interesting

2 as tall as

3 The most exciting

4 the tallest

5 brave enough

6 too hot

C It was the best vacation I've ever had!
I think it's the largest public square in the world.
It's not as expensive as the food in the restaurants, and I think it's tastier.

The Real World

A Iran

B

1 F

2 T

3 F

4 NG

Reading

A b

B

1 b

2 c

3 c

4 c

5 b

C

1 T

2 F

3 F

4 NG

Vocabulary

A

1 goods

2 rely on

3 export

4 board

5 region

6 transport

B

1 trip

2 plane

3 round-trip

4 first-class

5 passport

6 tour

7 train

8 car

Writing

A

Building name: nicknamed the Gherkin; also known as 30 St. Mary Axe

Location: London, England; in financial district

Appearance/Height: modern design; looks like a cucumber; 180 meters tall

Year completed: completed in 2003

Cost to build: cost: £230 million ($300 million)

B Answers will vary.

C Answers will vary.

UNIT 9

Preview

A

Positive words: exciting, gorgeous, interesting, superb

Negative words: dull, predictable, overrated, unrealistic

B

1 c

2 e

3 a

4 d

5 b

C Answers will vary.

Language Focus

A

1 d

2 c

3 a

4 e

5 b

B

1 wasn't it

2 have you

3 can they

4 hasn't

5 will

C

1 didn't

2 spectacular

3 weren't

4 unrealistic

5 would

6 music

The Real World

A $75 million

B

1 T

2 T

3 F

4 F

Reading

A *Lord of the Rings*

B

1 b

2 c

3 c

4 a

5 b

C c; e

Vocabulary

A

1 curious

2 response

3 appeal

4 mood

5 identify

6 factors

B Answers will vary.

Writing

A

1 ;

2 —

3 —

4 :

B Answers will vary.

C Answers will vary.

UNIT 10

Preview

A

1 could find a cure for cancer

2 were an Olympic athlete

3 could make myself invisible

4 were able to breathe underwater

B

1 design

2 predict

3 cure

4 travel

5 set

6 make

C Answers will vary.

Language Focus

A

1 could; I'd

2 were; want

3 didn't; I'd be

B

1 If you were a time traveler, which time period would you go back to?; c

2 If you invented a robot, what would it do?; d

3 If you could give your mother any present, what would it be?; e

4 If you could be an architect or a lawyer, which would you be?; a

5 What do you wish you could do very well?; b

C

a 5

b 3

c 1

d 2

e 4

f 6

The Real World

A a

B

1 b

2 c

3 b

4 a

Reading

A a; d

B

1 c

2 c

3 b

4 a

5 c

C

1 d

2 a

3 c

Vocabulary

A

1 inspired

2 pressure

3 reality

4 event

5 represent

6 invention

B

1 luck

2 make

3 against

4 grant

5 dying

Writing

A

Longest sentence: My brother and sister both play well, but for some reason, I was told by my parents that I should learn the trumpet.
Shortest sentence: Unfortunately, I hated the trumpet!
Example of passive voice: was told

B In my opinion; Unfortunately; Of course; For a third wish

C Answers will vary.

UNIT 11

Preview

A

1 lied

2 cheated

3 lost

4 stole

5 damaged

B

1 d

2 a

3 c

4 b

C Answers will vary.

Language Focus

A

1 shouldn't

2 gave

3 was stolen

4 must have left

5 has been

6 couldn't

B

1 been doing

2 was taken

3 been watching

4 was designed

5 were painted

6 been feeling

C Anyone could have come in here and taken it from your desk.
I've been looking forward to eating it all day.
Well, you could ask the people in the hallway.
If someone took it, they probably wouldn't admit it.
I think you should keep your food inside your backpack next time.

The Real World

A a

B

1 c

2 b

3 b

Reading

A c

B

1 c

2 a

3 b

4 b

5 a

C

1 piracy

2 hurt

3 Netflix

4 books

5 fined

Vocabulary

A

1 caused

2 joins them

3 stealing money

4 divides into two or more things

5 test if something is true

6 steal money from it

B

1 b

2 a

3 b

4 b

5 a

Writing

A Answers will vary.

B Answers will vary.

C Answers will vary.

UNIT 12

Preview

A

1 whole grains

2 protein

3 sugar

4 Healthy

B

1 exercise

2 red

3 sugar

4 vegetarian

5 minerals

C

1 Answers will vary.

2 Answers will vary.

3 Answers will vary.

Language Focus

A

1 healthier

2 hot enough

3 eating

4 which

5 as important as

B

1 Eating less salt can lower your blood pressure.

2 Lean meat—like chicken and turkey—is healthier than red meat.

3 My sister Louisa is the fittest person I know.

4 The bakery is just around the corner, isn't it?

5 I'm not fit enough to run five kilometers.

6 My doctor, who helped me improve my diet, also suggested I join a gym.

C

1 c

2 a

3 d

4 b

The Real World

A grasshopper; crickets; Ants; Waxworms

B

1 T

2 F

3 F

4 T

Reading

A

1 c

2 b

3 a

4 d

B

1 b

2 c

3 a

4 c

5 b

C

1 c

2 b

3 e

4 a

5 d

Vocabulary

A

1 c

2 d

3 a

4 b

5 f

6 e

B

1 senses

2 sensational

3 sensible

4 sensation

5 sensitive

Writing

A

1 M

2 S

3 M

4 S

B Answers will vary.

C Answers will vary.

CREDITS

Photo Credits